# Organizing Higher Education for Collaboration

# Organizing Higher Education for Collaboration

## A Guide for Campus Leaders

Adrianna J. Kezar
Jaime Lester

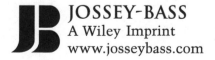

JOSSEY-BASS
A Wiley Imprint
www.josseybass.com

Published by Jossey-Bass
A Wiley Imprint
989 Market Street, San Francisco, CA 94103-1741—www.josseybass.com

Readers should be aware that Internet Web sites offered as citations and/or sources for further information may have changed or disappeared between the time this was written and when it is read.

Limit of Liability/Disclaimer of Warranty: While the publisher and author have used their best efforts in preparing this book, they make no representations or warranties with respect to the accuracy or completeness of the contents of this book and specifically disclaim any implied warranties of merchantability or fitness for a particular purpose. No warranty may be created or extended by sales representatives or written sales materials. The advice and strategies contained herein may not be suitable for your situation. You should consult with a professional where appropriate. Neither the publisher nor author shall be liable for any loss of profit or any other commercial damages, including but not limited to special, incidental, consequential, or other damages.

Jossey-Bass books and products are available through most bookstores. To contact Jossey-Bass directly call our Customer Care Department within the U.S. at 800-956-7739, outside the U.S. at 317-572-3986, or fax 317-572-4002.

Jossey-Bass also publishes its books in a variety of electronic formats. Some content that appears in print may not be available in electronic books.

**Library of Congress Cataloging-in-Publication Data**
Kezar, Adrianna J.
    Organizing higher education for collaboration : a guide for campus leaders / Adrianna J. Kezar, Jaime Lester. — 1st ed.
        p.   cm.
    Includes bibliographical references and index.
    ISBN 978-0-470-17936-9 (cloth)
        1. Universities and colleges—United States—Administration.   2. College environment—United States.   3. Student participation in administration—United States.   I. Lester, Jaime.   II. Title.
    LB2341.K453   2009
    378.1'01—dc22
                                                                2008042587

Printed in the United States of America
FIRST EDITION
HB Printing   10 9 8 7 6 5 4 3 2 1

The Jossey-Bass
Higher and Adult Education Series

# Contents

*Part Three: Conclusion: Bringing the Strategies
Together for Collective Action*

# Preface: Organizing Higher Education for Collaboration

Perhaps you came to this book because you suspect something is wrong with the way that your unit is operating on your campus. Or maybe you intuitively believe in the power of collaboration but have had difficulty gaining support from others around you. You might also have heard people within your college or university talking about the importance of collaboration and you are unsure about the benefits or how to accomplish this task. Or perhaps you were part of an unsuccessful collaborative effort and want to understand why it failed and how you can avoid a similar experience in the future. Although this book is aimed at helping you understand some of the benefits of and barriers to collaboration (and providing you with more detailed resources to pursue these topics), the main purpose of the book is to provide a framework for how to reorganize campuses to fundamentally be better able to engage in collaborative work. But before getting into these details, it is important to review some basic assumptions and purposes that will help set the stage for the rest of the book.

Collaboration embodies a paradox. It seems to be the most natural and perhaps easiest activity that we can imagine. As human beings, we are constantly engaged in relationships, we often envision the world as interdependent, and in society we live in a cooperative fashion. It is hard to imagine societies or an organizational world in which collaboration would not exist. However, as demonstrated throughout this text, collaboration can be one of the most difficult and challenging human endeavors. Part of this difficulty is related to Western philosophies and values (to speak in the most generic terms) that celebrate the individual and structure institutions to support individual activity (Bar On, 1994; Loy, 2002; Russell, 2004). American values celebrating the rugged individualist further compound and solidify this perspective in organizations. Typically, individuals are rewarded, individuals are held accountable, individuals hold a spot within institutional hierarchies, and the like. Although this book does not review the broader philosophies and values that have shaped our generic working and living patterns, it is nonetheless important to keep in mind that this deeply held value system creates a paradox for enacting collaboration. Whereas our intuitive day-to-day interactions might suggest that collaboration is natural and easy, the tacit assumptions heralding the individual that underlie institutions and societal norms fly in the face of this assumption and disrupt even the best efforts to collaborate. It is this paradox that is important for leaders to understand as they engage this text. Even if you meet other people who want to collaborate or believe in its value, you are likely to run into difficulty. Unconscious norms and institutional processes and structures may trip up efforts. This very paradox makes the ideas presented in this book important to creating successful collaborations.

For those who are interested, there are a variety of texts that deconstruct Western value systems, describe other value systems, historically review the evolution of Western values, propose new value systems, and try to reconcile varying philosophies (Bar On, 1994; Loy, 2002; Russell, 2004). We highly recommend these books to you, but our purpose is different—we are focused on helping leaders create environments that support collaboration in the face of this paradox. Understanding the details of the paradox is not necessary. The hope is that someday collaboration will not embody a paradox and will simply be synergistic and bring out the best in contributors. Until that time, we all need to struggle with the contradiction that is collaboration. With the overarching theme of paradox in mind, we now move on to describe the origin of the book, its purpose and organization, the need it fills, its significance and contribution, and the intended audience.

## Origin

This book emerged from many years of research on leadership, change, and institutional effectiveness within postsecondary institutions. In particular, Adrianna Kezar's experience working on the Project on Leadership and Institutional Transformation of the American Council on Education (ACE) and on the Documenting Effective Educational Practices (DEEP) study at Indiana University (Kuh et al., 2005) solidified her understanding of the importance of collaboration to the future success of colleges and universities. Although these two studies were not focused on collaboration, it emerged as pivotal to institutional effectiveness. Collaboration was a critical component to institutional change and learning in the ACE project and was shown to facilitate creation of a successful learning environment for students in the DEEP study.

From her studies of student and academic affairs collaboration, service learning, learning communities, collaborative learning, and a variety of other types of collaborative campus endeavors, Kezar has been impressed by the range of student outcomes that these activities provide, activities that create a more holistic, rich learning experience for students. Because she found collaboration to be central to the learning mission of postsecondary institutions and to so many critical higher education outcomes and processes, it seemed essential to learn more about how to guide institutions in becoming more collaborative.

Jaime Lester's interest and background in collaboration stems from her active participation in several research projects (such as the Transfer and Retention of Urban Community College Students and the Transfer Success project) that brought together local and state community college districts and researchers across different institutions. Through the sharing of resources, both physical and intellectual, coalescing of expertise, and an interest in learning, collaboration emerged as essential to examining and understanding how to assist community college students to be more successful in achieving their educational goals. In addition, Lester has cotaught several courses, instigating dialogue around the complexities of teaching in collaborative and experimental formats within traditional higher education structures. Despite the positive outcomes from these collaborations, it became clear that many structural difficulties arise because departmental structures (e.g., budgets and teaching assignment structures) do not support faculty team teaching, collaborative research and publications are not valued in the tenure and promotion process, and collaborative research that does not include grant monies is not supported by the university. What emerged from these experiences is an understanding of the need to reexamine the mission, values, and rewards that either help or hinder successful collaborations.

This book evolved from the long-term research agenda of both Kezar and Lester to provide a framework for higher education institutions to create more collaborative campus contexts and facilitate collaboration more broadly.

## Purpose and Organization

The three main purposes of the book are to (1) describe the benefits, necessity, and barriers of collaborative work in higher education, (2) provide a vision for what a collaborative postsecondary institution looks like, and (3) guide educational leaders in efforts to redesign their campuses for collaborative work by presenting the results of a research study of campuses that have been successful in recreating their environments to support collaboration. This book is unique in its focus on how to reorganize and redesign the organizational context; it examines how to make all collaborations successful by rethinking the overall organizational structure and culture.

These three purposes are met in the following ways. Part One, Setting the Context for Moving Toward Collaboration, provides background for why leaders might want to engage in a change process and consider redesigning their campus. Chapter One, The Collaborative Imperative, briefly synthesizes the literature on the advantages of working collaboratively within organizations. The literature base has been created over the last thirty years, but few have attempted to pull together this information to build a cohesive argument for why collaboration has become an imperative. This section complements books such as *The Fifth Discipline: The Art and Practice of the Learning Organization,* by Peter Senge (1990), that, although not solely focused on collaboration, describe some of the benefits of collaboration. Chapter Two offers an overview to the challenges of collaboration, providing the context for understanding why campuses may need to be reorganized.

Chapter Three, Taking Advantage of Collaboration, outlines a vision for what a campus that has reorganized for collaboration looks like. This extended example of a campus from our study demonstrates how the campus changed its teaching, research, service, governance, and management. This chapter also gives examples of collaborative work in higher education and describes trends. Although texts have been developed focused on specific collaborative endeavors, such as the work of Smith and McCann (2001) on learning communities, Austin and Baldwin (1991) on collaborative teaching and research, Jacoby and associates (2003) on community service learning, Kuh (1996) on academic and student affairs collaboration, and Keig and Waggoner (1994) on collaborative peer review, there is no text that examines collaborative work as a trend by analyzing patterns across these activities or how various efforts could be leveraged together to transform campuses for collaborative work. Exploring these trends together will help institutional leaders make connections and synergize reform initiatives. Rather than work on collaborative issues separately, leaders can begin to see how they can save time and resources by combining efforts to develop collaborative work on campus, making one change to enable all these efforts rather than approaching them one at a time. This also means that readers who are focused narrowly on setting up a learning community or encouraging multidisciplinary research may want to go directly to those focused resources. This book is an important complement to but not a substitute for such resources.

Part Two, Strategies for Reorganizing Campuses, reviews lessons for institutional leaders about how to reorganize campuses to conduct collaborative work—the primary goal and the largest section of the book. These lessons were developed from intensive case study research of four campuses with extremely high levels of collaboration. We spoke to them about structures and vehicles they had created to support and enable collaboration. The study involved interviews with administrators, faculty, and staff; document analysis; and observation of meetings related to collaborations. The organizational features that facilitated collaboration and were found across the campuses involved in the study were (1) mission or vision and educational philosophy, (2) values, (3) social networks, (4) integrating structures, (5) rewards, (6) external pressure, and (7) learning.

Part Three puts all of these elements together. Chapter Eleven presents a model in which all the strategies are linked together and can be used to guide the work of institutional leaders. Chapter Twelve explores the roles of various constituents in supporting collaborative work within the higher education sector.

## Need, Significance, and Contribution

This book provides needed guidance and advice for how colleges and universities can reorganize to foster more collaborative work. There are many books and articles on the value of specific types of collaboration; however, there are few resources that help leaders understand how to create an environment supportive of all the various types of collaborative initiatives being advocated. Furthermore, this book is one of the few research-based resources on this topic. Occasionally, anecdotal articles are written with advice from leaders about creating collaboration around a specific initiative such as service learning or interdisciplinarity, but these ideas are not supported by research.

In a time of declining resources, institutions are looking for ways to maximize their resources while continuing to be effective. Collaboration is always a key strategy for leaders to consider in hard financial times for achieving goals with fewer resources. Furthermore, governors are demanding reforms (e.g., P–16 initiatives, learning communities) that require collaborative work. Federal agencies are pressuring postsecondary institutions to undertake new accountability efforts such as improved student retention, which requires a more collaborative approach to institutional operations. The state and federal policy imperatives are clear, but the guidance for institutions does not exist. The findings from the case study research of exemplary institutions involved in high levels of collaboration provide the necessary tools to guide leaders in redesigning their campuses.

## Intended Audiences and Uses

Presidents, administrators, faculty, and individual change agents can use this book to gain familiarity with the necessary strategies to redesign campuses for collaborative work. The stories from successful campuses will make the recommendations provided easier to use by allowing readers to operationalize and concretize the ideas for action. First, individuals who are planning various change initiatives or who have failed at particular changes such as the move to multidisciplinary research or P–16 partnerships will benefit by further understanding the hurdles they face in developing a new and better strategy for moving forward. Second, legislators and policymakers will find this book useful for developing state and federal initiatives and to better understand what type of language should be included in requests for proposal and grant applications in order to help campuses redesign for collaborative work. Third, national and professional associations will be interested in this book because it focuses on an area, collaboration, that is part of their national dialogues and for which they are seeking knowledge and resources.

## Acknowledgments

Adrianna would like to thank her various collaborators–Jaime Lester, Peter Eckel, Melissa Contreras-McGavin, Rozana Carducci, Tricia Bertram Gallant, Doug Toma, William Tierney, George Kuh, Jillian Kinzie, Vasti Torres, Hannah Yang, Lynn Gangone, Tony Chambers, Jay Dee, Kevin Kruger, Jeanne Narum, Donna Bourassa, and Sally Lubeck. In particular, I dedicate the book to Donna and Sally who are no longer with us.

Jaime would like to thank all the people that she has collaborated with over the years. Each collaboration has been a rich learning experience that has taught us much about how to collaborate in an environment that is not necessarily conducive to team-based work. Specifically, Jaime would like to thank Linda Hagedorn and the TRUCCS team, Jeni Hart, Pam Eddy, Scott Cypers, Scott Lukas, Margaret Sallee, Frank Harris, Melissa Contreras-McGavin, Rozana Carducci, Tricia Bertram Gallant, and Adrianna Kezar. Also, Jaime would like to thank her daughter, Mackenzie, who was very patient in the early days of her life as her mom completed this book. Lastly, this book is dedicated to Craig Hayden, who was part of my greatest collaboration: Mackenzie.

# The Authors

**Adrianna Kezar,** associate professor for higher education at the University of Southern California, holds a Ph.D. (1996) and an M.A. (1992) in higher education administration from the University of Michigan and a B.A. (1989) from the University of California, Los Angeles. She joined the faculty at USC in 2003.

Kezar was formerly an assistant professor at the University of Maryland and George Washington University. Kezar was editor of the *ASHE-ERIC Higher Education Report Series* from 1996 to 2004. Previously, she was an administrative associate for the vice president for student affairs (1992–1995) and coordinator for the Center for Research on Learning and Teaching (1995–1996), both at the University of Michigan.

Her research focuses on change, leadership, public purposes of higher education, organizational theory, governance, access, and diversity and equity issues in higher education. She has published over seventy-five articles and books and is featured in the major journals for higher education including *The Journal of Higher Education, Research in Higher Education, The Review of Higher Education,* and *Journal of College Student Development.* Her most recent book is *Rethinking the "L" Word in Higher Education: The Revolution of Research on Leadership* (2006). In 2005, she had two new books published by Jossey-Bass, *Higher Education for the Public Good* and *Creating Organizational Learning in Higher*

*Education,* and a national report published by the American Council on Education, *Leadership Strategies for Advancing Campus Diversity.* She is currently working on a grant from the Lumina Foundation related to a federal financial program called Individual Development Accounts.

Kezar has participated actively in national service, including being on the editorial boards for *The Journal of Higher Education, The Journal of College Student Development, Change,* and *The ERIC Review* and serving as a reviewer for eleven journals in and outside higher education. She has served on the AERA-Division J Council and Association for the Study of Higher Education Publication Committee and Dissertation of the Year Committee. Kezar also serves or has served as a board member for the American Association for Higher Education; Association of American Colleges and Universities' Peer Review and Knowledge Network; National TRIO Clearinghouse; and the American Council on Education's CIRP Research Cooperative. She volunteers for several national organizations, including the HERS/Bryn Mawr Summer Institute, Pathways to College Network, and the Kellogg Forum on Higher Education for the Public Good. She has received national awards for her editorial leadership of the ASHE-ERIC report series from ASHE, for developing a leadership development program for women in higher education from ACE, and for her commitment to service learning from the National Society for Experiential Learning.

---

**Jaime Lester,** assistant professor of higher education, George Mason University, holds a Ph.D. and M.Ed. in higher education from the Rossier School of Education at the University of Southern California. Lester also holds a dual B.A. from the University of Michigan in English and women's studies. Prior to George Mason University, she was an assistant professor and co-director of the Research Center for Community College Inquiry in the Department of Leadership and Counseling at Old Dominion University from 2006 to 2008.

Lester maintains an active research agenda that examines gender equity in higher education, retention and transfer of community college students, socialization of women and minority faculty, and leadership. She has published articles in the *Community College Journal of Research and Practice*, *Community College Review*, *Journal of Higher Education*, *Liberal Education*, *National Women's Studies Association Journal*, and *NEA: Thought & Action*. She also has two forthcoming books on gendered perspectives in community colleges and family-friendly policies in higher education. Currently, she is completing a project on nonpositional leadership and change in higher education.

In addition to her research, Lester has participated as a reviewer for several academic journals inside and outside higher education, including the *National Women's Studies Association Journal*, *Community College Review*, *Journal About Women in Higher Education*, *Journal of Women and Minorities in Science and Engineering*, and *New Directions for Community Colleges*. She also serves as a board member for the national association the Council for the Study of Community Colleges, who granted her an award for her dissertation work.

# Organizing Higher Education for Collaboration

# Part I

# Setting the Context for Moving Toward Collaboration

## Understanding the Logic, Barriers, and Need to Reorganize

L eaders will not be able to successfully enact the strategies
for reorganizing campuses (offered in Part Two) unless they
understand the advantages of collaboration and the systemic barriers to creating collaboration, which we describe in Part One.
The foundation and building blocks presented in Part One provide the essential logic to motivate people to engage in the reorganization process. A leader is not well-equipped unless he or
she can describe the type of service provided when individuals
collaborate, the benefits of cognitive complexity, and how collaboration can help organizations innovate. Most important, however,
is that higher education leaders make the case for how collaboration enhances the teaching and learning mission of the institutions
with which they are entrusted. The benefits and logic supporting
collaboration are fully reviewed in Part One.

Higher education leaders and change agents must also possess
some understanding of the paradox of collaboration: why it can
be so challenging no matter how compelling the logic, how many
external agencies and groups desire higher education to embrace
collaboration, and how many internal champions (faculty and
staff) seem devoted to the idea. A general understanding of the
norms and values that are embedded in and that shape current
educational structures and processes demonstrates why it can be

so challenging to collaborate and why these systems need to be altered. Because colleges and universities are generally large and stable institutions, they are not the most nimble organizations, so collaboration will not happen easily or overnight. Collaboration is an endeavor that leaders need to address with patience, recognizing that to overcome the paradox major systems need to be reorganized. The model for reorganized campuses outlined in Part Two offers leaders a framework for how to engage in the process of creating a campus supportive of collaboration.

Important to maintaining patience is to have a vision of where the institution is going—one that embraces many different types of collaboration and can create synergy between the various types of collaboration to get there more quickly—so people do not lose faith, hope, and energy. One of the reasons leaders often fail to move forward is that they do not capitalize on the natural synergies that can occur when multiple, similar initiatives come together. We describe how all these reforms in teaching, service, research, management, and governance can be captured in an overall vision of a collaborative campus. We hope this example helps change agents solidify a vision for their own campus by providing the context to move to the next step of reorganization to support and enable a range of collaborative endeavors.

# The Collaborative Imperative

*People collaborate when the job they face is too big, is too
urgent, or requires too much knowledge for one person
or group to do alone. Marshalling what we know about
learning and applying it to the education of our students is
just such a job. This report makes the case that only when
everyone on campus—particularly academic affairs and
student affairs staff—shares the responsibility for student
learning will we be able to make significant progress in
improving it.*

Powerful Partnerships, *Preamble (American Association for
Higher Education et al., 1998)*

*Achieving this vision (of learning) will require concerted
action among all stakeholders. Learning-centered reform
cannot be accomplished by any one institution or even
by the higher education sector alone. Collaboration with
secondary school leaders will help ensure better preparation
of all high school students for rigorous college learning.
Collaboration among policy makers at the state and federal
levels will focus public policy and resources on the quality of
students' liberal education.*

Greater Expectations: A New Vision for Learning as a
Nation Goes to College *(Association of American Colleges
and Universities, 2002)*

In the last two decades, there has been increasing recognition
among organizational leaders more broadly and higher education change agents specifically about the importance of collaboration

among functional areas (e.g., student and academic affairs) to achieve their organizational mission and be effective. Collaboration seems to be an intuitively good idea to many people. We do not need a research study to illuminate how having more than one faculty member design a course can enhance the quality or complexity of ideas. We see the benefits of scientists working together in labs, creating breakthroughs that are unimaginable without cross-disciplinary work. These examples have become accepted wisdom on many campuses across the country. In fact, collaboration has moved from an intuitively good idea to an imperative because of the overwhelming evidence of its benefits (Frost, Jean, Teodorescu, & Brown, 2004; Katz & Martin, 1997; Loan-Clark & Preston, 2002).

A variety of external organizations and sectors are encouraging higher education to become more collaborative in its approach to teaching and research, including accreditors, foundations, business and industry, and government agencies such as National Institutes of Health and National Science Foundation. These organizations have been espousing the importance and value of collaboration for knowledge creation and research, student learning, and improved organizational functioning (Ramaley, 2001). The recent "Spellings report" (U.S. Department of Education, 2006) suggests that higher education needs to work in collaboration to increase access, lower costs, and improve performance. If you look at the conferences announced in the *Chronicle of Higher Education* they often have collaboration within the title: "Collaborating to Embrace the Changing Dynamics of Higher Education," "University and Community Partnerships: Improving Access to Higher Education," "Collaboration for the Advancement of College Teaching and Learning," "Using Technology to Create Greater Cross-Campus Collaboration," and "Diversity: A Shared Responsibility—Getting Student and Academic Affairs to the Table."

Yet collaboration is not widespread in the academy, and if one attends a professional conference in the field, one is likely to hear about the difficulties of trying to implement a plan for student and academic affairs collaboration or a campuswide research center. Learning communities and student and academic affairs partnerships struggle to become institutionalized because higher education institutions are generally organized in departmental silos and bureaucratic or hierarchical administrative structures. Even though there is great difficulty in implementing collaborative initiatives, the imperative to collaborate and logic supporting collaboration are very strong. As a result, we see campuses attempt one collaborative effort after another, often with limited success. For example, one year they may try to develop a first-year transition program, the next year a transfer center, followed by a research collaborative, but each project struggles to get off the ground. We need to better understand how to support this work and make it successful.

Much has been written about the barriers to collaborative work, but little has been written about how to foster collaboration within higher education. (For barriers to collaboration see Frost, Jean, Teodorescu, & Brown, 2004; Love & Love, 1995; Schroeder & Hurst, 1996; Sobol & Newell, 2003; Stein & Short, 2001.) This is the challenge that is undertaken in this book: to provide a working framework for institutions interested in creating a context in which collaboration can flourish. Currently, each college or university independently attempts to determine its path to collaboration. This approach can be extremely problematic, as research suggests that without intention and design, over 50 percent of collaborations fail (Doz, 1996). Furthermore, tinkering with collaboration on the edges—that is, trying out an innovation in a pocket (although better than no collaborative work because it can lead to collaborative efforts)—will not allow institutions to meet the promise of a collaborative advantage; campuses will experience more success if they redesign their campuses. But before getting too far ahead of ourselves, we want to describe more about the reasons that collaboration has become so important and why it is often difficult. This background on the logic of collaboration establishes a context for understanding why institutions should undertake the work, how to move to a collaborative environment, and why fairly major reorganization is necessary.

## Defining Collaboration

First we provide some thoughts on and definitional distinctions related to the concept of collaboration. People are constantly working together, but what makes an effort collaborative? Research that we cite in this text about the advantages of collaboration often does not differentiate clearly among teamwork, collaboration, coordination, partnering, or networking. Although these studies may not be clear about terminology, what is clear is that they are examining different ways of working together that involve a more collective and interactive approach. The study we conducted focused on campuses that were involved in collaborative efforts, and we were interested in these types of working relationships. We briefly describe some of the differences between these terms so the reader understands some of the dissimilarities, but they are not essential to understanding our argument. Whether you are interested in increasing the amount of teamwork, coordination, networking, or collaboration within your campus, the framework described in this book will help you succeed.

Now let's examine some definitions of collective and interactive work. Networks are not deliberately designed, do not necessarily have shared goals, and depend more on the exchange of information and ideas. Cooperative arrangements are usually more formal than networks and may involve a memorandum of agreement or other formal structure (Hagadoorn, 1993; Lockwood, 1996). They typically involve coordination in which partners share information or work on tasks together but usually do not fundamentally alter their work (Hagadoorn, 1993; Lockwood, 1996). Partnerships and collaboration involve joint goals and a reliance on each other to accomplish the goal. Collaborators try to align goals and identify a similar mission, such as student character development. They then try to work at a more fundamental level, which entails joint planning and power sharing (Hagadoorn, 1993; Lockwood, 1996). In order to be considered collaboration, it is essential that the process entail an interactive process (relationship over time) and that groups develop shared rules, norms, and structures, a task that often becomes their first work together (Wood & Gray, 1991).

Also, there are two types of collaboration commonly referred to (usually called alliances)—internal and external (Wood & Gray, 1991). Internal collaborations include areas such as cross-functional teams, interdisciplinary teaching and research, and student and academic affairs collaboration. External collaborations include steering committees, P–16 partnerships, campus-community partnerships, research parks with industry and business, and regional health collaboratives. External collaboration has received a great deal of attention in the business literature because alliances and mergers are considered a key aspect of surviving in difficult financial times (Saxton, 1997; Whetten, 1981). In the higher education literature, more research and writing has been developed on external collaboration, including work on university and community partnerships and school and university collaborations (Brisbin & Hunter, 2003; Johnston, Wetherill, High, & Greenebaum, 2002; Timar, Ogawa, & Orillion, 2004). The study of collaboration reported in this text explored both external and internal collaborations, but focused more on internal collaborations as there is generally less literature in this area.

Is collaboration always necessary? No. There is nothing worse than people forcing collaboration on a situation that simply does not require it. Not all decisions need multiple forms of expertise; sometimes a program can be better offered by one unit, some policy issues cannot be broadly shared because of privacy, and sometimes learning needs to be focused within a specific discipline to master a competency. We want to make sure this book is *not* interpreted as denying the value of individual efforts, efforts within a department or function, or discipline-based work.

## The Logic of Collaboration

Why are so many external constituents interested in having higher education become more collaborative? These external groups (accreditors, the United States Department of Education, state policymakers) are all responding to research conducted in the last thirty years within government and business. In the 1980s, American businesses suffered from competitive challenges that forced them to look at their operational structures and to examine ways to be more successful (Cole, 1999). One of the main lessons learned from this research and reflection is that the hierarchical and bureaucratic structure of American businesses (and organizations more broadly) was preventing them from innovating and responding to customer or client needs (Damanpor, 1996; Kingston, 1995). Products were more costly, and therefore less competitive, because of the lack of collaboration across functions, which has been found to be more efficient. Under pressure from difficult financial times, changing demographics, globalization, and increasing complexity, "siloed" work with duplicative activities and a lack of communication and synergy across function was not working anymore. Under these new conditions, organizations were forced to rethink their work. In the business literature, the main strategy for addressing these many new challenges has been through collaboration and partnership. For example, partnerships help combine resources and identify new solutions to problems by combining expertise. Rosabeth Moss Kanter (1996) coined the term "collaborative advantage" to describe the way that private sector organizations had begun to engage in strategic partnerships that enhance institutional capacity to meet the demands of the new environment. In addition, the now famous term "learning organization" coined by Peter Senge (1990) is centered on collaboration (teamwork, cross-functional work) to increase effectiveness and meet external organizational challenges. Government agencies and units also began to reexamine hierarchical structures and implemented Total Quality Management and other techniques to create more cross-functional work (Cohen & Brand, 1993; Osborne & Gaebler, 1992).

As these sectors (government and business in particular) began to re-examine how they function and change how they fundamentally operate, it was only natural that they would want to encourage this type of collaboration within other organizations. Accreditors and state policymakers began to suggest that colleges and universities work across units in order to effectively conduct student assessment, for example. In addition, various funders such as government agencies and foundations began to encourage joint submission of grant proposals to enable cross-sector solutions to societal problems (Ramaley, 2001). The various benefits that accrue to collaborative activities made government and businesses feel compelled to try to encourage this activity on college campuses.

## Advantages of Collaboration

In this section, we review the collaborative advantages that convinced Kanter (1996) and Senge (1990) that successful organizations are ones that can encourage collaborative activities, especially related to their main functions and mission. These collaborative advantages are reasons that business and government have supported and will continue to support collaborations.

### Innovation and Learning

Perhaps the most important and cited advantages to collaboration are that it creates innovation and learning (Senge, 1990;

Googins & Rochlin, 2000). Study after study demonstrates that bureaucratic and hierarchical organizations reinforce the routine following of policies and procedures (Austin, 2000; Barringer & Harrison, 2000; Googins & Rochlin, 2000; Kanter, 1996; Senge, 1990). If people are focused on routines and follow policy exclusively, they will not question ineffective practices and policies or work to innovate. However, organizations that are set up in a matrix fashion (have both horizontal and vertical linkages and connections among staff), with cross-functional structures (different functions within organizations work together and report to each other), or are team based (units work collaboratively rather than individually and in various functional areas) and encourage more interaction, information sharing, communication, and collective problem solving result in innovation and learning. Although there are other outcomes from collaboration, such as increased communication, which can be advantageous itself, collaborative efforts are typically touted for their relationship to innovation (Paulus & Nijstad, 2003). As Mohrman, Cohen, and Mohrman (1995) note: "innovation occurs when different perspectives and knowledge bases are joined, resulting in the reframing of problems and solutions that would not have been likely or possible from within one perspective" (p. 8). Although many college campuses may not see the importance of innovation as easily as businesses that create new products and respond to the changing market, there are many functions on campus that do require innovation. For example, research often involves innovation, particularly applied research. In addition, campuses are being asked to conduct assessment of student learning and institutional effectiveness. Campuses are more likely to innovate and learn if they are set up to create novel solutions. In general, campus environments have changed dramatically (more diverse students, additional technological demands, increased need for security and safety, new skills needed for student success), but processes have not necessarily evolved. Some researchers

(Chafee, 1998; Ewell, 1998; Keith, 1998; Tierney, 1998) suggest that this inability to innovate is compromising higher education's effectiveness and quality.

## Cognitive Complexity

Another important outcome of working in collaborative ways is cognitive complexity (Bensimon & Neumann, 1993; Googins & Rochlin, 2000). Cognitive complexity is a perspective of a problem or issue with nuanced solutions that represents multiple perspectives. Problem solving might not always result in innovation or new ideas, but having a more complex perspective to address problems can enhance solutions. Research on teams, in particular, demonstrates that having individuals that represent different types of expertise (functional area) or background (gender or race or social class) enhances the number of perspectives offered and develops a complex picture, analysis, and resultant solution (Bensimon & Neumann, 1993; Denison, Hart, & Kahn, 1996; Eisenstat & Cohen, 1990; Neumann & Wright, 1999). Collaboration ensures that the needed expertise to problem solve an issue is available and addressed. How many times have you been on a committee that had to address complex problems, such as understanding rising attrition rates or difficulty recruiting a diverse student body, and realized the need for different types of expertise to address the issue? Campuses need to pay more attention to establishing teams with appropriate expertise.

## Better Service

Collaboration also creates better service within an organization (Ascher, 1988; Brown, 2000; Bloland, 1997; Fried, 2000; Denison, Hart, & Kahn, 1996; Hyman, 1995; Swanson & Weese, 1997; Wohlstetter, Malloy, Hentschke, & Smith, 2004). Although organizations create individual units to handle and manage discrete sets of activities, processes cut across organizational units. Organizations that work across functions better address students' needs, for example, by eliminating the need to send a student from advising to financial aid to the TRIO program to obtain a solution to a problem. Because information is shared between offices and communication is open, each office has a better chance of serving students and helping them understand what other office they need to be directed to in order to resolve a problem. This also helps address student concerns more quickly, thus creating greater efficiency and effectiveness. Service offered through siloed organizations typically involves more time to resolve a problem, sending the client to multiple locations, and often leads to incomplete or inaccurate resolution.

### Cost Effectiveness and Efficiency

Collaboration can also decrease costs and lead to greater efficiency (Googins & Rochlin, 2000; Hagadoorn, 1993). If every unit within a college campus decides to set up a separate unit to conduct assessment of student learning, the cost to implement this function will be quite high. However, if a variety of similar units work together to conduct student learning assessment, a cost savings can be obtained. In addition, these units can learn from each other and share ideas about outcomes assessment. The time saved through information sharing also saves money because less time and fewer human resources are used to address common issues on campus. Furthermore, collaboration often leads to learning among people who work together and hence can save professional development money and create greater efficiency as the staff in various units become more effective in conducting their work. Collaborating in this fashion is not an argument for greater centralization of resources, but it is an acknowledgment that collaborating can create cost savings for certain organizational functions. Also, hierarchical organizations tend to be a costly way of integrating complex work. Having a proliferation of managerial and control rules can also result in delays and lack of responsiveness as decisions have to move up the organizational chain.

**Employee Motivation**

One of the least described advantages of collaborative organizations (but a very important one) is that employees tend to be more motivated and committed and have greater job satisfaction. Working in teams can increase desire for personal development, and employees tend to enjoy having more interaction and access to greater information (Denison, Hart, & Kahn, 1996; Googins & Rochlin, 2000). Because individuals work on a variety of projects of interest and share ideas with other people who are interested in similar initiatives, they tend to be more satisfied in their positions. Working with a team or any matrix organization enlarges an individual's experience and usually involves increased responsibility and involvement in decision making, which are all results generally related to improved morale (Denison, Hart, & Kahn, 1996). In short, collaboration can lead to much greater effectiveness, efficiency, and a better work environment.

## Higher Education and the Logic of Collaboration

There is a plethora of evidence from other sectors such as business and government about the advantages of collaboration, as well as increasing research support from within higher education for the need of campuses to rethink their organizational structures in order to reap the rewards of collaboration (Knefelkamp, 1991; Love & Love, 1995; Stein & Short, 2001). It is these rewards and opportunities that compelled leaders such as Donald Kennedy, former President of Harvard, in his book *Academic Duty* (1997), to state that reorganizing higher education institutions for collaboration is one of the primary challenges and has the greatest promise for ensuring excellence in the future. Kennedy and other higher education leaders and scholars have documented how undergraduate education has become impoverished, a decline often exacerbated by siloed departmental structures (Arnold, 2004). Departmental specialization has resulted in students' receiving a fragmented knowledge base with the consequent difficulty in thinking in multifaceted and problem-based ways. Undergraduate education, the primary mission of the higher education system, is impoverished as faculty focus on upper division courses within their disciplinary area of specialization. The departmental structure represents a barrier to creating quality education by stifling collaboration and providing few rewards for focusing on general and liberal arts education. Kennedy has been joined by other major educational leaders such as Derek Bok (1986), and many national associations have critiqued higher education for its individualistic and siloed structure. Perhaps the most well-known document to articulate the benefits and need for collaboration is *Powerful Partnerships: A Shared Responsibility for Learning* (American Association for Higher Education, American College Personnel Association, and National Association of Student Personnel Administrators, 1999). The report makes the case that: "only when everyone on campus—particularly academic and student affairs staff—shares responsibility for student learning will we be able to make significant progress for improving it" (p. 1). The Association of American Colleges and Universities report, *Greater Expectations* (2002), also notes that the future success of higher education is dependent on collaboration across disciplines and units and between higher education and other sectors.

Although much of the concern and pressure to collaborate has focused on the impact of a fragmented learning environment, there have also been critiques to how fragmentation has affected and limited knowledge production (NAS, Institute of Medicine, & NAE, 2005; Paulus & Nijstad, 2003; Rafferty, 1994; Sobol & Newell, 2003). Thus, there has been growing concern that current organizational structures prevent higher education from meeting its mission of providing a quality learning environment, ensuring value added to students by increasing their learning, and creating valuable knowledge for society. Research suggests that collaboration can enhance student learning, enhances research production, improves governance and management, and creates more productive services (Conway-Turner, 1998; Eyler & Giles, 1999; Kezar, Hirsch, & Burack, 2001; Knefelkamp, 1991; Lenning & Ebbers, 1999; Love & Love, 1995; Smith & McCann, 2001).

## Student Learning and Teaching

In their book entitled *Student Success in College*, Kuh, Kinzie, Shuh, & Whitt (2005) identify shared responsibility (collaboration) for educational quality and student success as being associated with campuses that have high levels of student engagement. One of their main conclusions is that leaders should encourage collaboration across functional lines. Colleges and universities with strong levels of student engagement were organized similar to high-performing organizations in business with multiple partnerships, cross-functional collaborations, and teams. Some of the key elements that they note are faculty collaboration across disciplines and units in developing curriculum; student and academic affairs collaboration to develop first-year experience and transition programs, residential programs, and service learning; and inclusion of educators from the library or distance learning into the creation of educational activities. Their research found that students are more likely to thrive and learn when support comes from multiple sources that are working together.[1] For example, summer bridge programs are particularly successful on these campuses because they include expertise from multiple student affairs offices (advising, tutoring, safety), faculty from a variety of units, librarians, students, and key administrators across units.

Although Kuh et al. (2005) examined campuses that are designed to encourage collaborative work and have an overall ethic of collaboration, there is research from studies of specific collaborations (e.g., service learning) that also support the impact of collaboration on student learning. For almost two decades, there has been a concerted movement to create greater collaboration between student and academic affairs. For example, Kuh et al. (2005) concluded that academic and student affairs collaboration helps create innovative solutions and programs that enhance student learning, such as learning communities and undergraduate research experiences; brings a broader expertise and set of perspectives to programs and services offered to students; and provides greater alignment and synergy between the academic mission and services and support of academic mission (Kezar, Hirsch, & Burack, 2001; Schroeder, 1999b).

Higher education institutions are realizing the importance of enabling internal collaboration to create a better learning environment and as a result a variety of new collaborative practices have emerged and studies have been conducted on their effectiveness. Several recent studies of interdisciplinary teaching (Barkley, Cross, & Major, 2004; Conway-Turner, 1998; Smith & McCann, 2001), learning communities (Smith & McCann, 2001), and community service learning (Eyler & Giles, 1999) illustrate that these collaborations enhance student performance on many learning measures. Interdisciplinary teaching has been found to promote greater student engagement in learning, increased likelihood to develop higher cognitive skills (i.e., problem solving and critical thinking), promotion of creative thinking, increased sensitivity to ethical issues, and a greater tolerance for ambiguity (Hursch, Hass, & Moore, 1983; Newell, 1994, 1998; Newell & Green, 1982). Furthermore, collaborative learning contributes to an openness to diverse perspectives, fosters persistence in college, and promotes greater faculty-student interaction, which has a notable impact on student success and learning (Astin, 1993; Cabrera et al., 2002; Pascarella & Terenzini, 2005). Similar to interdisciplinary learning, partnerships among multiple departments and units have a positive impact on student learning (Bosworth & Hamilton, 1994). The study of Kuh et al. (2005) on student engagement also found that shared responsibility among multiple groups (i.e., student and academic affairs, staff, and faculty) enhances student learning and success. Students experience increased student engagement and a greater sense of integration into the college, experience that also leads to student success (Nesheim et al., 2007).

## Research

Collaboration has the opportunity to improve research and knowledge production. A variety of authors have noted how interdisciplinary research, which draws on the expertise of faculty across various units, creates innovative and holistic knowledge that improves our understanding (NAS, Institute of Medicine, & NAE, 2005; Paulus & Nijstad, 2003; Rafferty, 1994; Sobol & Newell, 2003). For example, studies demonstrate how interdisciplinary research enhances research production and improves understanding of how to address issues of poverty, infectious diseases, environmental degradation, and health care (Bradshaw et al., 2003; Frost & Jean, 2003; Frost, Jean, Teodorescu, & Brown, 2004; Mattila, 2005; Ramaley, 2001). Similarly, faculty who have developed multi- and interdisciplinary research centers to address pressing problems of our times often obtain greater funding from external sources and develop richer knowledge (Boardman & Ponomariov, 2007; Frost & Jean, 2003). The National Science Foundation and National Institutes of Health have been encouraging higher education institutions to create interdisciplinary research institutes to draw on the expertise across campuses and to create more innovative and holistic research. The benefits of interdisciplinary research and multidisciplinary research centers are many. Researchers note that interdisciplinary research centers allow for the sharing and synthesis of knowledge across a wide set of disciplines, enable more rapid sharing of information, forge external and internal networks, raise prestige, promote faculty productivity, and stimulate the production of new and innovative research (John-Steiner, 2000; Frost, Jean, Teodorescu, & Brown, 2004; London & Walsh, 1975; Younglove-Webb, Gray, Abdalla, & Purvis Thurow, 1999). Multidiscipline, multipurpose university research centers (MMURC), which are specifically funded by the National Science Foundation's Engineering Research Center and

Science and Technology Centers programs, are attributed with increasing technology transfer (Boardman & Ponomariov, 2007). MMURCs have contributed the promotion of technology sharing between universities and industry, which often leads to new technologies available to the general public.

In addition to the overall benefits of interdisciplinary and multidisciplinary research centers, there are also benefits to the individuals who participate in this form of research. Boardman and Ponomariov (2007) note that faculty who are involved in MMURCs not only gain access to additional resources and are able to associate with the prestige of these centers, they gain a sense of satisfaction by contributing to society. Sharing their skills and research often leads to the development of new technologies that industry is able to produce and make available to the general public. In turn, academic departments become more problem based as MMURCs involve more faculty and integrate into the academic culture. MMURCs are important research centers; they have afforded substantial federal funding and serve as a model of the potential benefits of collaborative interdisciplinary and multidisciplinary research.

Interdisciplinary and multidisciplinary research is not without its challenges. A lack of reward for collaborative research in the tenure and promotion process (Arreola et al., 2003; Bozeman & Boardman, 2004; Frost, Jean, Teodorescu, & Brown, 2004), expectations to complete work in both the department and research centers (Frost, Jean, Teodorescu, & Brown, 2004), and challenges to academic norms often lead to conflicts between disciplines and interdisciplinary work (Bohen & Stiles, 1998). However, the benefits of interdisciplinary research—the development of innovative and creative research, technology transfer with industry, increased likelihood of receiving external funding, and individual satisfaction for contributing to society—underscores the necessity that teams working together overcome those obstacles (Ancona & Caldwell, 1992; Austin & Baldwin, 1991). Simply put, the benefits of interdisciplinary and multidisciplinary research outweigh the challenges.

## Improved Governance and Management

It is significant that collaboration not only fundamentally improves the core mission of postsecondary institutions (teaching, learning, and research), but it is also helpful in improving governance and management. Although higher education institutions have a history of shared governance (in contrast to the individualistic approach to teaching and research), the range of stakeholders involved in shared governance has been limited. For example, staff, students, and nontenure track faculty, which make up over 50 percent of the faculty, are often not involved in the governance of the institution. Collaborative efforts that involve people across various units usually result in a broadening of governance on campus to include new groups (Astin, Astin, & Associates, 2001; Kuh, 2006; Kuh et al., 2005). For example, in the effort to create a learning community, new stakeholders are brought to the table, such as librarians, clinical staff, and students (Bourassa & Kruger, 2001). These new stakeholders are usually recognized for having important ideas and input. As a result, campus leaders often realize the need to alter governance structures to be more inclusive. Research on governance in higher education demonstrates how increasing stakeholder groups' input leads to several important outcomes: it (1) increases the complexity of analysis, (2) results in stronger decisions, (3) develops greater buy-in and trust, and (4) tends to improve morale (Birnbaum, 1992; Bensimon & Neumann, 1993; Ferren & Stanton, 2004; Kezar, Carducci, & Contreras-McGavin, 2006).

## Operations and Service

Collaboration also can create greater effectiveness and efficiency in day-to-day operations (Ferren & Stanton, 2004; Fried, 2000; Hyman, 1995; Muraskin & Lee, 2004; Schroeder, Minor, & Tarkow, 1999). For example, management is more effective on a campus that establishes a budget process in which all units work together to create the overall budget and have input on the budgets of other units. When this process is well structured, resource allocation matches more closely the needs and priorities of the campus rather than being overtaken by politics and personal relationships. Many college campuses have to make difficult financial choices. State budgets have provided few increases for postsecondary institutions in the last few decades. Funding is shrinking for higher education as foundations and corporations provide fewer resources (Ehrenberg, 2006). However, corporations are more likely to give funding if higher education can demonstrate its accountability by providing services in the most efficient and cost-effective way. Campuses that can demonstrate how they work in nonbureaucratic and responsive ways attract attention from philanthropy and business.

## Summary

This chapter has described how collaboration has become an imperative for higher education. A variety of influential external groups and agencies are encouraging higher education to reconsider the way it operates. The stakes are high, as many of these external groups provide funding to higher education. The chapter also outlined the many opportunities and advantages that result from working in a collaborative fashion based on research from a variety of sectors and also specifically within higher education. But to meet this imperative, it is necessary to understand some of the challenges to creating partnerships. This is the topic of the next chapter.

### Notes

1. Kuh et al. (2005) can only measure proxies for learning outcomes. National Survey of Student Engagement (NSSE) measures areas such as educational challenge, active and collaborative learning, faculty-student interaction, support services, and enriching educational experiences.

# 2

# The Challenges of Collaboration

*No matter how many good ideas emerge on this campus,*
*they fail in the face of the history and approach to doing*
*things. People retreat into their routines.*

*Faculty member, community college*

*Faculty and administrators cannot work together, and at*
*times work at odds with each other. The plethora of units,*
*divisions and departments is staggering. I have given up*
*on the idea of collaboration or people working together in*
*meaningful ways.*

*Staff member, research university*

These remarks voice the frustration of faculty and staff at colleges and universities who have tried to partner and collaborate. They represent the struggles of people with a desire to break from current organizational habits who are nevertheless locked into particular institutional structures and cultures. Most people are unaware that these structures and processes represent an institutional and academic history that goes back a hundred years and reflects norms that reach far beyond the campus walls and borders. Leaders will not be effective in creating partnerships unless they understand that the structures that undergird most postsecondary institutions prevent collaboration. One of the first steps in helping to eradicate these barriers is to be aware of the structures, processes, and routines that prevent collaboration. Through this consciousness, leaders can intentionally change these processes and structures to better support collaborative work. In this chapter, we review individualistic structures and processes that make collaboration difficult and present a model for redesigning campuses that helps overcome these barriers.

## Higher Education as a Siloed, Bureaucratic, and Hierarchical Organization

Campuses across the country have attempted to develop a host of initiatives (service learning, learning communities) to improve education without taking on the challenge of reorganizing, often only to find these entrepreneurial efforts thwarted by traditional structures and processes. We hope to fill a gap in our understanding by presenting the results of a research study of institutions that have broken free from their historical structures and been exemplary in organizing for collaborative work. However, many institutions are still struggling to develop a collaborative context and promote collaborative work. If collaboration is so important, why is it often so difficult? Also, why is collaboration more difficult on certain college campuses?

One has to examine the history and development of higher education to understand how the structures and cultures that emerged support and reinforce individualized rather than collaborative work. As Philpott and Strange (2003) note, college campuses in the 1800s were structured for more collaborative work, but changes over the course of the last hundred years have created a situation in which "faculty and other campus constituents may have all but forgotten how to collaborate on common educational goals and programs" (p. 78). This does not suggest that all universities are the same. Research universities, for example, are even more closely aligned with the individualistic model. The key areas to review are specialization, professionalization, disciplines and departments, paradigmatic differences, faculty training and socialization, loose coupling, reward systems, bureaucratic and hierarchical administrative structures, clash between academic and administrative cultures, staff subcultures, differentiation between academic and student affairs, and responsibility-centered budgeting, which are all structures that have historical roots as supporting individualistic behaviors. The focus in this section is on ways that higher education has been structured historically and how this structure can be altered.

### Specialization

Since the turn of the last century, one of the fundamental organizing principles of the academy has been specialization and fragmentation into new units (Knefelkamp, 1991; Schroeder, 1999b; Smith, 1982). As new areas of knowledge developed, new disciplines were created, separate from others. As a result, research and teaching became increasingly specialized. A sociologist, for instance, no longer has familiarity with history or anthropology or psychology, which were all related fields. In addition to specialization among faculty, specialization also occurs in administrative structures, with a profusion of new units ranging from advising to financial aid to the student union to housing, and so on. Each unit developed its own goals and values, as did each discipline. With specialization came differing goals and values, across the campus. Remember, our definitions of collaboration, common goals, and values are critical. Without any kind of common vision about the goals or values for the institution and educational processes, different units had an increasingly difficult time working together and understanding each other. Specialization became a value in itself, and faculty and staff on campus began to see their individual work or perspective as more important than the overall goals or mission for the campus or any agreed-upon set of competencies. Knowledge production and teaching were seen as discrete and fragmented processes rather than as holistic or integrated.

## Professionalization

As faculty and staff conceptualized themselves as having specialized knowledge, they worked to professionalize their areas of work. They developed standards of performance and accountability and also suggested that their knowledge and expertise should grant them power and authority over certain decision making. Faculty, for example, argued that they should have input and authority over the curriculum. Certain administrative areas asserted that they should have fiduciary responsibility or legal responsibility within the campus environment. As various groups laid claim to decision-making power, decision making became more decentralized on campuses. In addition, various groups made arguments for autonomy in their work, no longer seeking input from the general faculty or staff. Professionalization resulted in decision making becoming more isolated within certain groups and provided more autonomy so that the groups were not required to work together toward the overall benefit of the campus. Although the claims for professional autonomy made sense, they also served as barriers to collaboration by creating decentralized decision-making bodies and limiting coordination among units. Being aware of the decentralized decision-making structures and value of professional autonomy is key in overcoming these structures and moving toward collaboration.

## Disciplines and Departments

In the 1800s, faculty were part of the academic profession and felt great affinity as an academic group. However, with the rise of specialization, they began to segment and affiliate by discipline. Over time, disciplines have created specific cultures that differ dramatically between departments and may create tensions within and across disciplinary collaborations (Birnbaum, 1991; Bohen & Stiles, 1998; Clark, 1991). Tony Beecher (1989) has described how faculty members have become so divided they are like separate tribes with their own fiefdoms. These disciplines have distinctive goals for the profession and different ways of approaching teaching and research (described further under paradigms), working with students, and structuring their work together (Diamond & Bronwyn, 2004). Faculty in the physical sciences favor experimental and hands-on work with students whereas those in the humanities favor more abstract forms of learning. Faculty in the social sciences may work in a more democratic governance fashion whereas faculty in business may take more a authority-based form of governance. Faculty now define themselves and their identity by their discipline and often spend more time working within their disciplinary organization or affiliating with disciplinary colleagues. Faculty no longer have that sense of being part of the overall institution and faculty.

One result of specialization and disciplinary differences is the proliferation of bureaucratic and administrative structures to support particular areas of expertise. For example, in the early 1990s, faculty divided into departments based typically on disciplines that had their own decision-making structures and were responsible for the main work of teaching, research, and service within the specialization; the departments became increasingly disconnected from the overall university and its goals and values (Thelin, 2004). This further separated faculty, who were already meeting based on disciplines but were now moved into different buildings, met and worked separately based on discipline, and became isolated in departmental structures

Another result of the organization of disciplines and departments into silos is the lack of knowledge sharing between and among faculty exacerbated by "profound and extensive" difference among the disciplines (Boardman & Bozeman, 2007; Bozeman & Boardman, 2004; Braxton & Hargens, 1996, p. 35). Research collaborations often require faculty to come together under the larger umbrella of a research project or topic. The ability to draw from some common knowledge is important for moving the collaboration forward.

The separate department affiliations can also result in competition. Collaborative work competes with traditional disciplines for intellectual and financial resources (Frost, Jean, Teodorescu, & Brown, 2004). Establishing collaboratives across disciplines pulls faculty away from the work of the traditional discipline and into a "third sphere" where faculty expend their time and energy working in a collaboration that may, in fact, compete with traditional disciplines for grants or other institutional resources. Thus competition not only promotes more individualistic faculty work but also has the potential to create competitive departmental cultures in which departments and interdisciplinary collaborations compete for the same resources.

### Paradigmatic Differences

One of the consequences of disciplinary specialization and separation into separate departments is differences in inquiry paradigms. Defined as "the basic belief system or worldview that guides the investigator" (Guba & Lincoln, 1999, p. 105), inquiry paradigms guide how faculty think about and conduct research. If different paradigms exist among faculty in a collaborative project, collaboration becomes more difficult. For example, a collaborative team of faculty in the hard sciences, who generally adopt more experimental processes while seeking definite results, stands in contrast to a team of faculty in the humanities, who use more interpretive processes and more complex research results. Creamer (2003), in a study of collaborations that have extended over the course of many decades, found that paradigmatic differences can be overcome through strong personal relationships, respect for expertise, willingness to work through differences, and a commitment to creating a common inquiry. Yet these are fundamental differences that may take a long time of working together to overcome.

### Faculty Training and Socialization

Not only are faculty socialized into particular disciplines and paradigms, but they also are trained to work mostly in isolation.

Particularly in the humanities and social sciences, graduate students may spend many years working in virtual isolation on archival research or on an empirical research study. Dissertations are an individual activity and as graduate students become faculty members, they typically are encouraged to develop a research agenda that highlights their individual contribution. Collaborative efforts are highly discouraged before achieving tenure. For many faculty, this means working independently for at least fifteen years. After such a long time working alone, faculty are not likely to be inclined to work with others and have not learned the skills to work collaboratively. Although there are variations by institutional type, and some faculty at teaching institutions do not spend as much time in isolation from others, the culture of the academy reinforces individual work. The sciences have moved away from this model and work more in teams. However, the hierarchal arrangements of many of these teams and bounded roles often create an environment in which teams are not particularly collaborative and faculty do not necessarily learn collaborative skills.

## Loose Coupling

Another characteristic of higher education that makes collaboration difficult as a result of departmental growth, disciplinary and professional subdivisions, and professionalization is loose coupling (Weick, 1991). An institution with loose coupling is characterized by decentralized systems and processes, limited coordination among units, greater structural differentiation, limited connections between people, and specialization and redundancy of work and functions (Weick, 1991). Loose coupling reflects how organizations operate under the conditions of specialization, professionalization, and decentralization of power and demonstrates how these structural factors operate to reinforce each other, creating an environment that is even more challenging for collaborative efforts (Frost, Jean, Teodorescu, & Brown, 2004). Academic units of colleges tend to be even more loosely coupled than administrative units. Collaboration is typically inhospitable within a loosely coupled system, because of the lack of connections between people and increased specialization—especially large-scale campuswide initiatives. When collaboration does occur, it is likely to occur in pockets at local levels (Salter & Hearn, 1996). Small-scale, improvisational, synchronistic, and local collaborations are encouraged within a loosely coupled system but often have high rates of failure and often may not spread out of the marginal area (Weick, 1991).

## Reward Systems

Reward systems on campus overwhelmingly support individualistic work, particularly for faculty who are judged on their single author publications, individual teaching evaluations, and singular leadership efforts. Tenure and promotion systems, which are historically based on the German university system, are focused generally on the work of individuals and not the contribution to a collaborative process, such as interdisciplinarity (Diamond & Bronwyn, 2004; Lattuca, 2001). Staff and administrators are also rewarded on their individual performance. Merit is obtained by individuals who create new programs, meet individual goals, and demonstrate personal development and growth. Some campuses might include contribution to collaborative efforts in a reward system, but these are typically not weighed as heavily as individual work. In addition to institutional reward systems, other merit systems have also traditionally lauded individual work. Patents, for example, which are commonly sought after in the hard sciences, are often rewarded to one individual and not to a collaborative team. This lack of external support and funding often reinforces individualistic work over collaborative work. In the last few years, some funding agencies such as the National Science Foundation have made efforts to increase collaboration by requiring that grants and research be formed via a collaborative team. We have yet to see the impact of collaborative funding on patents and other external funding sources, however.

Faculty grapple with conflicts that devalue or do not recognize collaborative work. Bohen and Stiles (1998) in a study of collaborative interdisciplinary initiative at Harvard found that faculty who participate in collaborations add this responsibility on top of their traditional academic work. The expectations of traditional academic disciplines are not substituted by collaborative work. Faculty must fulfill responsibilities in their departments as well as in the context of the collaboration. Collaborations that result in team-teaching or other curricular reform rarely result in monetary rewards or course releases. Often, team-teaching is above and beyond normal teaching expectations. Therefore, disciplinary and department structures instantiate rewards within these processes by making work outside of them mostly unvalued and unrecognized.

## Bureaucratic and Hierarchical Administrative Structures

Colleges and universities developed complex administrative structures during the twentieth century. They followed the example of businesses and corporations of the time, which created increasingly vertical organizations shaped by command-and-control leadership and standard policies and procedures to dictate behavior and ensure uniformity of activities (Knefelkamp, 1991; Schroeder, 1999a, 1999b; Thompson, 1965). Bureaucratic and hierarchical structures limit communication flow across the organization by making horizontal work more difficult as people communicate and interact less often (Schroeder, 1999a, 1999b). People are encouraged to share information up the chain of command but not across the organization to other similar units; horizontal communication is often cut off. Bureaucratic structures also self-proliferate by hiring more layers of individuals to oversee and standardize work rather than perform specific tasks, thus creating greater costs, separating people, and causing communication challenges. Vice-presidents, deans, and other high-level administrative positions were created to oversee areas of service and work.

Many middle managers were hired to oversee staff. Department chairs became managers within the faculty to ensure that certain work was conducted in a uniform fashion that fit within the norms and structures of a vertical hierarchy. Hierarchy, in particular, limits communication flow horizontally, as communication chains emphasize that information should flow up through the chain of command. Bureaucratic structures also limit the flow of information to only the relevant group within the specific silos or areas of work. Individuals become more focused on their limited area of work, whether it be legal issues, athletics, or auxiliary services, rather than thinking about the institution as a whole. As people become more isolated within the bureaucratic silos, they have more difficulty seeing the overall goals of the organization and contributing to collaborative work.

## Clash Between Academic and Administrative Cultures

Over time, the governance of colleges and universities has shifted from being largely in the hands of presidents and boards (1800s to early 1900s) to being shared with faculty as they professionalized (1920s) to even greater degrees of involvement of faculty after World War II. In more recent years (1980 to present), however, administrators have centralized governance again. The shifts in power and attempts by faculty to have input have resulted in a clash between faculty and administrators who are competing for power and influence within institutional decision making. A divide has developed between academics and administrators (typically senior administrators) as their foci have become substantially differentiated. Academics-faculty and administrative units have different priorities, perspectives, and competing domains (Birnbaum, 1991; Cohen & March, 1976; Kuh, 1999; Rice, Sorcinelli, & Austin, 2000). Moreover, administrators and academics are positioned differently within the organization and are under different institutional expectations (Bok, 1986).

The work of administrators is bureaucratically defined with legal and fiduciary concerns; it is focused, however, on specific goals such as efficiency and effectiveness that require a more holistic approach to the institution.[1] In some situations, administrators might foster collaboration because of their holistic view of campus in which they see the value of learning communities. However, based on their financial perspective, they might decide that the endeavor is too costly to support.

Academics and faculty, however, are more autonomous and more focused on their scholarship and less concerned with collective decision making. In short, they are often disconnected from larger institutional priorities. Also, academic units and leaders may be more concerned with values underlying decisions rather than outcomes. They also tend to favor rationale outside of efficiency, emphasized within staff culture. Although they may be less able to view the institution and decisions holistically from their standpoint, they have special knowledge from often being placed closer to the issues of teaching, learning, and research. Also, their ability to examine underlying values and alternative rationale can develop complex solutions. Academics and faculty may support collaboration when they see a strong rationale for it, but they might also block collaboration based on their interest in autonomy and decentralization (Engstrom & Tinto, 2000). Situations vary, but in general, the different perspectives and positions of academic and administrative cultures create a clash in values that may lead to differences in the need for beliefs about and values of collaborative work.

## Staff Subcultures

Staff are broken up into various subunits and develop their own cultures and approach to their work. Business affairs, student affairs, planning officers, institutional researchers, financial aid, librarians, legal staff, secretaries, and development and alumni affairs all have very different approaches to the way they conduct their work. They each belong to separate professional associations and are part of different networks on campus. Many of these offices have little interaction and operate in silos. A lawyer or business officer on a campus may have more connections with lawyers or business officers in other sectors than they do with other staff on campus. Although staff often do not have the power of decision making within their own units, the multiplicity of subunits creates difficulty in integrating across services and processes. These subcultures were created from several of the conditions noted above, including their move to specialize and professionalize and the bureaucratic structures that emerged to support the various areas.

## Differentiation Between Student and Academic Affairs

Although various subcultures and differentiation among areas of expertise have developed over time (including the division between academics and faculty and administrative staff), the differentiation between academic and student affairs is another of the pronounced divisions that prevent collaboration on campus. The development of student affairs decades ago signaled a shift from institutions that were entirely focused on the mind of the student to an understanding of the social and psychological needs of the student. To accommodate student needs beyond academics, student affairs offices (i.e., orientation, student activities, counseling services, and residential life) were created with the mission of supporting students outside the classroom. Student affairs programs have grown in significance and size as they integrate the student into the social world of the college and provide a large number of support services. However, the differentiation between student affairs as responsible for the social welfare of the student and academic affairs as developing the mind of the student has created a substantial divide between the two units of a university. Despite the call from policymakers to create a more seamless learning environment, student and academic affairs do not collaborate extensively.

## Responsibility-Centered Management

Responsibility-centered management emerged more recently as a trend across the academy, but it can have a profound impact on collaboration nonetheless. Responsibility-centered management is a fiscal system in which various units or schools are responsible for their own revenue developments and covering costs. The units pay a tax to the overall institution to pay for certain infrastructure (e.g., campus administration, student affairs). Previous fiscal models, operating at the overall campus level, might have certain units that were more profitable and others that were less profitable and the institution just looked at the overall bottom line. However, some institutions want to create incentives for all units to be profitable, and by making units responsible for their own expenses, this ensures that none have losses. This form of management also creates incentives for units that make profits by sharing revenues. One of the disadvantages of responsibility-centered management and budgeting is that schools end up competing for students and course units in order to increase their revenue stream. Collaboration that would benefit students and learning (such as team-teaching) can be compromised as units focus on creating additional revenues and not giving revenues. Also, faculty resource sharing is discouraged, which is often a part of interdisciplinary teaching and research. A sociologist will not be encouraged to teach a course in the policy program because the salary of the faculty members paid out of sociology and the income for a course in policy will only go to school policy. Grant projects across multiple units have to divide out revenue, so deans and administrators encourage faculty to obtain grants individually rather than work in cross-campus collaboratives.

## Summary

In order to change the field of higher education, it is important to understand the structures and culture that have been created within it. Historical vestiges of an emphasis on individualistic work are the key areas that need to be altered in order to enable or support collaborative work. But what has become the norm—departments, disciplines, and siloed units—is not easily changed. Some campuses have tried to eradicate departments, but the individualistic values that supported the rise of these structures still remain. Given the current structure of most college campuses (shaped by their histories), collaboration will not happen easily and needs to be consciously designed. In this book we describe a set of campuses that have fundamentally reorganized and challenged the normative structure of higher education. Thus we hope to illustrate the potential for redesigning higher education to support collaboration.

## Addressing the Challenges: Reorganizing and Redesigning for Collaborative Work

With the study results presented in this book we hope to demonstrate how campuses overcame the challenges noted throughout this chapter. Before moving into the results, we present the framework, assumptions, and methodology for the study. This book focuses on a major gap in the literature and in our understanding: how the overall environment or organizational context can enhance collaboration. The *organizational context* refers to major structural, process, human, political, and cultural elements such as institutional policies, organizational charts, decision-making processes, leadership, training, climate, and politics. It is a comprehensive term and includes the major elements of an organization. Liedtka (1996) found that a supportive context that provides commitment, processes, and resources to facilitate collaboration was critical to making collaboration a reality within organizations. All the advantages to collaborative work described in the last chapter are likely to occur only in collaborative efforts that are well designed to overcome the barriers described in this chapter thus far. Many studies have shown that without the proper supports, whether they are training or rewards, collaborative initiatives do not reap the benefits, and poorly implemented cross-functional efforts can even worsen morale, exacerbate divisiveness, and elevate cynicism. So although there is substantial promise in working in collaborative ways, if organizations do not carefully design these processes, they will not obtain the benefits and could create even greater problems. Understanding the organizational features that support collaboration in higher education—a topic about which there have been very little research and virtually no publications in higher education—is the original contribution of this book.

Because researchers have realized that collaborative efforts need to be well designed to obtain the benefits, a variety of studies have been conducted to help guide the work of teams (the most collaborative unit). The work on teams focuses on an assortment of issues ranging from group composition and dynamics (Bensimon & Neumann, 1993; Denison, Hart, and Kahn, 1996; Jassawalla & Sashittal, 1999) to task design (Denison, Hart, and Kahn, 1996; Holland, Gaston, and Gomes, 2000) to the attitudes and beliefs (Liedtka, 1996; Tjosvold & Tsao, 1989) necessary for collaboration. Researchers have historically emphasized individual and group dynamics but have missed the systemic elements of the organization that need to be changed in order to make collaboration successful (Denison, Hart, & Kahn, 1996; Kidwell, Mossholder, & Bennet, 1997; Stewart & Manz, 1995). We recommend that readers obtain these texts to complement (Bensimon & Neumann, 1993, for example) the macro organizational issues we are presenting in this book.

This research builds on Mohrman, Cohen, and Mohrman (1995), who conducted one of the first studies of how organizations can enable collaborative activities. Mohrman, Cohen, and Mohrman claim that one of the main reasons collaboration fails is that organizational leaders cannot impose collaboration within a context designed to support individualistic work (most earlier research tries to "fit" collaboration within traditional organizational boundaries—the proverbial square peg into the round hole). They hypothesized that to make collaboration successful, organizations need to be redesigned to enhance group and cross-divisional work, which otherwise typically fails. They suggest that if organizations want to be serious about creating more cross-functional and collaborative work, they need to move to a team-based organization or design. The organizational context features that need to be redesigned to enable collaboration include structure, processes, people, and rewards. Although how these features might be changed varies based on institutional culture or context, these same essential features tend to be important, regardless. They reinforce that the transition to an organization that supports collaborative work is pervasive (that is, involving change in almost all aspects of the organization), involves the whole organization (cannot be contained in particular units), and is deep (requiring changes in the assumptions and beliefs of organizational members). This approach was created to understand the creation of a collaborative context in the corporate sector and it is the most comprehensive model to date.

Their model identifies six specific areas that need to be altered to successfully design an organization that can support collaboration. First, the *strategy* or what the organization is trying to accomplish (in higher education this would be akin to *mission*) needs to be adjusted. Second, the *tasks or the work of the organization* need to be reexamined—in higher education this would be equivalent to the teaching process. Third, the *structure* will need to be changed in order to create integrating mechanisms; therefore, a centralized division might need to be created to link several currently disparate activities. Fourth, the general *processes* such as goal setting, management, and decision making need to be modified to support collaboration (e.g., teams and collaboratives need to be able to develop a set of objectives from the bottom up that fit in with the overall organizational goals). Fifth, *rewards* need to be developed to provide incentive and accountability systems that recognize teams rather than individuals. The major system within higher education is the promotion and tenure process. Sixth, *people* need to be trained and given skill development in the area of collaboration. The strength of this model is its emphasis on comprehensive redesign of the organization from its strategy, processes, human capital, type of work, and rewards.

There is a heavy emphasis on management, rewards, and accountability within this model.

## Study of Collaborative Contexts

We used the Mohrman, Cohen, and Mohrman (MCM) model as a point of departure for studying collaboration in higher education, specifically by examining whether campuses that had high levels of collaboration had reorganized in some way and documented the key elements that allowed collaboration to flourish. Because the MCM model was developed within the corporate sector, we imagined that not all aspects of the model may be applicable to higher education and that new aspects might emerge within postsecondary institutions for fostering collaboration. Organizational theory suggests that models should be altered to the particular context to which they are applied. Theories often transcend contexts, but models should be examined within particular settings. Therefore, the MCM model was tested in this study within four higher education institutions where collaboration flourished. In order to test the model, we decided that intensive case study design would be best. We provide a brief summary of the methodology here; for more details please see Appendix A.

In order to identify institutions for case study, we requested nominations from national higher education associations. Our criteria were relatively simple: we wanted to identify institutions with high levels of collaborative work but that were not created with a specific mission or structure to support collaboration. For example, campuses such as Evergreen State that were specifically developed with collaboration as part of their underlying philosophy and structure from the beginning were not chosen. We identified four institutions that had initially been developed within traditional norms of higher education based on individualistic norms and bureaucratic structures. We wanted institutions that represent the typical postsecondary institution but that had shifted in more recent years to support more collaborative work. We examined institutions that had gone through this transition and documented what changes they had to undergo in order to make this significant change. These institutions can be helpful to other institutions across the country that need to make this same transition. Another criterion was that the institutions have a variety of collaborative initiatives occurring. Some campuses have one or two collaboratives that have been successful through the sheer charisma and leadership of a single individual. Although these are important to document as well, we were more interested in campuses that support collaborative work, rather than merely documenting the work of a single charismatic leader. We also chose to focus on one institutional type: comprehensive, regional publics. This is among the largest sectors and the one most directly affected by recent budget cuts. These institutions are in even greater need for strategies for collaboration. Consequently, four public comprehensive institutions were explored.

After a set of institutions was identified, we contacted them to find out what type of collaborative activities were occurring on campus to be sure they were involved in high levels of collaborative work across a variety of practices including teaching, research, management, and service. Once institutions were identified, we conducted case site visits to each institution, conducting interviews with approximately thirty to forty people on campus who were active leaders in collaborative initiatives. We also spoke with administrators and faculty who were not involved in establishing collaboratives in order to understand how typical individuals on campus view and participate in collaboration. On each campus we made sure to talk to faculty across a variety of disciplines, staff in multiple units, and administrators at various levels. In addition to interviews, we obtained documents related to the campus context and its collaborative work, including mission statements, strategic plans, accreditation reports, and minutes from meetings. We also reviewed their Web site for reference to collaboration and took campus tours and analyzed the physical environment to determine how it might enable collaboration. Finally, we attended meetings of certain collaborative groups to understand how they work together and interviewed them to identify in what ways they felt the institutional context enabled or hindered their collaborative work. During our observations and document analysis, we concentrated on describing what collaborative activities they were engaged in and assessing what systems were in place to support their collaborative efforts and what they believed contributed to their success in collaboration. Through these multiple data collection techniques, we were able to develop a model of how higher education institutions need to reorganize in order to support collaborative work.

## Note

1. Even though colleges and universities adopted many business principles as they developed their administrative structures, many faculty today are concerned about administrators adopting management trends because faculty feel these are faddish practices that harm the institution. Business approaches such as total quality management or reengineering attempt to create fewer hierarchical and bureaucratic structures and were used to transform business environments into more team-based and innovative organizations. Business process reengineering allows organizations to review their processes and to adapt structures for more effective work (Davenport, 1993; Hammer & Champy, 1993). Many campuses have tried to use some of these

business models to make changes on campus and are moving away from bureaucratic and hierarchical structures, but there is great resistance. Also, much research has been conducted on the failure of efforts such as total quality management (Birnbaum, 2000). Even if colleges or universities currently resist business models, they need to acknowledge that these very models created the current structure of campuses and locked them into processes and structures that do not allow much vertical communication and blending of functions.

# 3

# Taking Advantage of Collaboration

## *Synergizing Successful Practices*

You may be wondering what a campus that has reorganized itself for collaborative work looks like or what exemplary collaborative practices you might want to integrate on your campus. In this chapter, we describe a campus that demonstrates the activities and processes that you can expect to see on campuses that are meeting the collaborative imperative and becoming more effective institutions, reaping the benefits of the collaborative advantage. The difference between this campus and campuses across the country that have a single or small number of initiatives such as an interdisciplinary research center or service learning program is that the campus we describe has made organizational changes in order to facilitate collaborative work, conducts this work with greater ease than other campuses, and believes these efforts are sustainable.

Instead of viewing an assortment of collaborative practices that higher education should consider to improve student learning (such as learning communities, service learning, or team teaching), enhance research (interdisciplinary and cross campus research centers), revitalize campus service (community and university partnerships), or improve campus management (business process reengineering or cross functional teams), in this chapter we demonstrate how just one change—toward a reorganized campus— can facilitate all these initiatives. People need a vision for a new collaborative approach that they believe can be implemented on their campus. But some campuses are forward thinking in the area of teaching, for instance, but not in research or management. In this chapter we show that collaboration can be important to transforming all of these areas on campus (if so desired).

What campuses are lacking is the *vision* for a collaborative campus. This chapter illustrates, through a case example, how the specific elements outlined in this book can be used to successfully create a collaborative culture. All of the important reforms we discuss are currently touted as important teaching, learning, and management innovations, but campuses often have difficulty in making these changes and do not realize why. We hope the example of "Collaborative University" helps other campuses see how they might rethink their current work.[1] This example is culled from the research study and is a real, nonfictionalized example. It is not meant to be a prescription for what a collaborative campus should look like; we acknowledge that the specific types of collaboration in teaching, research, and service will probably vary by institutional type and culture. Every campus will need to individually develop its own vision. We hope this example helps with this process. Chapters in Part Two of the book provide specific guidance on how to achieve this vision and provide more specifics.

## Collaborative University

Collaborative University is a public university located in the eastern part of the United States. As a young university (founded in the 1970s), Collaborative University has a strong reputation in the areas of law, economics, and public policy. The enrollment at the university is quite large, with over 25,000 students in both undergraduate and graduate education. Collaborative University is distinct in that it focuses on interdisciplinary research, collaborative forms of teaching, integration of traditional academic structures, distributed leadership, and an active process of rethinking physical space. However, a focus on collaboration was not an inherent aspect of the university, but a value that emerged over time due to external pressure and the university mission.

A major factor in the development of a collaborative ethic at the university was external pressure that came in the form of federal funding agencies, national trends related to teaching and learning, individual funders interested in supporting multidisciplinary work, and statewide resources for innovative programs. Specifically, federal funding agencies (i.e., National Science Foundation and National Institutes of Health) began to require that grant awards have faculty from across disciplines working in a collaborative fashion on projects. Collaborative University was also approached by several philanthropists with an interest in funding interdisciplinary research centers, thus adding pressure to focus on a cooperative model. Moreover, statewide programs and national trends emerged with a focus on innovative teaching practices. Also, Collaborative University was exploring ways to differentiate itself from other state institutions. A focus on collaboration and innovation in teaching and learning would distinguish it from state institutions with a greater distance education and research focus. All of these factors synergistically led the university to considering how to become more collaborative. The result is the collaborative ethic illustrated in this chapter.

In today's higher education climate, these same external pressures are still in place. Thus Collaborative University is a timely example of the ways that campuses can infuse a collaborative ethic into their mission and activities. Also important is that Collaborative University did not just have set funding or gifts to create collaboration but made the shift with existing operational funds, as most institutions will need to.

The focus on collaboration is embodied in the mission statement of the university, which serves as a guidepost for all activities within the university, as well as an indicator of the value placed on collaborative activities. The mission statement calls for the university to respond to the call for interdisciplinary research by rethinking traditional academic structures and specifically mentions a value placed on responding to the needs of the community. The university mission statement was established in the early 1990s during a pivotal time in which the university began its focus on collaboration. The mission is, therefore, the starting point for many of the activities presented in this chapter.

The mission of the university has guided the rethinking of traditional academic structures. Rather than having a division of academic affairs and another division of student affairs, Collaborative University has recognized that these two areas should not be distinct. The integration of students in academic affairs has led to a closer collaboration between areas that are traditionally isolated. Partnerships have evolved between academic and student affairs with the realization that individuals from academic and student affairs have specific expertise that, combined, can provide a more enriching educational experience for students. For example, faculty are becoming more involved in service learning and student advising, which traditionally were activities reserved for student affairs professionals. The highly rated study abroad and service learning programs have resulted from such partnerships and offer a variety of opportunities for students to become active in local and international communities.

Student involvement in service and volunteerism at Collaborative University also differs from that on traditional campuses as a result of the university's integration of structures and mission of collaboration. Whether it is embedded in the curriculum through service learning or offered through an office of volunteerism, service at Collaborative University is constructed as an activity that faculty, staff, and students are involved in collectively. On many traditional campuses, service learning may involve as few as one student volunteering for a particular project. In contrast, at Collaborative University large-scale, joint projects are developed that involve hundreds of students, faculty, and staff in one-time or ongoing service opportunities. Service projects are planned by a community—faculty staff, and students—and there is campuswide commitment to service learning and community-based research. Service learning has moved beyond single course offerings in a couple fields or disciplines to a much larger commitment across the campus.

Another area that characterizes Collaborative University and affects teaching, research, and government is its participatory style of leadership. Distributed leadership as practiced by Collaborative University allows innovation and ideas to emerge at multiple levels; administrators can encourage people to innovate and provide support for leadership at any level. If there are reasons for certain organizational boundaries in certain instances, they just make sure to establish cross-campus committees that can bring individuals together on joint work. The campus has a large number of campuswide committees, and their work is reported to members across campus on a regular basis. For example, at Collaborative University staff and students are encouraged to lead efforts to change policy or to create new programs. The staff developed a proposal for a new accounting and computer system that was adopted by the campus. Students developed a plan for a new orientation program that was then brought to governance groups; the groups adopted their proposal, which radically changed the nature of the program. The campus also believes in shared governance, and this is demonstrated in their budget process.

In order to rethink the traditional disciplinary boundaries found in research and respond to external pressures, Collaborative University sought external funding that promoted the mission of collaboration. Currently, Collaborative University has a variety of externally funded research institutes that require cross-disciplinary collaboration. For example, an external funder made it possible to create a research institute that brought together the fields of cognitive psychology, neurobiology, and artificial intelligence. This innovative research institute exemplifies the culture of collaboration that has developed over the last several decades at Collaborative University. As will become clear throughout this book, external pressures, as well as an external funding, can push forward a collaborative value more easily than a singular reliance on internal pressure.

Another hallmark of Collaborative University that stems from the mission to rethink traditional academic structures to facilitate collaboration is the focus on physical space. In the 1990s, the university sought to create a new student center that brought together the library and the student union. In the structure, an open-stack library houses a restaurant, a coffee shop, a movie theater, and a bookstore. Students are able to sit among the books, meet in many of the group meeting rooms, use the computer labs, socialize with other students, and purchase food from the restaurant. Unlike other campuses, students can prepare for academic work and socialize with fellow students all under one roof. The structure serves as a symbol for the approach that Collaborative University takes in all of its activities.

The following sections—teaching and learning, research, service, and governance and management—outline some specific examples of collaborative activities at the university with a focus on how each element of the model presented in this book served to assist the development of a collaborative ethic. The process of creating a collaborative university illustrates how a reorganization of structures and intentionality can transform a traditional university into a highly collaborative university.

## Teaching and Learning

Campuses that embrace a collaborative ethic toward teaching and learning operate in very different ways. These include team teaching, interdisciplinary or multidisciplinary teaching and programs, service and experiential learning, first-year experience programs, team-based advising, and cross-functional assessment. Although there are other collaborative teaching and learning innovations, these represent some of the most prevalent experiments on campus. Let's take a look at how Collaborative University experimented with teaching and learning.

A major example of collaborative teaching and learning techniques is the creation of an experimental unit (school) on the Collaborative University campus. A set of faculty are specifically hired for the unit who desire to work with innovative pedagogies and in a multi- and interdisciplinary fashion. Administrative staff have also been hired to support the school. The innovative unit, which offers interdisciplinary learning opportunities, relevant problem-based curriculum, service and experiential learning, and an outcome-based education, was first offered in a learning community before it became popular on many campuses. The curriculum and classes are jointly constructed in a team approach with faculty from across the disciplines. Rather than having learning goals established within a particular discipline, the unit at Collaborative University has an outcome-based approach to learning with established goals that all courses are aimed at meeting. Students have a capstone experience in which they demonstrate how they have achieved these goals. Students and faculty teach and learn together in a learning community; collaboration and working together in dialogue is embedded into the curriculum.

Over the years, this unit has operated as an experimental site for a variety of teaching innovations that have been integrated across the campus, such as team teaching, learning communities, first-year interest groups, collaborative student assessment, and interdisciplinary courses. For example, first-year students now take a series of courses that have been jointly constructed by faculty across a variety of disciplines to address an issue such as war and violence, globalization, or the human experience. Students report that these interdisciplinary courses help them better see the contribution of various forms of knowledge to understanding real-world problems and issues. In addition to jointly constructing courses, faculty across a variety of disciplines team teach the course. A sociologist, historian, and biologist might work together to teach a series on war and violence. Faculty note how their own research and teaching is improved by working with other academics in different units; they report that they are more creative and are learning in ways they have not in years. Faculty also learn different approaches to teaching (business faculty might use cases whereas a biologist might use field techniques for experiments, for example). Students get the opportunity to learn about a topic from a variety of disciplines and perspectives and begin to understand the complexity of how the world operates.

As discussed previously, the experimental unit emerged from a statewide initiative geared toward funding new innovative programs on college campuses. Whereas other universities in the state chose to develop distance learning programs, Collaborative University recognized the success of new learning-based experiential units across the country. Collaborative University learned from the emerging research on new learning methods and was able to sense the national trend toward the new experiential teaching methods. The experimental unit brings faculty together from across disciplines and integrates notions of student success found in student affairs (i.e., faculty and student engagement and academic integration). Networks and a strong commitment by a few visionary pioneers created institutional support for the development of the experiential unit, which has also been found to be essential in creating a collaborative campus. Finally, bringing together faculty from across disciplines required a rethinking of rewards. Collaborative University sought to establish policies that would allow faculty to teach interdisciplinary courses and receive course reductions in their home discipline. In addition, faculty were hired specifically as interdisciplinary faculty whose primary department was the experiential unit itself, thereby eliminating competition with other reward structures.

Another example of innovative teaching and learning structures at Collaborative University is the integration of academic and student affairs into one unit. This integration has created opportunities for new partnerships between faculty and student activities. For example, in service learning at Collaborative University, faculty develop the syllabus and assignments related to activities and student affairs staff often meet with community agencies to establish the service or experiential program and maintain connection with the community agency. Faculty are trained on reflection and other pedagogical skills that help enhance service learning in the classroom. The integration of faculty expertise and student affairs connections with the community maximizes the student learning experience.

Collaborative University also has first-year experience programs that are jointly or collaboratively planned with input from academic affairs, student affairs, and students. At Collaborative University, a student, faculty member, and staff from student affairs jointly teach the first-year seminar. The student offers expertise about his or her own adjustment to college, student affairs staff present data on study skills, and faculty talk about their expectations and offer tips on how students can be successful over their academic career.

Finally, academic advising and mentoring (traditionally a task of student affairs) at Collaborative University requires joint responsibility of faculty, staff, and students. This ethic extends to special support programs for historically underserved students, commuter and adult students, and transfer students. Collaborative University encourages faculty and staff to work closely together to develop orientation programs for transfer students who have been unsuccessful in moving from community colleges to a university. The university realizes that it needs to draw together more expertise to help students be successful.

The integration of student and academic affairs has proven to be a significant factor in the success of a partnership model at Collaborative University. As will become clear in later chapters, integrating structures is an essential activity in sustaining collaborative efforts. Without the structures that support collaboration, many partnerships fail or recede to become smaller projects kept alive by charismatic and committed individuals. As seen with Collaborative University, integrating structures leads to a practice of partnering with constituents across the university and within many of the activities in student and academic affairs. The integration of structures, however, does not always naturally lead to involvement. Networking is needed to identify faculty and staff who are interested in collaboration and to foster long-term partnerships. Collaborative University relies on the community-based networks of individuals within student affairs and the ability to seek out faculty with an interest in service learning to promote collaboration in the classroom.

## Research

Higher education institutions that want to help solve complex social problems and create a difference in communities and the world often find working collaboratively essential to meeting this goal. Collaborative approaches to research include interdisciplinary, multidisciplinary, or transdisciplinary research, community-based or action research, and undergraduate research teams.[2] Collaborative University shared this desire and has systematically changed the nature of its research.

One of the most important factors in creating innovative research at Collaborative University was the introduction of resources (both internally and externally) to fund collaborations. Initially, administrators on campus developed incentives for working across departments and schools and set up a series of research institutes focused on particular problems such as health care, immigration, or homeland security. The institutes involved faculty from several schools across campus and received seed money and support to start up the centers. Other centers were established through individual donors who had a commitment to creating interdisciplinary centers, such as the center focused on cognitive psychology, neurobiology, and artificial intelligence. As described earlier, many other institutions have relied on funds by the National Science Foundation, Department of Defense, and National Institutes of Health to establish interdisciplinary research centers that bring together a variety of faculty to work internally on major issues or to work together in partnership with outside industry. Collaborative University, however, established internal support through resources and incentives to create interdisciplinary work to illustrate the commitment to faculty and external funding agencies.

Many faculty are also beginning to engage in community-based or participatory action research in which groups of faculty and community members work collaboratively to address a complex research problem and make a direct impact within the community and world of practice. For example, at Collaborative University faculty members across a variety of disciplines have developed extensive research collaboratives with community members to address local, national, or international community issues. This involves a large network of faculty who are supported in their work. Creating solutions to complex social problems such as poverty and homelessness requires faculty to work across disciplines in coordination with various staff members and many community agencies.

Similar to strategies adopted in the area of teaching and learning, Collaborative University fostered partnerships in research by integrating structures through the research centers and establishing rewards for faculty involvement in research across disciplines and within the community. Breaking down disciplinary silos through campuswide funding and support structures helped establish interdisciplinary centers in which faculty have the opportunity to collaborate on various projects and participate in interdisciplinary, federally funded grants. In order to facilitate faculty work in the centers, the university actively altered reward structures by giving faculty course release time, establishing a value of collaboration and interdisciplinarity in tenure and promotion, and providing seed money for the research. Each of the rewards provided the time, money, and support required to help make faculty collaboration possible.

## Service

Although campuses have not given as much attention to transforming service as they have to teaching and research, there are some novel practices emerging and there are likely to be others in coming years. At Collaborative University, service takes on a very different character. Service is envisioned as a collective activity and tends to include off-campus as well as on-campus activities. In the past, individual faculty members might work in the community or provide service to a community agency. Campuses that envision service in a collaborative fashion, however, have developed university and community partnerships that involve faculty, administrators, students, and staff from across campus working in conjunction with community members. Traditionally campus constituents tend to think of service as committee work and involvement in governance. In the section on governance, we describe how committee work and governance has shifted as well. Here we highlight how the notion of service has expanded and taken on a different meaning on collaborative campuses.

Collaborative University took an approach that was highly focused on the community. Realizing that its service efforts in the community were not as powerful and effective as they could be, Collaborative University instituted a plan called "The Engaged University," which involves partnering with many off-campus groups. This plan is directly linked to the mission of the university through the commitment to provide service to the community, both local and international. Through a needs assessment with the community, campus leaders have identified target areas for community development, including economic development, education, community health, citizenship, and homeland security. This has also led them to expand their activities into other areas identified as having unmet need. For example, Collaborative University's expansion into another county is based on determining that this area had regional workforce needs that were unmet. Through these partnerships, the Collaborative University off-site campus offers an opportunity for faculty and students to be involved in current research and to gain access to facilities and employment opportunities at the companies in the area. In turn, the university will provide workers at these facilities with training opportunities to enhance their communication skills and job proficiency. Partnership leaders have discussed and developed the requirements to improve workforce development in this region.

Another new collaboration was a service program focused on college access and youth development with several community and business organizations. Using networks within the community, the program brought high school seniors to the campus, where they role-played in a "game" that taught life responsibilities. Each student assumed the identity of a twenty-five-year-old in various career fields. They proceeded to stations staffed by local business volunteers representing different life responsibilities. For instance, one station, "the IRS," took a portion of the student's salary; then students moved on to banking, where they opened a checking account, then to health insurance, then to housing costs, and groceries, and so on. The campus is actively involved in many similar community programs. By working collaboratively with other groups off campus, their service work has reached more individuals and had a greater impact. The campus also has more students and faculty participating in service because the programs and opportunities are better designed.

Collaboration within services is supported by the mission statement of the institution, which provides a value and framework for facilitation of community-based service. The mission statement also places an emphasis on experiential learning, which supports community service among students and in the classroom as well. Backed by a clear mission statement of the goals and values of the university, collaboration is more readily achieved and more easily diffused throughout the university, as well as between constituents across the campus and community organizations. Capitalizing on existing networks and creating new partnerships all facilitate collaborations within the community, a function that is highly valued within the university.

## Governance and Management

Campuses with a collaborative ethic tend to integrate various stakeholders into the function of management and governance via practices such as cross-functional teams, student and academic affairs collaboration, distributed leadership, shared governance, and joint planning and budgeting. One way that Collaborative University established a collaborative environment was by revamping its governance and management. Collaboration in governance and management is not a simple task. Universities have developed structures that separate managerial and administrative tasks from faculty academic interests. Therefore, creating an ethic of collaboration within a university requires a rethinking of traditional structures and an openness to including more stakeholders in the decision-making process.

Collaborative University has been able to establish partnerships in governance and management by relying on networks to identify individuals who should be involved in all aspects of the college. For example, when Collaborative University sets up any committee, such as a committee on student assessment, they think about every unit on campus that might have expertise or that is a stakeholder in the issue. Therefore, in addition to the "usual suspects" such as institutional researchers and faculty, they include librarians, students, technology staff, and staff from a variety of student affairs units. The process of identifying those units and individuals relies on networks, as well as the commitment to listen to others and take the time needed to get buy-in and feedback from all individuals at the table.

Other efforts that have used a similar collaboration style include assessment, accreditation, and curriculum. Assessment efforts on campuses that value collaboration tend to include individuals from units across campus, not just the institutional research office. The assessment movement has also resulted in meaningful collaboration among faculty related to student outcomes. For example, faculty members across a variety of disciplines will confer to jointly construct ways they can meet the quantitative reasoning competency that is a part of their general education curriculum. At Collaborative University, they have established several campuswide committees to create assessments of certain competencies. Their writing-across-the-curriculum planning group that brings faculty from almost every discipline jointly develops competencies and assessment to ensure that students learn to be strong writers.

Another example of collaboration in decision making concerns the budget process. Collaborative University has revised its budget process so that each unit has input on every unit's budget process. Although it is difficult to completely eradicate the competition for funding that characterizes most campuses, the sharing of budget information among different units and the joint setting of priorities with input from people across campus helps create greater buy-in for each unit's budget. As several people noted: "It's great to be at the budget table and hear someone else argue for your budget priorities, and this happens quite often." Campus constituents also note that they have input into planning through a variety of mechanisms from the campuswide teams, the open budget process, retreats, and feedback mechanisms (they often do internal assessment of people's views and perspectives). The university has a very active institutional research office that does much more than government reporting or even student learning outcomes; it also focuses on improving communication and input to governance and planning through internal surveys and feedback mechanisms.

## Visioning the Collaborative Campus

One barrier to creating more collaborative work environments (beyond the individualized and hierarchical structures and processes) is that campus leaders do not necessarily have a vision for what a collaborative campus might look like. Collaborative University, as a campus that has undertaken the challenge of reorganizing and is reaping the benefits of collaborative work, provides an example for leaders.

Collaborative University is among a growing number of campuses that are no longer willing to continue to be constrained by academic tradition or prior institutional norms that do not help create the best learning environment, produce the most innovative research, assist in providing powerful service experiences, serve students well, or be the most appropriate governance and organizational structure for the campus. We hope that this example provides other leaders in higher education with a vision for how they might transform their campuses to support collaborative work. We acknowledge that the specific types of collaborations in teaching, research, and service will be likely to vary by institutional type and culture. This example is only meant to help develop a vision for other campuses that will adopt particular, collaborative practices that fit the mission and niche of the institution. The rest of the book explains how Collaborative University (and others in the study) achieved this vision.

### Notes

1. As part of the Institutional Review Board process, we promised anonymity to the institutions in the research project; therefore, we do not specifically list the names of institutions.

2. There are a variety of publications that distinguish between work that is interdisciplinary (happening between two or more interacting fields), multidisciplinary (insights from various fields brought together), and transdisciplinary (based outside any particular discipline). We do not explore these differences in depth in this book, but the reader should understand these differences if he or she wants to work at any of these levels.

# Part II

# Strategies for Reorganizing Campuses

*The problem is that we keep trying to force collaborative
innovations into a structure and culture that supports
individual work.*

Provost of a large comprehensive university

This insight could be applied to almost any community
college, research or comprehensive university, or liberal
arts college in the country. Campus leaders and change agents
struggle to institutionalize collaborative initiatives because the
higher education environment, as structured, is not conducive to
it. As described in Part One, these structures reflect the culture
and history of how "things get done" in academe and the legacy
of what has been valued as a way to approach work. In order to
overcome the long history and prevalence of conducting individualistic work and establish an ethic of collaboration, we contend
it is necessary to reorganize the features of the campus. Many staff
feel these individualized structures and environments are unique
to their campus and choose to leave one campus for another,
hoping to find a more collaborative context and a new job, only to
be disappointed. Others realize how prevalent the individual model
is and believe there is no other way that work can or will get done
on campus. After seeing initiative after initiative fail, they now
believe it is impossible to transcend this approach to work.

As noted in Part One, because institutions are generally
not structured to support collaborative approaches of learning,
research, and organizational functioning, the context needs to be

reorganized. How can higher education move from bureaucratic administrative structures and siloed, disciplinary units to institutions that support collaborative work? The chapters in Part Two examine this question, focusing on the elements of the organizational context that need to be redesigned.

As a reminder, *organizational context* refers to major structural, process, human, political, and cultural elements of the campus such as institutional policies, organizational charts, decision-making processes, leadership, training, climate, and politics. Chapter Two in Part One described seven key context features that must be altered in order to develop an environment that is conducive to and that enables collaborative work in higher education institutions: (1) mission and vision and educational philosophy, (2) values, (3) social networks, (4) integrating structures, (5) rewards, (6) external pressure, and (7) learning.

Although these seven context features all support collaboration, a few of them are essential: mission and vision, a campus network, and integrating structures. Without them collaborative activities will fail.

Each chapter in Part Two begins with a definition of a context feature, gives a brief overview about why it is important and how it enables collaboration, describes the background of and literature on the context feature, offers advice and examples from various campuses, points out the challenges to revising the feature, and provides a summary of key issues. Although some of these seven contexts overlap, they nonetheless represent distinct areas for organizations to consider as they redesign for collaboration. Campuses need to address all of these areas in order to be successful. If an institution changes its mission but does not change its rewards it will not be successful in the long term. While not all of these will be reorganized at the same time or in the same pace, faculty and staff need to see that progress has been made in each of these areas to believe that the campus will truly support collaborative work.

# 4

# Mission, Vision, and
# Educational Philosophy

*The mission of an institution articulates its purpose and
organizational character. Mission is distinctive from
other organizational processes or structures, such as
planning, in that it creates institutional meaning. Vision is
aspirational and expresses where an organization hopes to
be in the future.*

Because mission creates institutional purpose and articulates
priorities, it is not surprising that it is a critical organizational
element in helping a campus be successful in developing
collaboration. There are several reasons that mission is so important
as a context for facilitating collaboration: it helps people reflect on
values, develop a shared vision and sense of purpose around why
collaboration is a good idea, create a sense of priority around that
good idea, and provide specific direction and logic for undertaking
the work of collaboration.

Mission and philosophy are reflections of the underlying values
of organizations. Although values are central to framing what
work we do and how we do it, they are often taken for granted
and become invisible. For example, individualism has become
a taken-for-granted value within most campuses. But without
consciously bringing these values to the surface, it can be difficult,
if not impossible, to change them.

Mission also creates a shared vision and sense of purpose for
members of a campus. People are looking to understand what

the priorities, values, and norms are; if there is no articulated statement then they look to existing structures and rewards to try to understand what the institutional values are. As noted in Chapter Two, existing structures tend to reinforce individualistic patterns of behavior. Therefore, it is extremely important that campuses that want to support collaborative work articulate this desire within their mission and values statement, include it in the vision for the campus, and describe it in relationship to the educational philosophy of the campus, thus ensuring that employees clearly understand the value of collaboration, even if existing structures do not yet support it.

Campuses in the study have strategically used a mission statement (and resulting strategic plan) to create a sense of urgency and commitment to do work differently. For these campuses, working collaboratively was a new direction, and they knew that it would be a difficult one unless there were "real teeth" to the new mission statement. This meant that budgeting, planning, and evaluation processes were aligned with the new mission, thus making sure that everyone knew it was a priority.

The various campuses we spoke with for our research understood the power of mission to provide direction for campus employees. It can be used everywhere. Campus employees use the mission to drive hiring processes and discuss it at orientations and campus events. The mission is included and referred to in key institutional documents. Mission is used to anchor important processes such as accreditation or assessment and is part of campus decision making. By invoking mission in these many situations, it becomes a guide and compass for people doing work in new ways.

Furthermore, campuses specifically spoke about the important role of educational philosophy in providing the logic and ideas for creating collaborative work. The educational philosophy supports the implementation of a collaborative mission by providing specific ideas for how to work in different ways. The philosophy of collaborative learning offers guidance to faculty on how to revise their classes and syllabi in order to create opportunities for students to socially construct knowledge together. Members of collaborative research projects can draw on the educational philosophy in order to obtain specific advice about the challenges and opportunities of working in teams. Articles about the philosophical underpinnings of management teams give advice for establishing cross-functional teams. As a result of a collaborative educational philosophy, collaboration becomes more tangible and concrete for members of campus and easier to implement.

Mission is also powerful because it appeals to people's need for meaning and purpose. People seek meaning through their work. Collaboration can enhance the sense of meaning and actually help employees become more committed and motivated within the workplace. In this sense, mission and collaboration reciprocally reinforce each other. There have been many critiques of the modern workplace as providing little purpose and sense of meaning because people are separated from directly creating a product or providing a service. For instance, bureaucracies tend to disconnect people from the overall service or product. But through collaboration, employees can see how their part fits into an overall whole—thereby giving them greater meaning.

Now that you have some sense of why mission is such an important part of organizational context, we introduce you to some literature that provides more background on how to think about mission.

## Background of Mission

Several key concepts from the literature help shed light on the context feature of mission—how it captures meaning, character, and philosophy; whether it is espoused or enacted; ways it can be sustained and nurtured; the need for reexamination; and the way it has an impact on campus operations.

Tierney (2002) reminds us that mission and vision have been part of our collective culture and dialogue for thousands of years and that religious texts such as the Bible often reference mission and vision. In addition, new trends such as branding that focus on product definition and distinctiveness are processes put in place for ensuring that organizations have a mission. Although this mission can be articulated in a formal statement, it can also be observed in the behaviors and practices of people on campus. For example, campuses with a commitment to developing citizens should see this commitment in teaching and cocurricular programs.

One of the key elements of mission is that is helps create meaning for an organization. Many psychological studies have documented how human beings intrinsically try to seek out meaning in the various experiences of their life (Bolman & Deal, 1997). The workplace is one of the most prominent organizational contexts in which people find themselves. Institutional meaning is created when a mission answers questions such as, Who do we serve? What is our work? How do we accomplish our work? It differs from a strategic plan, in that the mission includes and focuses on the values and core beliefs about education and human existence. A mission statement falls short if it does not shape values and resonate with core beliefs held institutionally. Institutional identity is also related to this process of meaning-making and values (Kuh & Whitt, 1988). Just as people develop over time, deciding which values will guide their lives and creating an identity or character, institutions also need to create dialogues about values and make decisions about what the character of the institution will be.

Furthermore, the mission helps articulate abstract philosophical beliefs. Philosophy relates to the particular logic and assumptions that educators use to guide their work. Although philosophy is strongly related to mission and is often used to develop the mission statement, it is distinctive. Kuh et al. (2005) describe the notion of an operating philosophy in which, consciously or not, colleges "develop a philosophy that guides thought and action as it pursues its educational mission" (p. 27). A philosophy is typically a tacit understanding of what is important and institutional participants rarely consciously think about these deeply held values. The mission statement serves as a written expression of the philosophical beliefs and values that may or may not be explicitly understood by institutional participants.

Although people typically think of the mission and vision statement as an articulation of the character of the institution, they are less likely to think about the dialogue and conversation necessary to create the mission. A process of collective dialogue should be undertaken every five years or so to ensure that beliefs have not changed and to remind people about their core values. People who are successful in living their values tend to have a strong sense of personal purpose (Senge, 1990); the same is true of organizations. Institutional purpose is strengthened through dialogue, which needs to occur periodically. A mission statement is successful when it articulates what participants would say about themselves and their identity (while also being aspirational); in other words, people should see themselves in the mission. Tierney (2002) cautions that institutions should not treat the mission statement as a marketing document written for an external audience and that says what the institution would like others to think and say about it.

Kuh et al. (2005) make a distinction between the espoused mission (often seen in mission statements) and the enacted mission, which can be seen by walking into classrooms and observing people at work. Ideally, if an institution says that interdisciplinarity is part of the mission, you will see team-taught courses, interdisciplinary research centers, and other work that suggests interdisciplinarity is part of the day-to-day work of the campus. One of the findings of the research of Kuh et al. (2005) examining campuses with high levels of student engagement is that campuses that are successful in meeting their mission have only a small gap between their espoused and enacted mission, whereas institutions that have less engagement tend to have a larger gap. Some gap between espoused and enacted mission is natural, as institutions often create a vision that is aspirational in order to "stretch" institutional participants to move in important and new directions. But one of the important aspects to understand about mission is that it is more than a formal written statement.

Research also demonstrates that the mission needs to be nurtured and sustained. One of the most typical processes for making the mission come to life is ongoing communication about the mission statement. For example, as Tierney (2002) notes: "the real power of Martin Luther King Jr. was not only that he had a dream but that he could describe it, that it became public and therefore accessible to millions of people. A leader's job is to follow in King's communicative footsteps. Print the mission on a one-page sheet of paper and memorize it. Speak about it at every talk you give" (p. 55). Creating an ongoing dialogue about whether the institution is meeting its mission and ways it can reconsider its work is another way to nurture the mission. Furthermore, most scholars writing about mission agree that it should be stable enough to provide consistency but flexible enough to change with new context and circumstances (Kuh et al., 2005). Tierney (2002), for example, suggests that an institution that revisits its mission statement every year is probably missing a core purpose, but a campus that does not revisit its mission statements every five or ten years is probably missing opportunities for renewal: "although an institution that dramatically reformulates its mission every year is one that I assume has no identity, we also ought not fool ourselves into thinking that the mission is so rigid that in a decade's time there will not be reconsideration and renewal" (p. 56).

---

Tierney (2002, p. 57) provides advice for institutions that are trying to make sure their mission supports activities that are listed. He suggests that leaders answer the following questions:

1. Describe two examples of when an outsider would see the mission at work.

2. Ask new faculty at the institution what they see as the mission.

3. Ask longtime faculty what they see as the mission. If the faculty's responses differ radically from yours, you have a problem.

4. What are the three central projects that took place over the last twelve months and how do they relate to the mission? If they do not relate to it, then the mission needs to be realigned or internal processes realigned for the mission.

Mission is more successfully enacted and sustained if institutional priorities (strategic plans) support and provide ways to bring the mission into action. Also, institutional budgeting and resource allocation should be prioritized for the central activities of the mission. Rewards and programs should be developed based on the mission. Ideally, all institutional activity should be tied back to the mission. Similarly, all evaluation practices should be related to the mission.

We do know that certain higher education institutions are much more driven by their mission statements. The following generalizations can be made. Liberal arts college employees often think about the mission of their institutions on a more regular basis and tie it to their daily work. These institutions will be readily able to use their mission in order to create change toward a commitment to collaboration. Community colleges often rely heavily on their open access and workforce development mission, which defines all organizational processes, as well as the populations they serve and the academic programs they offer. Larger and less distinct colleges and universities that have not spent much time in dialogue about their missions and see themselves as meeting a generic goal may have less success appealing to the mission and educational philosophy. Therefore, some campuses may find it easier to more immediately appeal to mission and others may need to take more time to build the significance of this aspect of their campus.

## How Campuses Use Mission and Philosophy to Create Collaboration

---

**Sample Mission Statement**

1. Institution X embraces its diverse community by providing excellent and unique educational programs in a collaborative, nurturing safe environment that promotes student success and lifelong learning; or

2. Institution Y is connected to societal issues through civic engagement and community involvement. *We lead* by providing a unique combination of liberal arts and professional education in a challenging, scholarly, and culturally diverse academic community. *We engage* our students through collaborative teaching, team-based scholarship, and cooperative and experiential learning. *We inspire* our students to be citizens of character who demonstrate professional and civic leadership for their communities. *We contribute* to the vitality and well-being of the communities we serve.

---

Mission is one of the most important context features for collaboration because it formally articulates the underlying value system of institutions. In this section, we describe how campuses have used mission statements to establish, create, and support collaboration—specifically, embedding collaboration into the written mission statement, creating a philosophy of collaboration, communicating the mission, continuing dialogue and socialization, and allocating resources.

### Including Collaboration in the Mission Statement

On campuses that have created a collaborative context, collaboration is part of the mission statement and, as several senior administrators noted, "defines who we are." In the process of developing the mission statement, dialogues on these campuses determined that collaboration is necessary to achieve their approach to learning, whether integrating or transformative. Through these discussions, people on campus realized they needed to add collaboration to the mission statement. In the words of one staff member:

> It kept coming up, again and again, how we needed to work across campus and with people off campus and then finally some one stood up and said, I think collaboration needs to be part of our mission statement. It would seem obvious but until she synthesized all our comments, it just was not apparent to us. This generated excitement—because people supported collaboration, but making it part of our mission and identity, that was new, this captured what we cared about, but were not really practicing consistently. It made us realize that it could be part of who we are.

Campuses included collaboration into the mission in a variety of ways. Some included collaboration within their core mission statement: "Our campus works collaboratively to develop servant leaders who will become change agents nationally and internationally." Others cited a collective responsibility to meet the mission: "Our mission of being a premier urban institution can only be accomplished by working collaboratively across units, bringing the expertise of faculty, staff, and administrators together." Some campuses included a values statement, listing collaboration as a core value. In descriptions of the collaborative value system being embraced in the mission, specific types of collaborations were usually cited, such as between academic and student affairs partnerships, joint planning processes, learning communities, or interdisciplinary work.

While each campus made changes to the institutional mission and vision statement, changes were also made to unit, departmental, and school-level mission and vision statements. Senior administrators encouraged other units to examine their own ways of doing work and determine where it made sense to align their values and mission to institutional priorities. One faculty member commented on the importance of rethinking mission and vision statements throughout the institution:

> There were a lot of junior faculty who were excited about collaboration because this had been a part of our graduate experience. Unfortunately, the overall campus was emphasizing collaboration, but our school chose to ignore it. A new dean came in and started having conversations and realized we were out of alignment with the overall university. He also spoke to many junior faculty, like me, who impressed on him their interest in working more collaboratively. We then began the process of changing our school mission statement and had a series of retreats over a year. But without that change here at the lower level, things were still not moving in the direction we hoped.

This story illustrates how larger campuses may often have particular units, departments, or schools that can evade change, even if some of its members desire such change. Thus, making changes at the department or school level is particularly important on large campuses. For these larger institutions, a campuswide mission is often too distant to be meaningful.

Each campus agreed that the reasons for and advantages of collaboration need to be part of the mission and values in order to ensure that the logic is compelling. Important documents that describe this logic include *Powerful Partnerships*, by the American Association for Higher Education, the American College Personnel Association, and the National Association of Student Personnel Administrators (1998), and *Learning Reconsidered*, by the National Association of Student Personnel

Administrators and the American College Personnel Association (Keeling, 2004); and *Greater Expectations*, by the Association of American Colleges and Universities (2002). Any campus interested in moving toward collaboration should obtain copies of these documents, some of which may be available online.

## Creating a Philosophy of Collaboration

Many people explained that a philosophy of collaboration that is tied to the mission of the institution made collaboration a systematic process and part of all the work they engaged in. For most campuses, the philosophy that guided their work—a belief in collaborative learning—is infused into their mission statement. Most campuses had already formally adopted a philosophy of learning that challenged traditional, individualistic views of learning. In order to achieve a particular kind of learning environment and meet the institutional mission—whether it was innovative teaching, community-based learning, interdisciplinary research, or a true liberal arts education—collaboration was necessary. In the words of one faculty member:

> Well what connects our work more than any unit, person, rewards, or value is a philosophy. What I mean by philosophy is that we all share a common understanding in the notion of collaborative learning. We all discuss collaborative learning and what it is. We realize that it is this philosophy that helps us meet our mission, which focuses on active learning experiences and relational learning.

Also, the philosophy on these campuses was not tacit. Instead, the philosophy was intentional and consciously discussed. This is quite different from other studies, which found that the operating philosophy was part of the hidden layer of culture and usually unspoken among faculty and staff (Kuh et al., 2005). Perhaps collaboration will become an operating philosophy at such campuses at a later time. But at the campuses we studied, people reiterated from the beginning the importance of consciously holding a philosophical stance toward collaboration and articulating it on an ongoing basis. They noted the importance of discussions on campus about philosophies of education and learning and the role that collaboration plays. Some campuses also used research on teaching and learning that supports collaboration and enhances student learning. Campuses commented on specific documents, such as the *Seven Principles of Good Practice in Undergraduate Education* (Chickering & Gamson, 1987), the National Survey of Student Engagement, and *Powerful Partnerships* (AAHS, ACPA, & NASPA, 1998). They also pointed to research on learning groups, collaborative and cooperative learning, team learning, integrating and transformative learning, learning communities, and experiential and service learning. These documents and research helped campuses develop an educational philosophy in support of collaboration. Several texts have been developed on collaborative learning and research and can serve as a resource for campuses working to create a philosophy of collaboration. See the resource guide in Appendix B for some of the texts mentioned by campuses we studied.

One promising strategy that campuses used to foster discussion of the educational philosophy was to form a campus reading group. Research on reading groups has demonstrated that if cross-campus teams read articles and information in common and then have discussions on the material they are more likely to develop a shared understanding of concepts, problem solve how to integrate a novel concept into the setting, and move toward change (in this instance, collaboration) (Eckel, Kezar, & Lieberman, 1999).

Some campuses had many faculty and staff that already adopted a philosophy of collaborative learning, and including it in the mission statement was a way to formalize and support these employees. However, on other campuses discussions around the mission statement resulted in the development of a philosophy of collaboration. In the words of one administrator:

> We were excited that our mission now supported collaboration. But we needed to do more to bring that mission to life. What did we really mean by collaboration—was it just finding opportunities to work together? Several people mentioned that there were frameworks of collaborative knowledge and learning and that these might serve as guidance for how to enact this new aspect of our mission. And it really worked. We started reading and our understanding of what collaboration meant to us became much deeper.

Whether it comes before the mission statements or as a result of the mission statement, the educational philosophy provides the level of detail necessary to translate the mission into action. With a collaborative philosophy of learning in place that related to the core activities of teaching and learning, all employees regardless of area began to conceptualize collaboration as part of their work. A staff member describes how the core activities of the institution changed as a result of the philosophy:

> After the change in the mission statement, many people were wondering how different the campus would really be. We had some collaborative work going, but then we started to have dialogues about what it means to be a collaborative learning environment—where everyone on campus supports learning. Lots of us in student affairs decided we needed to make more overtures to academic

affairs, and that's how the learning communities got started and then we worked to change service learning and integrate it more into the classroom. We also started to work more directly with the library on some of our student programs. I can give you lots of examples, but the key point is that the mission demonstrated a priority, and the philosophy helped us to think through how we would actually reconstruct our day to day work and processes. And this did not happen overnight, it took many different planning sessions and lots of brainstorming. But it is certainly worth the time.

### Creating Documents About Collaboration That Express a Vision

Although the mission statement is helpful in articulating a sense of priority, some people needed more detailed documents to help them envision collaborative work. Several change agents had developed concept papers to describe their own vision of how collaboration can enhance the teaching, research, service, and governance and management of the organization. These documents of ten to fifteen pages highlighted innovative collaboration and how it fit into the mission of the institution. For instance, if a campus has a religious orientation and history of having faculty and student volunteers, senior administrators might describe the development of a broader service learning program developed jointly by student and academic affairs. An urban campus, with a long history of outreach, might recommend the development of stronger university and community partnerships that involve faculty and staff from across the institutions. On a campus committed to developing student leaders, change agents might describe the expansion of a leadership development program that includes faculty and staff with expertise in leadership to create a national signature program.

The concept papers developed by change agents helped create more enthusiasm from people who may not have clearly understood the collaborative mission. One faculty member describes his experience reading a concept paper:

> I have been involved in a variety of collaborations in research and I was open to the idea of collaborative work, but as we were reviewing the mission statement, I just didn't quite get how this would change the nature of my day-to-day work. The concept paper that our provost wrote about seamless learning, borrowing from *Powerful Partnerships*, gave me 10 or 15 ideas about how I can change my teaching, advising, and service. So it all came together for me while reading the document.

Administrators often developed these concept papers jointly with other members of campus (again, the importance of modeling collaboration). They encouraged colleagues to reach out to the network of individuals on campus who were already conducting or supportive of collaborative work and ask for their input. They also contacted influential faculty and staff to get their feedback on the emerging concept paper. Many different drafts were written before the concept papers were released more broadly to the campus.

### Communicating and Articulating the Mission

Every campus described how a well-articulated and well-publicized mission fostered collaboration. Leaders on campuses that had created a collaborative context took every opportunity to reiterate the importance of collaboration to the institutional mission and future direction. One administrator describes her efforts:

> Any meeting that I went to, no matter the constituent group, I kept referring back to the need for collaboration, the way this was a part of our mission statement, and

the importance of translating this mission into our everyday work. If I was meeting with academic advisors, I would check to see if they had the appropriate contacts in student affairs and academic affairs. When I met with faculty, I asked about interdisciplinary work, involvement in curricular activities, and partnering with the community. I managed to integrate this concept into all of my conversations. It made a difference, over the next year, I saw people fundamentally change the way they were working.

Various campuses described the litmus tests they had for determining whether they had communicated the mission and educational philosophy. For example, on one campus it was noted: "Our mission statement can be repeated by any faculty, staff, or student on campus. That familiarity is also important for building collaboration." Making sure that the mission is articulated repeatedly and understood by faculty and staff changed the nature of work within these institutions. In the words of a faculty member: "People understand the work of the institution and it serves as a foundation for discussion and common understanding. So a clear understanding of the mission actually helps us in doing the collaborative work."

Faculty and staff on campus believed that senior administrators had committed to collaborative work when collaborative initiatives were included in the strategic plan and other strategic documents. According to one staff member:

I had heard people talk about collaboration for five or six years, and I had not seen anything happen. So I was not holding my breath, and I certainly wasn't volunteering for any of the collaborative initiatives. But then the strategic plan came out and several collaborative efforts were highlighted and provided resources. It startled many of us and we realized that we were finally going to get the support we wanted. I just did not want to get involved with something that was not going to be supported again.

Faculty and staff also noted the importance of documents that went to the campus board. They found that if ideas were discussed with the board and codified into new documents, action usually took place. Reports prepared for external audiences such as accreditation reports also signaled whether collaboration was being taken seriously. The more numerous the official documents that mentioned collaboration were, the more likely faculty and staff were to believe that planning and resources would be available.

## Continuing Dialogue and Socialization—Living the Mission

Although the strategy of continuously articulating the mission helps get buy-in from individuals, it does not necessarily result in changing day-to-day practices so as to actualize the mission statement. As most faculty, staff, and administrators are aware, simply having a mission statement does not ensure that it is lived or becomes part of campus operations. However, institutions in our study that fostered the mission by including collaboration as part of annual evaluations, creating specific mentoring sessions, and more prominently discussing collaboration in orientations were more successful than other campuses at creating a collaborative environment. Faculty members, especially those who had been on different campuses, commented on how the lived mission made a significant difference in the way they approached their work. In the words of one faculty member:

This is the first time I felt that collaboration was "real." On other campuses I have worked, occasionally a new administrator would decide we needed to work more collaboratively or a group of faculty would push for more interdisciplinary research or teaching, but then the tides

turned and the dialogue went away. On this campus, during the hiring process I was told about the campus mission
and the importance of collaboration. When I arrived collaboration was reinforced in the orientation and in all my
initial meetings with colleagues as "part of who we are."
Most public speeches by deans, department chairs, and
vice presidents refer to the mission and our collaborative work. And when I looked around, people were doing
work collaboratively—interdisciplinary teaching and
research, community-based research, working in teams,
it is all happening. So collaboration is lived here and the
socializing and conversations help to reinforce and create that environment.

As this faculty member's comment suggests, leaders take a
variety of opportunities to socialize people to the collaborative
context—hiring processes, orientation, staff and faculty development, tenure and promotion, evaluation, and planning all represent
key events in which a collaborative mission can be reiterated.

In addition, administrators set up dialogues to discuss how
various groups might work together in collaborative ways. On one
campus leaders hosted two retreats a year with the topic, "creating
new collaborations." On another campus, campus leaders organized a monthly speaker series in which they discussed collaborative learning and ways they could further integrate this approach
into the teaching and learning process. Formats and topics varied,
but the common principle was that people were brought together
to discuss the collaborative mission and make it come to life.

### Using the Mission and Philosophy to Allocate
### Resources and Conduct Planning

Each of these campuses committed to a strategic planning process,
created strategic priorities, and allocated resources based on the
plan to help realize collaboration across the campus. On one

campus, community-campus partnerships and outreach was a specific focus in the mission statement; on another, it was active learning. Both of these themes became the focal point of collaborative projects included in the strategic plan and were allocated funds because they were a strategic priority. In fact, many people noted how other collaborative efforts that were not aligned with the mission had more difficulty in gaining support, and the depth of implementation was also affected. They felt the lack of alignment with the mission was one reason the other efforts struggled while active learning and community partnerships thrived. One faculty member describes how resource allocation tied to the mission created new collaborative projects:

> There were several of us who were interested in creating a first-year experience seminar, but it was hard to get support for the effort. The argument always seemed to be that resources were tight and this was something new, and we cannot afford to do something new. However, once collaboration was included in the mission statement and part of our strategic planning, I appealed to administrators talking about how the first year seminar would be the perfect place for a collaborative program. I demonstrated how students could see collaboration in action as soon as they got to the campus and that it would establish and create the type of collaborative learning environment we're trying to achieve. But as I said, this didn't happen until the mission and resource allocation perspectives changed.

Faculty and staff on collaborative campuses also talked about the mission and vision as a guide for how funding was allocated. One faculty member describes this issue:

> I have been on many campuses where funding seemed pretty arbitrary. We would develop strategic plans and

funding never flowed for those initiatives. It was mostly rhetoric. But the reality is the plans were so generic, anyone could really make an argument for funding. The campuses operated fairly politically and resources were tied up in certain units with power. What was different when I came here is that people seem to have a really clear sense of mission, and our vision was to become a place where multidisciplinary research, learning communities, and other collaborative innovations thrive. And you can see how the funding process uses the mission and vision to guide making budget allocations.

## Challenges to Creating a Collaborative Mission

Although all of the campuses in our study were successful in including collaboration as part of their mission and philosophy for the campus, they did note that there were challenges, and they offered advice on the following topics to other campuses.

### Is Collaboration Always Necessary?

Certainly there are situations in which collaboration is not the best way to deliver a service, make a decision, or conduct research. Each of these campuses had concerned organizational citizens who feared that if collaboration was part of the mission statement, then individual work would no longer be respected. Campuses in the study recommended that leaders establish up front that embracing collaboration does not mean the demise of individual work. Instead, collaboration needs to be included in the mission because the historical preference for individualistic work over collaborative work has been the norm for so long that it is the default norm. This is an occasion when understanding the history of higher education and traditional structures (described in Chapter Two) can be helpful in assisting colleagues to understand how institutions are structured to support individualistic work with little, if any, support for collaborative work. By including collaboration in the mission, campuses are trying to create more opportunities for collaborative work.

## People Who Have Had Bad Experiences with Collaboration

On many campuses there will be individuals who come to dialogues or retreats who have had negative experiences with collaboration and who may discourage campuses from engaging in collaborative work. Listening to these voices is particularly important because they can be a source of information for how to think about ways to structure collaborative work on campus. In fact, leaders should try to include people who have had negative experiences in key discussions about the mission. The resulting dialogue will allow for a more holistic discussion of the barriers and challenges to creating a collaborative campus and establishing a collaborative mission. However, these individuals also need to be balanced with voices that describe the benefits and advantages of collaborative work, drawing on the information presented in Chapter One. Although you do not want to dismiss their concerns, you do not want their negativity to harm efforts to create structures and processes that can enable collaborative work.

## Key Leaders Do Not Buy into Collaboration or Are Unable to Be Champions

Although each of these campuses had leaders who supported the move toward a more collaborative context and worked to modify the mission, not all leaders were on board. Few administrators we spoke with were against collaboration per se, but they may not all have understood the advantages of collaboration clearly. Other administrators may not have had a successful or powerful collaborative experience. Without the lived experience of engaging in a powerful collaboration, leaders may not be able to be champions for collaboration. Trying to change a mission statement and to align all the faculty and staff of an institution to a new way of doing work is difficult if you do not have first-hand knowledge and experience. Campuses negotiated this problem in two ways. First, they identified leaders who had experience with collaboration and asked them to be advocates for the process. Second, they had heart-to-heart conversations with leaders who were sympathetic but did not have true buy-in and asked those leaders to support other champions on campus who could better articulate the power of collaboration. Although such discussions could be politically sensitive, they usually resulted in positive reactions.

### Institutions with Weak Missions

Not every institution initially had a mission that drove campus operations. Some of these campuses had to spend more time exploring the importance of mission and educational philosophy before they could make adjustments. This gave them time to generate dialogues about the role of mission on their particular campuses. Most of these institutions were on a course to create change, so they knew that discussing mission would be important. It may be important to first foster dialogue with institutional leaders about the need for an institutional mission to articulate the values of the college or university. Also, if there is not yet a sense of mission, you may want to locate other organizational sagas (stories about campus origins and goals) that serve to articulate institutional values. Even without a strong mission, these stories can create and articulate values that can be used to foster dialogue about collaboration and, eventually, mission.

## Key Issues

1. Ensure that collaboration is included in some part of the mission statement at the institutional level and throughout other units.
2. Include the benefits and logic supporting collaboration in supporting documents for the mission statement.

3. Make sure to talk about the advantages and approaches to collaboration during the discussions about revising the mission statement.

4. Continuously communicate the new mission statement as often as possible and make it relevant to particular stakeholders.

5. Help develop a philosophy of education and work that supports collaboration. Make people aware of key documents and research that can help form this philosophy.

6. Make sure that key campus events and activities include a reminder about the importance of collaboration.

7. Set up regular dialogues or a reading group about the collaborative mission.

8. Create a plan and allocate resources based on the mission statement.

# 5

# Values

*Values are beliefs that guide behaviors and shape underlying assumptions. Values are more moldable than underlying assumptions and are therefore important for creating change.*

Organizations are driven by values, and certain types of values have been found to be more effective in fostering collaboration. The values that appeared in our research to create a common ground in a postsecondary setting include being student centered, innovative, and egalitarian. Values also provide a common ground for people who generally do not work together but who are brought together to collaborate. In this section, we describe the important role that values play in creating a collaborative. But first, why are values so important to the creation of a collaborative environment?

Values cross bureaucratic organizational boundaries and give meaning to the actions and behaviors of individuals within the organization. In a sense, values promote collaboration inherently because they can bring people together to see a common purpose and way of approaching work. Values enable collaboration by giving shared meaning and relating the collaborative efforts to the history and mission of the college. For example, many community colleges are open-access institutions and have a history and mission devoted to success for all students. The mission and history represent the values of the college and provide a basis for defining and justifying individual actions and behaviors. For example, if student affairs professionals and faculty come together with the goal of increasing retention within a college, their actions and collaborative efforts are instantly given meaning as a result of the history and mission of student success on the campus.

Shared values create a sense of purpose and perspective that all organizational members share, which contributes to a sense of meaning, as well as an understanding of the way in which the collaboration fits into the larger organizational mission. For example, if a campus has a student-centered value, then a collaborative effort that focuses on creating access for low-income students relates directly to the student-centered value espoused throughout the organization. In this regard, collaboration assists in fulfilling the student-centered values. Bringing together people from student services, the faculty, and academic services appears to be a logical collaboration given the value of student centeredness.

Furthermore, shared values create a sense of trust and a cohesiveness in perspectives and values among collaborators. As we discuss in Chapter Six, on networks, a sense of trust and relationship building is essential in promoting successful collaborations. In postsecondary institutions where faculty come from diverse perspectives and may not share a common knowledge base or similar values, shared values within the organization take on increased significance. Beginning a collaboration from a sense of shared values creates a foundation on which individuals can build trust and move collaborations forward.

Finally, values promote practices throughout the institution that often require collaboration across disciplinary units and student and academic affairs. One of the important aspects of values in higher education is the power that values have in transcending loosely coupled units, as well as the boundaries and tensions inherent in disciplinary silos. By articulating collaborations as a value, institutions of higher education can transcend organizational boundaries to indirectly promote the creation of more collaborative projects. In addition, collaborations can be framed and shaped within the existing core values that are found to increase organizational performance. Collaborations can serve as an additional value and also as a vehicle to articulate, promote, and fulfill values that have yet to be realized in practice.

## Background of Values

Values are a part of organizational culture. Schein (1985) defines culture as comprising three levels: behaviors and artifacts (what people do), values (what people believe), and basic assumptions (what guides people's actions). Behaviors and artifacts include the physical environment of an organization, such as physical space, mottos, and stories, whereas values define the beliefs and are represented in the behaviors. The third aspect of organizational culture is basic assumptions, which represent the values. Therefore, values are central to organizational culture because they guide behaviors and assumptions.

Values are an integral part of understanding collaboration. Values not only represent organizational norms, they provide underlying meanings for organizational members. The research on organizational culture demonstrates the significant impact values have on organizational functioning and performance (Bolman & Deal, 1997). Organizations that have strong core values and maintain these values over time are found to perform better over the long term. This is not to suggest that values must be stagnant; rather, values need to be flexible. An organization must have both a series of core values that remain central to the organization and a set of flexible values that can be adapted over time. One of the ways that an organization can maintain core values is through the mission statement. For example, Southwest Airlines' mission statement stipulates "dedication to the highest quality of customer service delivered with a sense of warmth, friendliness, individual pride, and Company Spirit" (http://southwest.com). The mission statement directed to their employees states that the organization is committed to providing a stable work environment with equal opportunity for learning and personal growth. The statement continues with a discussion of the importance of creativity, innovation, and improvement of effectiveness of the airline, which are all values. Although the value statement may change over time, the core value of the commitment to providing high-quality customer service should remain the same. Therefore, the core value should be clearly represented in the mission statement, which represents the long-lasting core values.

---

**Examples of Value Statement in Higher Education:**

Respect for the rights, differences, and dignity of others

Honesty and integrity in all dealings

Conscientious pursuit of excellence in one's work

Accountability for actions and conduct in the workplace

Value high standards for learning, teaching, and inquiry.

Embrace the diversity of individuals, ideas, and expressions.

We foster personal growth within an environment in which every individual matters.

We uphold the responsibility of university citizenship.

Exercise stewardship of our global community.

---

Values are critical to collaboration because values often define the actions and behaviors of organizational members, particularly when they are faced with organizational changes. As external groups continue to demand that higher education consider forms of collaborative work, campus leaders may appeal to values to more comfortably lead discussions of what type of organizational change they feel is best. Kanter (1996) found that collaborations were much more like familial or dating relationships and worked based on the interplay of human dynamics much more so than based on contracts, structures, or processes. Research by Tjosvold and Tsao (1989) found values to be critical to collaboration; for example, if there was a sense of shared values between groups or a set of values that drew people together (e.g., passion to help the community), such values overrode other conditions in creating and sustaining a strong collaborative partnership. One recent study on collaboration in higher education demonstrated the role of values for initiating and implementing collaborative efforts (Philpott & Strange, 2003).

Not only do values define the actions of organizational members, they also serve as a foundation to organizational culture. According to Schein (1985), one of the most important elements of organizational culture is the values that are created during crucial incidences. For example, if a campus received a negative accreditation report for a lack of communication across administrative and academic units, the campus needs to evaluate core values to identify whether collaboration is antithetical to the mission and values of the organization. In turn, values serve as a roadmap for organizational norms perpetuated by organizational members through the process of socialization of new members into the organization (Tierney, 1988). In collaborations, individuals will rely on and refer back to the core values of the institution to situate the collaborative efforts within the context of the institution's mission. Individuals who are participating in the collaboration are reminded of the core values, and new organizational members are socialized into the organizational values. In order to foster collaboration at postsecondary institutions, organizational culture, particularly values, must be considered. In this chapter, we present guidelines of how to relate to existing values, capitalize on current values, and grapple with values in order to foster collaboration.

The values of higher education organizational culture are what separate it from corporate culture. Postsecondary education is said to have distinct and complex values that guide and shape culture, such as academic freedom, autonomy, professionalization of faculty and staff, shared governance, equity and access, and democratic engagement (Clark, 1983). The complexity of values in colleges and universities lies in the distinctive approaches of various university cultures. For example, in chemistry one relies on logic, mathematics, experimentation, and facts such as the periodic table, whereas in cultural studies one stresses interpretation and representation. Faculty, furthermore, are professionals who straddle two separate cultures—the culture of the institution and the culture of disciplinary societies. Moreover, students who enter higher education represent different generational values. These values may be in conflict with the values held by faculty and administrators; thus a number of value-based subcultures coexist within one higher education institution. In this chapter, we present guidelines of how to relate to existing values, capitalize on current values, and grapple with values in order to foster collaborations.

## Advice and Examples from Campuses

Values can be used to foster collaboration in higher education institutions to provide a common ground for understanding among organizational members, represent the history and mission of the institution, and promote practices across the institution. One caveat from institutions that have been successful: values were a helpful foundation to begin collaboration, but a sense of priority from people in senior positions, a reward system, and a campus network were noted as much more important for sustainability, particularly on larger campuses. However, smaller campuses that have a strong sense of shared culture could use values to sustain collaboration (see also the discussion under mission in Chapter Four about differences based on institutional type).

### Providing Common Ground

As mentioned at the beginning of the chapter, certain values seem especially important to encourage collaboration, namely, being student centered (putting student needs first in planning and implementation of all processes and structures), innovative (a willingness to experiment and try new processes), and egalitarian (various groups on campus have nonhierarchical relationships with each other). Campuses that embrace these three values seem to be able to foster collaboration more easily because they provide a common ground for collaboration (for students), an ethos to experiment (innovation), and an egalitarian ethic that allows people to value other people's work by eliminating some of the common barriers in an elite culture, such as hierarchies of disciplines, position (faculty and staff, administration), and administrative unit (academic versus student affairs). One faculty member reflected on this key point:

> We talk about our values here and they all have an underlying element of collaboration and help to foster it. It really is important because the mission seems so elusive, you may not interact with senior staff, rewards are often infrequent, but values are always there. They provide a stable foundation and seem very tangible since they guide our work and interactions, especially the student centered and innovative values.

In the words of another faculty member: "Our values system has really gone a long way to support a host of collaborations. I have heard people unprompted connect the values with the collaborative work they are doing."

Two other values—efficiency and capacity building—were also mentioned as providing common ground, but not quite as frequently. As state appropriations shrink, efficiency and capacity building are becoming more compelling values on campuses. One staff member told a story about the way that the values of efficiency and capacity building helped bring the campus together:

> We have gone through several really difficult financial years. Everyone was feeling the pain. But what really

> helped us to pull together and consider new ways of
> working together, more collaborative ways, was talking
> about how collaboration could build our capacity, even
> though we had less funding. Through our collaboration,
> we would be able to continue to meet students' needs in
> the ways that we believed in. Although sometimes it is
> hard to admit, we had some duplication of services that
> we could get rid of to free up funding.

Collaborations not only serve to bring people together to discuss common issues, they also serve as communities where people can began to identify overlapping services that work against the value of efficiency. Furthermore, collaborations can build capacity within an organization by using the time and resources of individuals more efficiently.

Most of these campuses appear to have had one or more of these values—student centered, innovative, and egalitarian—as part of their history and tradition. None of them set out to become more student centered or egalitarian before they set out to create collaboration on campus. Instead, these were existing values that they could capitalize on in support of collaboration. Campuses should strategically identify any such underlying values, as they have been proven to be powerful levers for collaborative work.

### Re-articulating Values

If you have these values, what are some of the strategies that you can use to ensure that people center their work on them? Leaders used several strategies to help make these values come alive. For example, change agents constantly asked questions about what values were used to guide decisions, planning, and campus efforts. A librarian explained:

> As we were starting the move to a more collaborative
> approach to management with campuswide teams,

I remember the head librarian would ask us to explain our rationale when we are making decisions. One of the primary reasons we were moving to a team approach was to be more innovative in our approaches—innovation has always been an important value on our campus, but we weren't always so consistently good about getting lots of different feedback. She would always ask how we had incorporated other people's ideas into our decisions. Were we broadly seeking input? Her questioning really helped remind us how working more collaboratively can help to create more innovation in our decision making.

Another strategy used, especially when conflict might have emerged in collaborations, was reminding people about the values that were being served by collaborating and working together. This is a particularly powerful strategy on campuses where people feel very attached to the culture and its underlying values—often at liberal arts colleges, religiously based institutions, or institutions that serve a specific population such as historically black colleges and universities or women's colleges. One faculty member talks about the way that connecting back to underlying campus values helped campus leaders continue to expand their collaborative work:

We know that we're helping students who just wouldn't make it anywhere else. We have a distinctive mission and our values of care, challenge and support, and high expectations for all have always been a strong anchor. But when we started to do more interdisciplinary work in our learning communities, and people who hadn't worked together before started to clash we went through sort of a dark period. However, there were people on campus that reminded us about why we felt interdisciplinary learning would be important for our students. This helped the biologist, sociologists, and an

art historian to see past their disciplinary cultures and
focus more on creating the best learning environment.

Conflict was a common occurrence on campuses that engaged
in more collaboration. Because people have been divided on
many campuses for a long time, they have created stereotypes
and misperceptions of each other. In addition, they have created
differing values. Reminding people of common ground shared by
educators across campus is essential work to build relationships
and trust.

The campus network and influential members of the
community was key conduits for communicating the values to
support collaboration. Articulating values only from "on high"
among senior executives or proclaiming them by just a few
believers was insufficient to build commitment (even if these were
values shared across the campus). Influential members of the community, who typically have a strong connection to campus values,
can be strong advocates for reminding others, who might have
forgotten in a time of turmoil, such underlying values as student
centeredness, egalitarianism, innovation, or other strongly held
values. These individuals are also trusted members of the community, and in times of change, people who are trusted and speak
up can be very influential and can provide a needed compass
to help maintain movement forward. Members of the campus
already committed to collaboration are also an important group
because they understand collaboration well and can demonstrate
the link between deeply felt campus values and collaboration.
A change agent making this link once or twice is not enough;
people need constant reminders during times of change.

In sum, leaders and the campus network reminded people on
campus about underlying values that are served by collaborating,
questioned people to ensure that their choices were based on a
valuing of collaboration, used values to generate common ground,

and connected and relied on the campus network of collaborators to spread the message as well.

## Create Leadership Teams to Connect Values to the Overall Institutional Mission

Although not a widespread practice, some institutions created a leadership team or made it the responsibility of the presidential cabinet to more formally try to connect existing values to the collaborative mission. This group created value statements and documents that formally described the new collaborative values or the values that they would use to lever a connection to a more collaborative environment. For example, at one college the president initiated a campuswide strategic planning process that included individuals, faculty, and staff from around the college. Organized in teams, the groups were tasked with the responsibility of identifying the underlying values of the college and articulating how each initiative would fit into the larger campus mission (which they also helped create). These teams were responsible for the planning process and not just an evaluation or ad hoc team that provided feedback for an ongoing process. In order to not exclude others, some of these groups also created opportunities for members of the campus to provide feedback on the value statements through town hall meetings or other types of forums. The strategic planning documents were widely disseminated and all individuals were welcome to become involved in the process either as team members or in providing feedback on an ad hoc basis. The teams also tried to work with other change agents on campus to provide them with strategies for articulating these values in the day-to-day management and decision-making context. By engaging others on campus, the new initiatives and values became part of the larger campus culture and were reinforced by those trusted individuals. Some of the strategies described in the last section were developed in these conversations between the leadership team and other change agents and leaders on campus.

## Challenges to Holding Values That Enable Collaboration

Existing organizational values can be used to support collaborative work. But having values that support collaboration will be a challenge for many campuses. We now review some of the major challenges noted by campus leaders in our study.

### Missing Shared Values

Perhaps the greatest challenge is for campuses that do not have any values similar to student centeredness, innovation, egalitarianism, capacity building, or efficiency that appeal to collaboration. This is a real challenge; manifesting new values on a campus is a very complex process that often takes years to develop. Individuals within the organization should come to a consensus on this new set of values, the values must be communicated regularly and in relationship to existing values, and individuals should adopt these values as a part of the organizational culture. Living the new values can take many more years as people become socialized to a new way to approach their work. Changing the values of an institution—either to value collaboration or the "lever" values—can take many years and may not be practical for some campuses.

It seems prudent for campuses that do not share the values discussed in this section to see whether there are related values they may be able to capitalize on. The process of understanding the relationship between long-standing institutional values and collaborative work may not be a simple or easy process. One method for attempting this goal or for evaluating its efficacy might be to establish a leadership team or ad hoc committee with multiple constituent groups for the purpose of deconstructing the existing value system and attempting to align those values with collaborative work. This long-term process of deconstructing values needs to be coupled with a short-term process for integrating collaborative work into the current value structure. Establishing organizational processes, such as rewards for collaborative work, articulates to the campus community that collaborative work is valued and potentially begins the process of integrating collaborative work as a value within the larger organizational culture.

### Lengthy Time to Alter Values

Ultimately, the goal of this work with values is to hold collaboration itself as a value—then collaboration will truly be part of campus culture and will be exhibited more naturally. However, there are several challenges (already described) to establishing and maintaining a new value system that supports collaboration. New values will take a long time to manifest. Another issue is that even if you have some of the lever values, they can be in direct conflict with deeply held existing values. For example, being student centered is extremely difficult on a research university campus, where the environment is largely faculty centered and most faculty are unwilling to admit that the values are structured that way. Other state colleges that are more teaching focused may have a difficult time establishing a value of research and external grant seeking for faculty because faculty in the college have traditionally maintained a focus on teaching and not research.

## Key Issues

1. Values are an important part of organizational culture and are essential in trying to establish collaboration in postsecondary education because they create common ground that transcends organizational boundaries.
2. Institutions need to use existing values that support collaboration such as innovation or student centeredness as levers for change until collaboration itself becomes a value.
3. Institutions should establish an ad hoc team to identify any other key values that support collaboration on their own campus.

4. Leaders and change agents need to be active participants in helping people connect existing values to collaborative work through questioning and re-articulating values.

5. Capitalize on the networks and trusted influential individuals who have existing relationships to the campus to communicate values to other individuals in the institution.

6. Establish leadership teams to focus on how collaborative work can be integrated into the core value structure while also supporting collaborative work within the institution.

# 6

# Social Networks

*Social networks are people loosely connected through some form of interdependency such as values, preferences, goals, ideas, or friends.*

Another critical feature of the organizational context for supporting collaborative work is an intentionally created campus network. The network is important for establishing collaboration, gaining initial support for collaborative efforts by leveraging collective influence, developing ownership, engaging implementation, providing diverse perspectives, and creating ongoing support of collaborative work. But why was a network so central to collaboration on the campuses we studied? Once the idea or concept was in place (through the mission, vision, and values), human resources became central to enabling collaboration and networks provided a "ready-made" source of connected individuals who were able to quickly engage a concept or idea.

Collaborations often fail because relationships have to be developed. Because of the tremendous amount of time that it takes to build relationships, in addition to getting the collaboration off the ground, relationship building can prove to be too much of a barrier. Preexisting networks with established relationships are useful when trying to launch a new collaboration. Often collaborations fail because groups do not undergo the necessary relationship building to create a trusting environment. Collaborations are defined by democratic decision making, debate, and discussion that is more successful when collaborative groups trust each other and feel they can be open and honest. Using an existing network that has undergone the relationship and trust-building exercises can propel collaboration forward quickly and give the network a unified purpose.

Networks are also useful in leveraging collective influence and power to navigate organizations. Established networks with knowledgeable and powerful individuals can propel collaborations forward by leveraging the knowledge of institutional policies and structures, capitalizing on institutional memory, and connecting people of influence who are able to navigate the power dynamics of the institution. Networks that have people of influence and knowledge provide the collaboration and capital necessary to move forward quickly and effectively.

Furthermore, networks provide the intellectual resources and cognitive complexity needed to overcome barriers that emerge. For example, one campus network helped the university determine that it needed to change its accounting and computer systems. The antiquated systems were desperately out of date and caused problems within the organization. The network not only identified a need but also researched and recommended new options for the campus to use. Creating new structures or rewards to support collaboration is a monumental task and often meets with failure. Networks, however, have the intellectual resources to overcome barriers and resistance to new structures and processes on campus.

Networks were also noted as the organizational context feature that helped maintain and generate more collaboration on campus. One faculty member commented on the synergistic power of networks:

> We started developing these really interesting interdis-
> ciplinary courses in the sciences and I was telling some
> of my friends in the humanities. They wanted to meet
> with the science faculty and hear more about our efforts.

> Within a few months, the humanities faculty were
> developing interdisciplinary courses as well. That is real
> network power!

As relationships developed through participation, one collaboration led to other activities. In terms of generating collaboration, the networks created opportunities for individuals to constantly come in contact or become aware of individuals who might be related to a new collaborative project or who could enhance an existing one, thus providing new and fresh energy to efforts on a consistent basis.

Networks in higher education foster dedication, decrease isolation, bring together different perspectives and help move initiatives forward. For example, on one campus individuals wanted to revamp their undergraduate curriculum; they began this effort by tapping into a network of faculty dedicated to collaboration and built a critical mass of people who took ownership and helped diffuse collaboration across campus. The network had evolved over several years and included faculty from the sciences, the social sciences, and humanities. Each had come to value collaborative work through different experiences—for some it was working in a lab and seeing the power of a research team, for others it was involvement in a community-based research project, whereas others had experiences outside the workplace such as involvement in athletics and volunteer work or in other workplaces that had valued collaboration. Before these individuals found each other, they felt that they were the only ones in the academy who valued collaboration. These networks were critical to create synergy by connecting like-minded people.

## Background of Social Networks

As stated at the beginning of the chapter, social networks are people loosely connected through some form of interdependency such as values, preferences, goals, ideas, or people (Wasserman & Faust, 1994). Because the structure is loose, it can be quite complex and involve people across various units, organizations, and outside the organization. Networks are typically viewed in terms of the nodes (people) and ties (relationships between people) (Scott, 2000), but people are at the center of the network, brought together by the relationships that exist between individuals and groups. Not all networks involve collaboration. A network is considered collaborative when people work together by sharing information, resources, and knowledge to achieve a common goal. Collaborative networks do not compete with each other and share all resources to achieve a goal. Otherwise, people can be interlinked within a network, but not have any shared goals or direction.

Another distinction is that networks can be formal or informal (Allen, James, & Gamlen, 2007; Golbeck & Hendler, 2006). An example of a formal network is a professional organization, such as the American Educational Research Association. People have a common interest and come together around formal organizational structures to support their communication and interaction. Typically, networks are visible in that others are aware of those formal networks. In contrast, informal networks typically do not have resources, organizational structures, and support and may remain largely unknown to other people within an organization or large system. In fact, informal networks are often characterized as the glue that holds together work that crosses typical organizational functions (Allen, James, & Gamlen, 2007). One reason informal networks are so powerful is that individuals feel a responsibility and trust for those involved in the network. For instance, employees may feel no particular allegiance to an organization but feel connected to interpersonal networks.

Whether establishing a formal or informal network, the literature describes the importance of trust, time and energy, mutual interests, a shared vision, selection of participants, and anticipation and planning for a long-term relationship (Axelrod, 2001; Keyes et al, 1996; Sabel, 1992). The first and most important aspect of networks is trust which binds people together when there are few other incentives (Adler, 2001; Buskens, 2002; Golbeck & Hendler, 2006). Networks are often created informally by individuals coming together and communicating because of an internal interest rather than an external mandate. Simply put, people become involved in informal networks because they have an interest and a willingness to invest the time and energy to assist others with the same interest. For example, a group of faculty may form a network because they are interested in promoting the hiring of more faculty of color. Their commitment to the network and the time and energy required to achieve the initiative is outside the bounds of their normal work. Trust in each other helps bond the group of faculty together and maintain the extra work required to participate in the network.

In order to establish networks, time and energy are required to bring people together and develop trust. Networks are not created quickly, but over the course of many months and years. Therefore, many networks result in long-term relationships because of the investment to establish them in the first place. When a network is functioning well, individuals may stay connected for many years, building long-term relationships characterized by trust and support (Adler, 2001).

Another important aspect of networks is a mutual interest and a shared vision. Some networks come together because they have a mutual interest, such as changing a policy in an organization; other networks are characterized by a shared vision. A network may have a larger vision for the organization that requires years or decades of work, such as wanting to increase the numbers of women and minorities in the faculty. In contrast, a network may have a mutual interest—helping low-income or students of color on a college campus—but not a similar vision. Although the network with a mutual interest may not meet regularly or have a particular vision for the future of the college, they pool resources and work together on an intermittent basis to help students. Whether networks are focused on a mutual interest or a shared vision, networks are more successful when there are commonalities that bind individuals together (Miller, Besser, & Malshe, 2007).

When establishing and expanding networks, the literature discusses the importance of selecting participants who are able to contribute to the network. Particularly in networks that rely on specific knowledge or collaborations that rely on a broad knowledge base (i.e., interdisciplinary teams), choosing the right combination of diverse backgrounds can make a difference in the ability of the network to achieve a common goal (Reagans, Zuckerman, & McEvily, 2004). For example, individuals from varying disciplines may bring unique perspectives and skills, thus providing more diversity as well as a larger knowledge base to draw from. Furthermore, the combination of individuals included in the network can have an effect on relationships within the network. Individuals within the network need to get along in order to have positive communication and experiences.

Several campuses in our study used networks to build successful collaborations. Let's look at the strategies they used for establishing new networks and capitalizing on existing networks.

## Building Networks for Collaboration

Successful collaborations on college campuses begin with strong existing networks. These networks can be drawn upon for a variety of purposes. For example, the network can create a formal coalition when a particular change is challenged by certain people on campus. The network provides expertise and human resources that can be drawn upon quickly and easily. The building of networks for collaboration, however, requires an intentional strategy to bring people together to form groups that are later capitalized on for collaborations. There are several strategies and practices: investing in network building activities, identifying and supporting natural network builders, creating incentives, capitalizing on committee work, using physical space, and opening up meetings—all are useful when considering how to build networks for the specific purpose of creating effective collaborations. The sheer number of techniques used reflects the variation among institutions studied that relied on a variety of techniques based on the institutions' individual histories, traditions, physical spaces, norms, finances, and existing structures.

## Invest in Network-Building Activities and Units

First, collaborative campuses had intentionally invested in building strong relationships through hosting different events for faculty and staff such as a leadership series for people across campus, social events, and symposia. The events were well-publicized, and campus leaders made sure to encourage involvement. It is important that a variety of different types of activities and events be offered because some faculty and staff are drawn more to intellectual events such as symposia or lunch speakers; others are interested in professional development opportunities such as leadership topics, while still others enjoy an opportunity to informally socialize and meet other faculty and staff. Institutions need to be aware that offering multiple opportunities for network building helps build the critical mass necessary for collaboration. Some campuses had a very strong culture where certain types of network building were more prevalent and multiple opportunities were not necessary. For instance, one campus had a very strong community outreach ethic, and the leaders were able to attract faculty and staff to network-building events by mentioning the connection to community outreach activities. Other campuses had a very strong intellectual environment, and symposia were the only type of activity needed to create a network. Some campuses had difficulty finding incentives that attract both staff and faculty, and they hosted separate network events for each group; however, they realized that over time they would have to find activities to attract both groups so that no one would be isolated from collaborative work.

Events served a variety of functions related to network building. They maintained the "existing" critical mass of individuals who are interested in collaboration and provided a way for them to sustain their involvement and interest. In particular, faculty doing collaborative work can become very isolated in departments or units that do not support their approach to work. Campuswide events bring together people who might otherwise become isolated and give up their commitment to collaborative work because it becomes too difficult and they lose their resiliency. In addition, these events offer an opportunity for new people to become part of the campuswide network of individuals interested in collaborative work and provide them with an immediate home for their interests. The networking activities also help informally connect people who might develop a new collaborative effort. Longtime faculty and staff can develop an interest in a particular collaborative effort such as a learning community and decide they are interested in working with others across campus. These events give them an opportunity to automatically connect to others who have done collaborative work and see how they can make this effort come to fruition. One faculty member describes how these networks operate on her campus:

> One of the most important elements of collaborative work is having relationships that have already been built which you can call upon at the needed time. I happened to meet with some different community agencies who are interested in developing some community based research projects. If I had to go back to campus and spend a year finding out who might be interested in explaining the importance of community based research, and all that background work, the

community agencies would have moved on to some other institution. Most places don't operate on our timetable. But I could actually say to them, I know lots of faculty who have this interest on our campus and was able to get the project off the ground within three or four months. If we didn't have people who are already networked and knew each other across campus, we would have missed out on this opportunity.

The networks often emerged at the departmental or school level, which had some limitations in that these levels do not directly facilitate campuswide collaboration. However, the benefit of network building at the local level is that it often resulted in more immediate collaborative work. Many campuses had a story of a school or department that hosted a series of lunches or a symposium and within six months they had several new team-taught courses, new interdisciplinary offerings, a revised advising structure, community service projects, or joint research activities that were immediately up and running. They all noted that the activity was primarily operating at the department or school level. However, these local efforts were often complemented by a centralized unit that hosted network-building activities to foster collaboration on campus—usually the faculty development center or human resources. Colleges that created an environment that enables collaborative work designated some offices for fostering campuswide network. The director of one center for teaching and learning describes this role:

> Several years back when we were meeting with adminis-
> trators about the future of the center, they suggested that
> we might play a larger role in helping build relationships
> across campus for both faculty and staff. Pretty soon we
> began to joke, any office that we were matchmakers
> work. . . . trying to connect people with similar interests

and see where that interest might take them. I see it as my job to know what faculty research interests are, those who are interested in community-based research, who are interested in innovative teaching techniques, and which staff have an interest in learning communities or service learning.

On another campus the human resources office used the metaphor of being a hummingbird, pollinating flowers all over campus with the seeds of collaboration in describing their role in encouraging and fostering networks.

The exact office responsible for hosting activities to intentionally create networks was different on every campus and depended on the campus culture and history. Community colleges often have strong human resources offices that both faculty and staff look to for support and opportunities. As mentioned earlier, centers for teaching and learning also often had the infrastructure and connections to play the role of network builder. On other campuses, it was a combination of several offices that had cross-campus functions such as assessment, community outreach, or interdisciplinary centers and institutes working together to host networking functions. But it is critical that the institution provide enough budgeting to support these networking activities and that senior administrators who establish roles and responsibilities make networking a formal activity of some office or offices on campus. One administrator describes the importance of making networking an institutionalized process:

> We wanted more collaborative work, and when we hosted events to attract people to particular initiatives, we often got some traction. But it seemed like we were recreating the wheel all the time. We always had to do a major campaign. One of the staff members mentioned that it would be a lot easier if we kept the momentum

going between people interested in collaborative work. This person was also going to take on the work, so we modified her role description and provided the funding. And she was right, ever since we developed the network on campus, our collaborative efforts are much more easily accomplished.

## Identifying and Supporting Natural Network Builders

In addition to formal units that saw their role as network building, there were also individuals who served as conveners who connected people across campus. These people usually worked in cross-functional units such as assessment, community service, community outreach, international affairs, and the like. Two conveners were mentioned by almost everyone at one campus as "routinely taking people out to lunch from across various units to develop new relationships." Typically these individuals were long-time members of the campus who had already developed extensive networks themselves. However, on some campuses such individuals were relatively new on campus but had had experience in network building a former position; for example, a faculty member who had led a nonprofit company or a staff member who had done public relations. Thus, key positions can be developed and capitalized on to build networks. One staff member talks about the work of the convener:

> Shannon is just amazing. I can go to her about almost any student issue, administrative concern, or political issue and she knows someone (usually several people) who can help me advance that issue. But she doesn't just stop there at giving you names. I think that's where it usually stops for typical networking. She usually makes an introduction, often offers to take people to lunch together, and when possible will host an event or meeting to bring people together. So she doesn't

just know people and have a network, but she actually convenes people.

On some campuses that convener was associated with or led the unit that provides campuswide networking activities (or they were placed in these positions over time based on their skills), but on just as many other campuses this individual was not a paid staff or faculty member doing this work as part of his or her role, but an individual who had natural networking skills and made this part of his or her day-to-day activities. What is important is that institutions identify these individuals and use their natural talents. Campuses that were successful in creating a collaborative environment sought out natural network builders, and administrators met with them periodically to inform them about strategic initiatives and to garner their support for new collaborative projects. Administrators were most successful when these meetings were open ended and allowed for the network builder to provide ideas and even question strategic directions. If the network builder perceived that administrators were merely trying to use their influence to create a particular direction on campus, the relationship could become strained. This strain might result in losing the network builder's or convener's support. One administrator talked about walking this difficult line:

> We're lucky to have several influential faculty who have invested their careers on the campus and who built a real reputation. Because they've been here a long time, they know faculty on every unit, staff across campus, alumni, and board members. Talk about individuals who can create collaboration. So we recognized these were key individuals to tap as we started our learning communities and were fundamentally altering our educational process. But we offended two of these faculty immediately. They needed time to understand where

we were going with the learning communities and we made the mistake of not including them in the initial planning process. We recovered and they were really supportive in the end. But you need to think through the relationships carefully because they have powerful networks that can be used to support or undermine your efforts.

## Creating Incentives

A third approach to developing the networks is incentives. For example, to obtain funding for an assessment initiative on one campus, applicants had to form teams within the school that would work with groups across campus. Almost every school and college took advantage of this initiative, and new campus networks are now in place as a result of creating an incentive system. Each of the initiatives needs to specifically target several constituent groups or have an overarching focus that will appeal to a variety of constituent groups. So tying funding initiatives directly to working with others across campus was a powerful way to get people to work in fundamentally new ways. A staff member commented on the success of using incentives to form networks:

> We had been trying to get people across campus to come up with ways to address the accreditation mandate around outcomes assessment. We needed to move away from the very individualized type of assessment that was going on. We set up a set of funding with some guidelines for assessment criteria in some groups that might naturally work together. What is exciting is that these initial networks have now resulted in other collaborative projects. It was important just to get people talking to other groups on campus. Because we had a real urgency around these outcomes assessment and provided a vehicle for creating these networks and some incentives behind doing it.

Another example of incentives to build networks among faculty is creating grant competitions on campus that require working with a group of other individuals such as a group of faculty from several schools or departments or both. One campus created a very large pool of funds that would only be allocated to units if they created cross-unit projects—typically working with several units. Some campuses had governance or curriculum committees that could provide course releases or summer funding, and they allocated these rewards based on collaboration-oriented proposals that intentionally described building networks on campus. By getting groups of faculty together with attached incentives, networks naturally developed. Networks can also develop by creating a committee or group on an ad hoc basis that has a mission that transcends constituent groups and provides some incentive for working together. For example, a committee that works on salary-equity issues can include individuals from all constituent groups, and the group can be rewarded with course releases, release of other administrative responsibilities, or other nonmonetary benefits, such as "face time" with the college president.

## Committee Work

Although college campuses always have committee work going on, many missed opportunities to create networks occur each day. The campuses that generated a great deal of collaborative work, however, knew how to capitalize on committee work for creating networks. These campuses realized that committee work needs to focus on particular purposes and goals but can also be capitalized on to build relationships, especially among key individuals who might help to move an initiative forward. Administrators on these campuses carefully chose individuals to serve on committees and encouraged involvement among faculty who might not normally serve on committees. Therefore, the work required to bring people together can also serve the purpose of relationship building to foster collaboration.

In addition to administrators realizing the importance of making strategic committee assignments to build networks, many faculty and staff were volunteering for committee work in order to build networks for bottom-up collaborative initiatives they were working on. A faculty member commented on how committee work helped build an interdisciplinary program she was working on:

> I decided it would be important for me to meet more people across campus. Such as other people in political science, anthropology, sociology, for example who had an interest on environmental issues. We did not have a committee on sustainability or environmentalism (which we are now setting up), but there was this cross-campus committee on scholarship. I know that sounds like a far reach, but I knew there would be representatives from across campus there. I got to know a few people and described my interests. They were not always particularly interested, but they introduced me to other people in their departments who were. I know I could've approach these people myself, but they might have been leery. After having spent some time together on committees, these people really trusted me and so they put a good word in for me.

Not all faculty and staff joined committees with the intention of building a network; instead, this was just a natural outcome. Campus service can build a comprehensive network that results in collaborations based on synchronicity. For example, a department chair commented: "This may sound strange, but as I think about the collaboration I have been involved with, many emerged from random encounters I had with people on campus committees. The more committees you serve on, the broader your network and over time, that serves to support initiatives and create new ideas." Committee work is a great opportunity for building networks because it does not require additional resources and it is expected that all faculty and staff will participate. Faculty maintain service as a part of tenure and promotion review, and campus administrators contribute to and organize a variety of committees to maintain democratic standards in decision making. By default, each individual on the campus works on many committees and meets individuals from across the campus, providing many opportunities for networks to develop. Institutions should maintain standards of service and work to keep individuals involved in a variety of committees across the campus because networks may develop just by getting people into the same room.

### Use Physical Space

Campuses used physical space in which to build networks, such as campus centers or faculty and staff dining areas. Dining areas become de facto meeting locations where people can eat together, bump into colleagues, and be seen on the campus. In addition, dining areas give faculty, in particular, reasons to get out of offices and laboratories, which isolate them from the larger campus community. Lobbies, courtyards, and common areas where people could interact were also important for facilitating collaboration. As one faculty noted: "If you do not see people, you lose touch and collaboration breaks down. The time it takes to set up meetings is crazy these days." Having spaces for people to bump into each other makes all the difference in terms of fostering collaboration. Individuals need to be encouraged to take lunch breaks, spend afternoons on campus, and interact with colleagues. Campus leaders can set a tone on campus through their own actions that meeting in common spaces is part of the campus culture and is expected.

Some campuses lacked adequate common space and had to designate a restaurant or local establishment where faculty and staff might meet, for instance, later in the afternoons or on Fridays. Administrators and faculty noted the need to be creative about finding physical space and not let the lack of space on campus dominate planning and block creativity. This is particularly true of urban institutions and community colleges that were not built with the amenities that are more typical of the liberal arts college or research university. Over time, campuses will have opportunities to rethink their physical space with capital improvement monies that come from the state or successful capital campaigns. But spaces are unlikely to be redesigned in ways that help build networks unless administrators make this a priority in working with architects and contractors.

---

**Ways to Rethink Campus Spaces**

Many campuses have deferred maintenance plans that provide an opportunity to rethink spaces in coming years and make them more collaborative. Facilities planners should be partners in the efforts to create a collaborative environment. See the Project Kaleidoscope Web site for samples of collaborative spaces, along with architects and other resources: http://www.pkal.org. Specific facilities resources can be found at http://www.pkal.org/collections/ PKALFacilities Resource.cfm.

---

## Opening Up Meetings

Another relatively easy strategy for creating networks is opening up meetings and processes to more people. One administrator described this strategy of building networks: "They never used to have divisionwide meetings, but then I thought, how are people going to meet and get to know each other so they can collaborate? So I began to invite everyone to the meetings and new initiatives have popped up as a result." Similar to promoting involvement on committees, developing an open door policy to meetings and events allows individuals to enter into a network and simply meet other people on the campus. As individuals volunteer to attend the open meeting, it can be assumed that those individuals have a particular interest in the content or topic of the meeting. Therefore, open meetings can connect people across the campus who share interests. These can be powerful and sustainable networks.

Similarly, faculty spoke about opening up governance meetings so all faculty could participate that had formerly been closed. They sent out meeting agendas early so people could plan in advance if there was a topic of interest to them and could connect with others at the meeting who had a similar interest. Junior and senior faculty came into contact more often on campuses that had opened up meetings, and more collaborations between these two groups consequently emerged.

### Hiring Staff and Reallocating Human Resources

Although many campuses could build a network with existing faculty and staff, some felt it was necessary to make strategic hires around a particular interdisciplinary initiative, learning community, or other cross-campus effort. They also felt these individuals could bring new energy to the network. One of the major barriers to collaborative efforts is having the right people on board who actually believe in collaborative work and have some experience with it. On campuses that are transitioning from a more individualized to a collaborative approach, senior executives may need to hire some individuals who can model this behavior for others on campus and build the existing network. Senior executives need to scan the campus environment to find pockets where individuals may need to be hired to facilitate collaboration. This strategy is used very sparingly, as creating new positions is usually difficult on most campuses. Most often senior executives only have the opportunity to hire a person with a collaborative orientation when there is turnover of a staff member, administrator, or member of the faculty.

Strategic hires not only provided more models of collaboration on some of the campuses studied, they also created more energy around the collaboration, as these individuals often had great enthusiasm for collaborative work. One faculty member describes the experiences and changes that resulted from the president's hiring of a new dean:

> You could really see the difference between our school of engineering or the business school who had deans that understood the new collaborative mission and had many projects under way. There is energy and excitement among the faculty in these schools—they received many campuswide grants; the president was talking about them every time he did a public relations piece. When our dean retired, it created an opportunity for the president to bring in someone who has the same commitment. Thankfully, the president saw this opportunity and hired someone who has now provided the leadership for collaboration.

## Challenges to Building a Network

Building networks is an essential part of fostering successful collaborations. As discussed, networks help by establishing trust, building capacity, and bringing together diverse perspectives that overcome barriers to solve problems. Not all campuses have networks to capitalize on, and these campuses must build networks internally. Building networks is a challenging process, yet it is essential for fostering collaboration. In this section, we outline a few challenges to building networks and suggest ways to overcome them.

### Faculty Networks

Fostering networks with faculty tends to be more difficult than with staff and administrators. Faculty pose a particular dilemma because their work takes them off campus and they have been socialized for years to conduct individualistic work (even if they value collaboration). To overcome these challenges, faculty and administrative leaders try to determine key areas of interest that will bring faculty together at social events, workshops, and symposia. One campus was able to generate faculty interest around serving the local community because many of the faculty had a personal investment in the community. Another campus generated interest by talking about regional concerns related to poverty and environmental challenges, describing how faculty could help address these regional concerns. Other campuses focused on the faculty's interest in being excellent teachers and developed workshops focused on improving teaching and learning across campus. These topics, though different, were all areas that faculty were passionate about and that could motivate them to show up at events. To choose these topics, administrators spoke with key faculty across campus and conducted surveys of faculty. Campuses can also capitalize on the external networks of some faculty; for example, professional or disciplinary groups. Collaborative campuses were aware that faculty, at times, realize the importance of networks (and are perhaps not averse, but do not see the benefits of on-campus networks), and they tried to explain why on-campus networks could be important for their career as well as external interests.

### Time to Develop Trust

Another challenge to building networks is the time, commitment, and energy required to develop relationships and create a trusting environment. Once created, networks are significant  structures in supporting and enabling collaboration. But creating those networks is a time-consuming process and many faculty, staff, and administrators are already overburdened with responsibilities. It is important to consider alleviating those time constraints by offering incentives to individuals for their participation in networking and in established networks. For faculty, campuses can place more emphasis on service in the tenure and promotion process, offer course release for involvement, or incentives by creating networks that lead to grant development or other intellectual exercises. Challenges may arise in trying to develop blanket policies that affect diverse disciplinary cultures and national academic standards. There may also be challenges in finding instructors to teach classes for which faculty receive course releases, yet the rewards for creating networks far outweigh the challenges.

## Lack of Incentives

Inflexible policies that maintain traditional structures and hierarchies serve as barriers to the establishment of networks and the development of collaborations. Policies that favor traditional departmental structures in higher education serve as barriers for faculty who wish to participate in collaborations. For example, faculty who want to contribute to cross-disciplinary groups do so without acknowledgment of their work in those collaborations; they feel as though they are taking on additional work rather than substituting the collaborative efforts for other aspects of their jobs. Consequently they are unavailable for creating networks that aid collaborations. Also, organizational structures may not value networks and incentives may be missing A lack of value placed on collaborative work in tenure and promotion practices, for example, creates disincentives for faculty to participate in collaborations.

## Poor Physical Environment

Many campuses are limited in the type of physical space they have and, as noted earlier, the physical layout of some campuses is antithetical to collaboration. Often urban campuses have few community and communal spaces because the assumption was that students would commute to the institution. In fact, several of the institutions in this study did not have physical spaces that were amenable to creating networks and community. However, as collaboration and creating networks became a priority, they were able to justify changing the purpose of certain available spaces. To overcome the challenges in physical space, campuses should consider using space for multiple purposes. For example, a faculty dining area can be created in a meeting space during lunch hours and used for meetings during other hours of the day. In redesigning and upgrading buildings, common areas and open floor plans can also be created that utilize space properly while also allowing for more interaction.

## Power Dynamics

Another challenge encountered among administration and staff is that when meetings are opened up to a broader audience, power dynamics sometimes emerge that often surprise people and need to be negotiated. Typically, meetings are reserved for senior staff and administrators. When a broader group of individuals is brought into the meeting, senior staff may unintentionally demonstrate that they do not value other staff members' perspectives. Mid-level and lower-level staff and administrators may find that some individuals feel they should be seen but not heard. Nonsenior staff may find themselves struggling to be full participants. People on each of the campuses studied said that if change agents had been aware that this problem would occur, they would have pulled aside the senior administrators to explain why opening up the meeting was important and to ask for their support and assistance. These administrators did not anticipate the power dynamics, however, which initially created some problems. The same power dynamics also emerged between junior and senior faculty on many campuses that opened up their meetings to a broader audience. Although they were able to overcome the tension, it resulted in some people not being as involved in the network as desired. As campuses open up meetings, change agents need to anticipate power dynamics that might emerge among faculty and staff of different status. Leaders and champions of collaboration need to pull aside senior administrators and faculty to make them aware of the need to create an inclusive environment and develop some strategies for making newcomers feel welcome to the meetings. They also need to be able to read the dynamics in the room and to protect individuals who are attacked and pull aside individuals who are acting inappropriately.

## Network as a Threat to the Status Quo

Sometimes networks can become "too" visible on campuses. On some campuses networks became a threat to the prevailing ideas and existing power structure, thus garnering some resistance to their work and to the notion of collaboration as a whole. Networks might include lots of innovators and individuals who think differently from the campus. Although this can be helpful for collaboration, it can also create political problems for the network. So tapping into the network of folks who already support collaborative work can be both a blessing and a curse. Creating networks should always be done politically, examining how people react to groups of innovators meeting. Some campuses decided not to tap this group of innovators until later, when they were brainstorming redesign issues or trying to navigate challenges.

## Key Issues

1. Create a centralized unit on campus with the specific mission of bringing together individuals with similar interests.

2. Encourage units and departments to establish network-building activities.

3. Develop incentives for individuals to become involved in networks such as competitive grants, course releases, and summer funding.

4. Create and capitalize on existing public spaces (faculty dining areas and green spaces) to build relationships and develop rapport between individuals.

5. Make it a priority to open up meetings to all interested parties.

6. Determine key areas of interest that would bring faculty together at social events, workshops, and symposia.

7. Anticipate collaborative needs and begin developing relationships to create trusting networks.

8. Identify individuals who naturally like to collaborate and bring them together as a support mechanism for collaboration.

9. Make sure to think about your own institutional context as you develop strategies for successfully building campus networks.

# Integrating Structures

*Integrating structures are restructured or new organizational
configurations that support collaborative and team-based
work such as cross-functional teams or a matrix structure.*

Integrating structures are another feature of organizational context that is extremely important for supporting collaboration.
Each of the campuses in our study established a central unit(s) or
initiatives for collaboration, developed a set of centers and institutes across campus, created cross-functional teams, and revamped
their accounting, computer, and budgetary systems. These structural
changes, oriented toward collaboration, helped create a very different campus environment.

Why were integrating structures noted as so significant? With an
idea (mission, vision, values) and people on board (network), structures were important to sustain collaboration. Integrating structures
assist collaboration by ensuring the health, vitality, and growth of
campus networks. They also help support the mission by making
institutional priorities around collaboration visible, tangible, and
concrete. Also, sustained collaboration seems highly dependent on
redesigning campus structures such as computing systems and divisional meetings and creating new structures such as research and
teaching institutes. Integrating structures ensure that there are not
any barriers in communication, budgeting, or technology. People
on campuses have noted how nay-sayers (those who do not believe
in collaboration) are looking for problems in order to provide evidence that collaboration will not work. Integrating structures are
one of the ways to make sure you do not hit the bumps along the

road to collaboration (or at least hit fewer). When information sharing is clear, when people problem solve together, and when technology works, nay-sayers have few problems to highlight.

Integrating structures, like mission, help develop a sense of priority related to collaborative work. These structures also create visibility about the value of collaborative work. For example, one integrating structure, the presidential initiative, usually received a great deal of attention across campus, thus highlighting the need for collaborative work. In addition, cross-institutional centers provided visibility for a core set of faculty and staff in order to coalesce and work together. The retention committee became very well-known on campus and was one of the most visible groups. All of these structures enable collaboration by creating visibility and a sense of priority related to collaboration.

Like the networks, integrating structures also helped connect people across campus. Faculty development centers, assessments units, and experiential or service learning centers became sites where teams of faculty came together based on their concern with improving teaching, improving student outcomes, or experimenting with new pedagogical approaches. People at these campuses spoke about how these units opened up lines of communication that created many new opportunities for collaboration. These integrating structures are important and pivotal mechanisms for creating networks described in the last section.

## Background of Integrating Structures

Integrating structures are a way to alter aspects of the organizational structure so that they support collaborative and team-based work (Mohrman, Cohen, & Mohrman, 1995). Perhaps one of the best-known integrating structures is the cross-functional team (Denison, Hart, & Kahn, 1996). Cross-functional teams bring together members from different units and divisions across an organization who typically do not communicate in order to work together toward a shared goal. However, there are also a variety of other integrating structures, including matrix management, project management, matrix organizations, and project units or organizations (Holland, Gaston, & Gomes, 2000). All of these terms refer to some type of cross-functional work that brings together people from two or more separate functional areas to undertake a task on a temporary or relatively permanent basis. These structures help create communication among individuals or across groups that typically do not work together (Holland, Gaston, & Gomes, 2000). Integrating structures are considered more important in complex and large environments that are prone to develop isolated, bureaucratic silos or become overloaded by multiple processes and can no longer process the information necessary to adjust to the changing environment. Therefore, smaller organizations may need fewer and less complex integrating structures.

Integrating structures have been found to solve information-processing problems (Holland, Gaston, & Gomes, 2000). When people are brought together in cross-functional teams or projects, they have the opportunity to share information about research, teaching, and service that has been trapped in siloed structures. Communication, improved information flow, and flexibility are enhanced by these structures. Some research has also demonstrated that integrating structures can increase individual motivation, job satisfaction, commitment, and personal development by providing employees with greater influence in their work, which makes them feel greater self-efficacy (Denison, Hart, & Kahn, 1996; Holland, Gaston, & Gomes, 2000). Cross-functional teams and other integrating structures have been related to greater technical excellence and stronger outcomes for the particular problem they address (Denison, Hart, & Kahn, 1996).

One of the key dilemmas discussed regarding integrating structures is the multiple reporting lines and how to ensure accountability (Holland, Gaston, & Gomes, 2000). One of the benefits of a hierarchy is that authority lines are clear and accountability by individuals to a superior is apparent (Jassawalla & Sashittal, 1999). The literature also suggests that miscommunication can occur when employees obtain input from multiple sources of authority and influence (Jassawalla & Sashittal, 1999). Input from multiple sources can also create ambiguity over resources both financial and human. When people and money are split between a team, centralized unit, or project and the traditional units of the hierarchy, often there is not a clear understanding of how much time should be allocated to the new structure. Integrating structures can also create conflict by bringing together people who do not have experience working together and who have very different backgrounds and goals. The conflict can become debilitating and thwart forward progress on the project or initiative. Research also demonstrates that the creation of integrating structures can be costly for individuals in terms of role ambiguity, conflict, and stress (Holland, Gaston, & Gomes, 2000; Jassawalla & Sashittal, 1999). Although leaders can help alleviate these concerns, there will be an adjustment period for many employees.

Some of the factors that are important to consider when implementing integrating structures are careful selection of the individuals involved, appointment of experienced leadership, and the culture of the organization (Holland, Gaston, & Gomes, 2000; Jassawalla & Sashittal, 1999). By carefully choosing individuals to participate in cross-functional teams, projects, and other integrating structures, leaders can help avoid conflict if they know certain individuals have difficulty working with each other. Also, it is critical to invite key stakeholders and influential individuals within the organization who can lend power and prestige to the process. The integrating structure needs careful leadership by an individual familiar with the dilemmas that can occur, as previously noted, so that they can negotiate these problems and maintain an effective structure. These leaders know how to anticipate role ambiguity, authority conflict, accountability problems, and budgetary concerns. They also help manage conflict that can emerge between the traditional units and the new integrating structures.

Organizational culture affects the success of integrating structures (Holland, Gaston, & Gomes, 2000; Jassawalla & Sashittal, 1999). If an organization has strong or charismatic leadership, a rigid bureaucracy, history of antagonism between units or departments, and authority invested in few individuals, then it will be unlikely to easily create integrating structures (Holland, Gaston, & Gomes, 2000; Jassawalla & Sashittal, 1999). However, a campus with a more open environment, collegial relationships between departments, some history of interaction, decentralized authority and decision-making processes, and an entrepreneurial spirit will more easily develop integrating structures. As organizations move to these new types of structures, they should examine areas of opportunity such as collegial relationships or entrepreneurialism and discuss these areas as sites for opening the culture up to a new way of operating and the formation of integrating structures. Similarly, they need to be careful to assess histories of conflict if they decide to combine several units or have them work together in more coordinated ways.

Integrating structures are often easier to create on smaller campuses or campuses with less complex structures (for example, multicampus systems can make integration more difficult). As campus structures become more complex, more planning, intentionality, and work may be needed to develop a structure that can work well in bringing work across campus together. For example, imagine yourself on a liberal arts campus; there are fewer bureaucratic layers, more communication across units, and fewer silos. Within these environments, not only may integrating units be less significant, but they can be easier to create. Presidential initiatives can take hold easier on a smaller campus where people across campus as a whole can physically be brought together because the size is smaller. Bringing members of an entire university together is not feasible in kicking off a presidential initiative. Interdisciplinary research centers might have an easier time being developed on a small campus where interaction among faculty, while not common, may have occurred naturally because of chance interactions more common on smaller campuses.

## Advice and Examples from the Campuses

Creating a collaborative campus requires a mission to articulate the value of collaboration, and networks to communicate the support and implement collaboration, and integrating campus structures to facilitate collaborations. In this section, we provide specific examples of ways to integrate structures to support and create a collaborative campus.

---

### Examples of Integrating Structures

Assessment Team—Many different campuses are developing assessment teams because of pressures from accreditors and the U.S. Department of Education. Assessment is an integrated activity that is hard to conduct well in institutional silos, so it represents an important area for helping demonstrate the importance of collaborative work. Although these teams often have a compliance and problem focus, on collaborative campuses they have become a hub for connecting people across campus who are interested in student learning and student outcomes. Because this is an area of interest for a great number of people on most campuses, the assessment team has allowed for connections to be created across all sorts of different units that typically have not worked together, including admissions, alumni affairs, faculty, academic administrators, student affairs professionals, and librarians.

Technology—One campus had developed a set of blogs related to different research interests, experimental teaching techniques, and issues related to student development. The blogs allowed people across campus who are interested in service learning to have a place to ask questions and raise concerns. The technology also allowed for people to connect regarding similar research interests and resulted in many more joint grant applications, increased collaborative research projects, and more joint publications. Various educators who are interested in issues of student retention, multiculturalism, or improving critical thinking among students are better able to work together and plan through the blog.

Faculty Development Centers—Although many campuses have a faculty development center or unit, most do not see their role as connecting people on campus. However, on collaborative campuses with a mission focused on working together, these units were encouraged to help create networks and foster the values of collaboration. Their orientation is quite different from traditional faculty development centers that focus on providing service for individual instructors. Instead, they connect their mission to broader goals (such as improving institutional student outcomes) that require collaboration among faculty across units to determine institutionwide outcomes. One campus we visited had hired a new director for their center on teaching and learning with a specific mandate to change the focus of the center to help bring people together for events and enhance collaboration around teaching, research, and governance.

A Multidisciplinary Institute on Urban Affairs—Campus leaders on one campus realized that they had a critical mass of researchers across campus that focused on urban issues. However, most of the faculty were not working together, had not done any joint grant seeking, and had not developed any courses together. In an effort to bring faculty together they created a Multidisciplinary Institute on Urban Affairs. Faculty were given seed money to participate in the development and growth of the institute. Operational money was provided to hire a director and host events that would bring new people into the institute who may not have a formal affiliation. Faculty associates were encouraged to develop several grant proposals that brought together expertise from policy, the arts, and various social sciences. The mission, goal, and purpose of the institute were clearly and intentionally designated at the beginning: to help create greater collaborative grant writing and teaching; to create networks and link people; and to better capitalize on the expertise that was formerly fragmented and create synergy to improve performance.

## Importance of Organizational Culture for Forming Integrating Structures

A variety of integrating mechanisms emerged that helped support collaborative work. Members of each campus noted that if these changes had not occurred, collaboration would have been slowed or thwarted in the long term. Although most of these campuses used all of the structures described below, they noted that it took time for them to develop them. Successful leaders who moved to a collaborative context had one overarching piece of advice for other campuses: be sensitive to the organizational culture in thinking through what type of integrating structures will work best and which to develop and experiment with first. For example, one administrator commented on the impact of organizational culture on the development of integrating structures:

> Our campus has a strong research focus, so it made sense for us to begin with research centers and institutes. But I've spoken to colleagues on other campuses and they started with their faculty development centers, because they focus more on teaching. More centralized campuses might be more successful with presidential initiatives. So it just depends; you have to think about your campus and the best way to begin creating structures to integrate work. Over time, you might have cross-functional teams, research institutes, and a strong faculty development center, but you want to put your best foot forward and start with an area you think you'll be successful.

With this initial advice, these campus leaders believe other campuses will be successful in setting up mechanisms that make collaborative work easier and more natural, instead of expecting individuals to collaborate within structures that have been created to support individualistic work.

## Creating Cross-Functional Units and Making Them a Priority

Each campus had one or more units that specialized in what might be termed cross-institutional work such as assessment, technology, service or community-based learning, interdisciplinary teaching or research, and the like. It was the work of these units to ensure that people were working together across campus on learning communities, team teaching, learning assessment, and other forms of collaborative work. The missions of the units or centers state that they will attempt to work with faculty and staff in every single unit on campus. These units typically report to the provost or president and have strong support from senior administrators. As one faculty member commented:

> We all know what is going on at the Smith Center. That is the one place everyone seems to read the informational materials and announcements. Plus, we know the work there is a priority for the institution, they work directly with the president. I like to serve on their committees or go to their events because I meet others, it is high visibility, and I know the work is seen as a priority.

The faculty development center was usually a second or complementary center on campus for cross-unit work, particularly among the faculty. As noted in the section on networks, faculty development centers have the opportunity to work with faculty across every discipline and department and are ideally situated to help create cross-campus work.

Although cost is always a concern in creating new units, most campuses had some strategic direction or priority with funding attached that provided infrastructure for the cross-campus unit to be established. Or the unit provided a needed service that was part of campus operations and was essential to day-to-day operations such as assessment. Cross-functional units that fulfill some day-to-day responsibility were generally favored, as units without another campus function found themselves challenged for operating funds once money dried up for kicking off new strategic, collaborative initiatives. The development of cross-functional units is a highly effective strategy—especially if they do daily operational work— but it is also a controversial one. We describe more of the dilemmas toward the end of the chapter.

### Presidential Initiatives

Campuses also used another, less permanent mechanism for creating collaboration at the centralized level—presidential initiatives. These initiatives became themes that provided focus for collaborative efforts and joint planning. On one campus every person interviewed could recite the areas of collaborative work—diversity, internationalization, student support, and assessment—as well as their contribution and involvement in these efforts. One faculty member talked about the role of presidential initiatives in creating collaborative work:

> Typically when the president takes on an initiative, it is one that crosses campus boundaries. So in my experience, over the years, presidential initiatives have been one of the most successful ways to bring together people around collaborative work. They usually require minimal cost and not a lot of administrative support. They are, generally, easy to establish.

One of the advantages often noted about presidential initiatives is that they incur fewer costs and require less administrative support than some of the other integrating structures discussed in this section. Many campuses saw this as a key mechanism for beginning collaborative work before they moved on to more complex integrating structures such as the cross-institutional institutes or cross-functional units.

## Cross-Institutional Institutes

Another integrating structure—cross-institutional institutes and centers—is important at all campuses that excelled in collaboration. Each campus had set up centers that brought together faculty and staff across disciplines and units to conduct research or outreach related to an area that many people on campus cared about. The topic might be immigration, globalization, digital media, or the human experience. What mattered was that they identified a topic that was important to the campus, often related to the core mission, for which they could bring people together to conduct work. One administrator referred to the way that institutes had transformed the campus and how cross-institutional centers and institutes differ from traditional centers and institutes:

> We made an intentional effort about twenty years ago that we wanted to be more collaborative—cross-campus collaboration, especially in the areas of interdisciplinary teaching and research. We examined ways that we might foster this work and we felt giving institutes a visible status was important—with independent budgets, high profile, and administrative support. Centers and institutes are on many campuses, at the departmental or school level. We didn't want that model; those tend to be shadow centers with little collaborative work going on. We wanted these to be high-profile that everyone on campus knew about and would want to be part of.

Often there are individuals who have a liaison role between the traditional academic units and the newly formed units that are provided release time or some compensation with the responsibility to ensure that the centers and disciplinary units come together as needed to work. Some campuses had success working with traditional departmental centers and institutes that were spread across campus. These centers did not connect people across the entire campus, but attempted to develop a meaningful assortment of individuals for joint research, outreach, or teaching. In fact, the traditional centers and institutes existed on all campuses as well and did serve to enable collaborative work, but most people thought the cross-institutional centers and institutes were more important, especially symbolically in demonstrating support for collaboration.

### Cross-Functional Teams

Campuses rely less on cross-functional teams than businesses and corporations do as a way to integrate functions and work, but they were used particularly in the administrative and staff settings. Administrators and academic and student affairs formed cross-campus committees. Also, each campus had a set of teams in place to address particular problems or issues on campus, such as assessment, retention, general education reform, and technology. These cross-boundary issues became the perfect avenue for beginning collaborative discussions and teamwork. One staff member describes how cross-functional teams support collaboration for their campus:

> We have been worried about retention for years, and our numbers have kept going down. We used to have a 87% retention range and then we were at 75%. The provost decided to set up a team of individuals from across campus to explore the issue. We collected data and talked to students and developed a report with a set of recommendations. The provost was really impressed because we identified issues that no one has considered before. As a result, he decided to make the committee a standing group which would oversee the implementation

of the recommendations and revisit issues of retention from time to time. Our retention rates have gone up over the last few years. I am sure we would not have been able to address this problem without the team.

Leaders on many of these campuses suggested that more cross-functional teams would be helpful, especially if they include faculty members. However, getting faculty to participate in cross-functional teams was a challenge that each campus experienced.

## Accounting, Computer Structures, and Innovative Technologies

Another integrating structure that is extremely important and appears key to enabling and sustaining collaboration is accounting and computer systems that allow for sharing of FTE (full-time equivalent credit) in team-taught courses, cross-listing classes, joint appointments, and in splitting indirect costs for research. To quote one interviewee: "If the administrative structures reinforce people staying in their boxes, then this makes partnerships difficult and most people do not need another difficult issue on their plate." Luckily, the timing is right and more sophisticated technology systems are emerging that allow for integration of services and support of collaborative work. In fact, the *Chronicle of Higher Education* regularly advertises new accounting and computing systems and showcases articles on new systems that enable better collaborative work. We know that technology has enabled collaborative work across a variety of industries and has created more connection among people more broadly in society through the Internet and the many related tools such as blogs and interactive media. Because technology is changing so rapidly, specific software is not recommended or mentioned in this book.

Many campuses noted that accounting and computing systems were the structures that they were likely to overlook but that ended up being a barrier time after time in efforts to team teach, conduct collaborative research, and work interdisciplinarily. Campuses recommended that the computer and accounting systems be examined at the beginning of efforts to develop more collaborative work. By exploring computing and accounting options one can avoid having unsuccessful collaborations, which make people cynical and avoid future participation in collaborative efforts. A more general missed opportunity is that campuses are not using technology to connect people across campuses on an ongoing basis.

In other industries, one of the key integrating structures is innovative technology that can connect people and bring them together for virtual work and meetings. Corporations use technology to create "Webinars" that bring people together across units to share information. Other forms of innovative technologies include: social networking sites, Weblogs (commonly termed blogs), and virtual online communities (such as Second Life). Social networking sites serve as virtual networks by bringing people together from a variety of nodes to form relationships. Often social networking sites are organized around an individual (or one node). Individuals can post interests, share information, and connect to others via the social networking Web site. Currently, many college campuses across the country are introducing campus-specific social networking sites. These sites can be introduced to faculty and staff to advertise interests, initiatives, and current projects with the potential of creating new networks and eventual collaborations.

Blogs, previously mentioned, are often focused on an issue or interest such as political issues, entertainment, and technology. Both social networking sites and blogs have the potential to enhance collaboration by connecting people with similar interest or goals, promoting the sharing of information, and creating opportunities for communication. Blogs, however, create an immediate connection because they are organized around an interest. Campuses may consider promoting the use of blogs as an interactive Web site where people can come together to virtually dialogue around a common interest. The potential of connecting people and promoting dialogue is endless in a virtual environment.

Another widely used form of technology that enhances the ability to communicate around a shared interest are podcasts or other forms of Web-based video. Podcasts allow individuals to share information by using video without the requirement of meeting at a specific time or location. Videos can serve as learning technologies, communication devises, and historical documents to aid in the creation and success of a collaboration. Videos can also serve to advertise the importance of collaborative work within the mission of the institution. Many campuses are creating videos for recruitment purposes. Including an emphasis on collaboration within these videos illustrates the importance of collaboration for the campus at large.

Finally, the more innovative technology of Second Life, a Web-based virtual world where individuals socialize via "avatars," can enhance collaboration by offering the opportunity to create more lifelike interactions in a Web-based physical location. Virtual worlds bring together the potential of many different technologies. For example, virtual worlds bring people together in a network (similar to social networking sites), help with the sharing of information (as with blogs), and provide a visual connection as seen in podcasts. Each of these new technologies is currently available for campuses to use to enhance, support, and create collaborations.

Although the use of innovative technologies to enhance collaboration did not emerge in the study, since we conducted the research this practice has developed on college campuses. Technology is evolving so quickly that by the time this book is printed, campuses may begin using more forms of technology to connect. This technique was a missed opportunity on these campuses, for the most part, but it is an area that campuses should explore in the future; it will be a key area for increasing collaboration. Some resources for keeping up on evolving ideas related to technology are included in Appendix B.

*Potential Advantages to Using Technology for Collaboration*

1. Stimulate multinational collaboration—Current advances
   in technology and the emergence of globalization has created the potential for multinational collaborations. Creating
   systems that create fast-paced and inexpensive Web-based
   communication systems will support existing and stimulate
   new multinational collaborations. For example, Skype provides
   a Web-based communication network with free computer-to-
   computer calls throughout the world. The ability to call an
   individual for free in another country will help make multinational collaborations possible.

2. Support interdisciplinary research—One of the major movements toward collaboration is within interdisciplinary research.
   The interdisciplinary requirement of many national granting
   agencies has created a plethora of collaborative groups on college campuses. Technology has the potential to enhance these
   collaborations by assisting people to communicate, network,
   and share information with ease. Technology also may help
   researchers in creating computerized models, processing data,
   and imagining new ways to represent and conduct research.

3. Allow for collaborative teaching across institutions—Another
   form of collaboration within the context of higher education
   is coteaching. Often, coteaching is done by two or more faculty at the same institution. However, podcasts and virtual
   worlds provide an opportunity for faculty from different institutions to coteach and create a collaborative learning experience. Imagine faculty (as their avatar) from across the world
   meeting students in a virtual world to share ground-breaking
   research.

4. Provide "on demand" access to information—When working
   with a collaborative team, information is regularly shared in
   documents (e.g., meeting agendas, research documents) and
   in verbal conversations (e.g., conference calls, team meetings).

Often, the information must be accessed at a later date. Web sites can store documents (such as YahooGroups), podcasts can store meeting recordings, and blogs can be locations to post agenda and meeting minutes. Each of these Web-based technologies allows for easy and quick access to all collaborative documents.

5. Create new networks—As discussed in our model of collaboration, networks are essential to collaboration within higher education. However, networks need to be created, supported, and nurtured. Each of the innovative technologies presented in this chapter can assist in the creation and sustainment of networks. Blogs and social networking sites create opportunities to connect people around interests or individuals. Virtual worlds help create more opportunities for communication, thus sustaining existing networks.

### Key Considerations for Using Technology for Collaboration

1. Security—One of the most pressing concerns of information technology (IT) professionals is security (*EDUCAUSE Quarterly*, 2008). IT professionals are under increased pressure to create and maintain systems that secure the personal and financial information of students, faculty, and staff. Creating new systems, integrating current systems, or opening up systems to people outside of the university to enhance collaboration further complicates the potential for security breaches.

2. Costs—New technologies are costly. Often new software and hardware is required, additional staff time is needed, normal business is interrupted for the integration of the new software, and consultants may need to be hired to provide assistance. Colleges need to consider ways to capitalize on existing resources (such as conference call systems and current campus-specific social networking sites) to enhance collaboration, as well as new technologies.

3. Fast pace of technological advances—The innovative technology of today easily becomes passé in just a few years. Virtual worlds, for example, are currently considered the new innovative technology for distance education and communication. Technology used for collaboration must strive to create meaningful networks and relationships but also capitalize on new technologies that offer greater communicative options. Understanding which technologies to invest in, particularly during fiscally difficult times, poses a challenge for higher education.

4. Overuse and dependency—One of the greatest hidden concerns with technology use is the potential for individuals to rely on technology exclusively for network and relationship building. Technology has the potential to enhance collaboration, but face-to-face interaction is also required to address difficult circumstances and to sustain a commitment to a collaboration. Therefore, there needs to be a balance between technology use and in-person interaction.

### Restructuring Units to Create Integration

Restructuring in higher education is not used often by leaders for fear of the political ramifications of doing so in a culture of autonomy in which people typically define their own positions and roles and middle-level leaders structure their own units. Although this autonomy is extremely important, restructuring positions or units so that they better support the collaborative goals such as learning communities and research institutes is a significant alteration for ensuring that work is done in the most efficient and effective way possible. One campus describes its decision to merge several units from academic affairs and student affairs into a broader division:

> For years we had struggled with problems at the career center where faculty were not as connected to programming as they needed to be. We also were not getting enough input from academic affairs staff on advising or

admissions. Under different leadership, some of these offices had even changed between student affairs or academic affairs. But that never solved the problems. Our new provost sat down and examined our structures and decided we needed to fundamentally change them to address the long-term problems. And these types of changes are never easy, many people knew that their positions might be threatened or that their work would be changed and some people were asked to leave, but it was the right thing to do.

## Challenges to Creating Integrating Structures

Integrating structures were developed on each campus, but not without some problems and bumps along the way. In order to integrate structures, existing practices must be altered and budgets aligned to support the integration. Here are a few of the potential challenges that campuses face while attempting to change institutional practices and integrate structures in new ways.

### Perceptions of Favoritism

When research institutes and centralized units are formed to conduct research or support teaching in a particular area (e.g., service learning or experiential learning), faculty who do not participate in this type of work often voice concern over nepotism, believing that certain projects or interests are being favored by particular faculty members. This can create rifts or divisions among faculty and antagonism toward the administration. Leaders on these campuses noted that this is where the mission statement and educational philosophy become crucial. They were able to overcome dissent by appealing to the mission and reiterating the agreed-upon educational philosophy. This approach was successful on most of the campuses. Campus leaders also relied on key influential individuals (those natural network builders) to speak up about the advantages of collaboration and the necessity of new structures and units. One administrator describes his experience dealing with tension as a result of developing a research institute:

> I had committed to five research institutes that represented the key work of a good number of faculty across campus. Interdisciplinary research is a key component of our mission statements and our future direction. But, of course, not everyone was included in the five centers and I started to hear grumbling. I brought together some of the key faculty members who were voicing concern. I talked to them about the new directions for the campus and the primary role of interdisciplinary work. I reminded them that we had committed collectively to this work and that we all needed to support it. And they weren't happy about it, but they understood it and in the end supported the centers.

### Budgetary Concerns

One of the major challenges cited for creating integrating structures is budgetary concerns. When a centralized unit is created to coordinate efforts across campus, it can take away money from departmental budgets unless additional income or revenue has been acquired. However, on most campuses additional revenue was not available and they had to work within existing resources. Successful efforts tended to funnel money back into the traditional departments and units; efforts to create centralized collaborative efforts with independent budgets usually met with resistance and sometimes resulted in failure. The institutes and centers were sometimes an exception as they did not require much financial resources, but they did meet with resistance on some campuses by certain constituents, especially at first until the full logic for their emergence was discussed and absorbed. One campus had an interdisciplinary unit that was downsized and lost most of its budget because it was perceived to be draining the departmental structures. These campuses recommended that budget issues be addressed carefully and politically. Budget allotment for integrating structures can create political fighting on campuses for resources. If discussions about how integrating structures will be supported over the long term do not take place up front, it can jeopardize the future of these centers, and some were closed by political pressure by people who believed the resources supporting integrating structures drained other units of campus.

## Getting Faculty Participation

Several campuses suggested that more cross-functional teams would be helpful, especially with faculty members. However, getting faculty to participate in cross-functional teams was a challenge that each campus experienced. Some of the campuses were successful in using "the network" to reach out to gain more faculty involvement in campus-based teams. Others had success with incentives, but that usually was more helpful with research and teaching and less successful when it came to institutional leadership and service. However, this remains a challenge on most of the campuses, one that they continue working to overcome.

## Isolation of Technology and Accounting

A challenge faced by some campuses is that collaboration was not used in the purchasing of the technology and accounting systems. Technology staff are often isolated on many campuses, and this was true of the staff on many of these campuses, particularly multicampus college and universities. Although administrators sent requests for technology staff to look into accounting and computer technology that would enable collaborative work, technology staff were not really sophisticated enough in their understanding of the teaching and learning environment to purchase appropriate software. Each of these campuses recommended that a committee be formed with people involved in team teaching, collaborative research, and programs with joint budgets to address concerns and issues with existing software, as well as assess future needs. All campuses acknowledged that this is an area that requires better strategies.

## Other Possible Challenges

Although the literature discusses leadership, team dynamics, role ambiguity, accountability, conflict, and concerns over lines of authority, these issues were not mentioned by people in the study. There was some discussion of the leadership within integrating units, but this was not mentioned as a challenge or particular concern. However, it may be that campus leaders are carefully choosing individuals to lead these units, so it did not emerge in discussion. Roles within higher education may be already more autonomous than in other organizations. Similarly, faculty do not have strict lines of authority in the way they are supervised.

Accountability has not traditionally been a strong value or principle within higher education and was not a problem mentioned in conducting collaborative work. It may be that campuses have not evolved enough to recognize accountability problems. Since accountability is a growing concern among external constituents of higher education, leaders should keep this principle in mind as they develop integrating structures. As people conduct work in more collaborative ways, what collective forms of accountability exist? How do we ensure that collaborative efforts are conducted in the most efficient and effective way? How do we know whether the integrating structures created are the best ones for facilitating work on the campus? Is assessment of collaborative work and integrating structures regularly occurring? What are the results of such assessments? Some leaders noted that an effort should be assessed for several years before making any definitive judgments because, like any new effort, initial assessments may not be accurate. At present, however, most collaborative efforts—and the integrating structures used to support them—do not have associated accountability mechanisms.

Finally, conflict was mentioned as a challenge, but mostly as a result of budgetary concerns when departments or units felt that integrating structures were siphoning off money.

## Key Ideas

1. Examine your computer and accounting systems to ensure that they support collaborative work. Create cross-functional teams to work with the technology office.

2. Discuss budget issues up front and come to consensus about how budgets will be handled and supported for integrating structures.

3. Begin with a set of presidential initiatives to kick off collaborative work and help bring a sense of priority.

4. Decide which integrating units make sense on your campus based on the organizational culture. For some campuses, creating institutional research centers might be more difficult than for others.

5. Make sure that cross-functional units, teams, and institutes have regular communication with traditional units.

6. Consider strategic restructuring to achieve integration.

7. Ensure that accountability mechanisms are in place so that if people question the need of an integrating structure there is support for it as the best structure for meeting its mission.

# 8

# Rewards

*A reward is a something given in return for performance of a desired behavior. Rewards for collaboration can be either extrinsic (e.g., seed money to establish a collaboration or monetary incentive for participation) or intrinsic motivators (e.g., working well with others and receiving praise for contribution to collaboration).*

Rewards are very significant for enabling collaboration. Particularly effective are changing promotion and tenure requirements, offering incentives, and making the intrinsic rewards of collaboration visible through the creation of "good" collaborative experiences.

One of the most fundamental ways that rewards enable collaboration is by creating opportunities. Opportunities can be created, for example, by restructuring the tenure, promotion, and staff evaluation requirements or by providing start-up funds that never existed before. When faculty are given start-up grants or staff are offered incentives to collaborate, the rewards may be time and resources that have not been previously available. Many faculty and staff on campus may have been interested in collaborating across disciplines or a division but had not had the time or resources to pursue collaborative initiatives. For example, student affairs professionals may have an interest in establishing learning communities but have not been able to release staff in order to create collaborations with academic affairs and faculty who are required for learning communities. Incentives in the form of more staff, release time for one or two current staff members, or institutional monies to support the development of a learning community create the opportunity where one did not exist before.

Rewards provide motivation. Individuals feel intrinsically motivated when their self-determination and competence are maximized. Intrinsic motivation is created in collaborations via rewards that target feelings of self-confidence, self-reliance, and contribution. Several individuals noted that intrinsic rewards to collaboration are found in meeting new people and accomplishing a task that could not have been done alone. In addition, intrinsic motivation is enhanced when individuals contribute to the overall goals of the collaboration, thus reinforcing those individuals' expertise and uniqueness. The key for the institution is to make sure that when it structures collaborative activities, it keeps in mind that people need to feel intrinsic rewards out of the experience or they are not likely to continue.

Rewards also extrinsically motivate individuals by granting incentives. Individuals and groups become motivated to work in collaborations when external rewards are established. Common examples of external rewards are internal grants for groups of faculty who come together to write grant proposals, funding of projects or student service centers that bring together multiple student affairs offices, or projects that collaborate with communities and community-based organizations. Each of these rewards requires that groups of people work together and collaborate in the development and establishment of the project or grant.

Rewards enable collaboration because they demonstrate for employees that the institution is willing to create support to meet its mission. The mission of the institution often seems esoteric to some campus constituents, and rewards are a way to make the connection between institutional values and purpose and people's everyday work. One important area that proved essential to supporting collaborations is the change in the tenure and promotion guidelines from devaluing to valuing collaborative work. Not only were faculty given the real rewards of receiving benefits from collaboration, the change in tenure practices symbolically represented the fact that the institutions were willing to alter practices to support the mission of collaboration. The definition of the collaborative mission became more concrete (i.e., working on collaborative grants, coauthoring publications) and it became clear that the administration was taking the mission seriously.

In addition to supporting the institutional mission, rewards can support the integration of structures. As mentioned in Chapter Six, the integration of structures is a challenging process that requires institutions to redirect resources, spend time getting buy-in from institutional constituents, and hire new staff. Rewards can help by creating incentives for individuals to consider integrating services and offices, such as providing new staff lines if students and academic affairs combine into one large office. For all these reasons, rewards were an essential contextual feature redesigned to help create collaboration on campuses.

## Background of Rewards

Some people may regard higher education as a higher calling and believe that rewards should not or do not have a major role in motivating faculty and staff. Faculty, in particular, often forgo better paying jobs in industry or corporations to seek out positions in higher education. So the notion that rewards—particularly monetary rewards—would be an incentive for employees in higher education may seem off base. However, even if faculty are not drawn to academic positions because of their high pay, they are often motivated people who want to be valued for the work they do. Also, one of the problems on many campuses is that collaborative work can actually detract from individual success, and faculty therefore feel less valued. Rewards need not be monetary, but they do need to appeal to intrinsic needs, such as being valued in the organization. Often the issue is not creating rewards for collaborative work, but ensuring that individuals doing collaborative work are not penalized. With this understanding, we examine some of the basics of rewards and how they operate.

Rewards have long been used to motivate employees. Highly motivated employees are said to be more satisfied, and therefore more productive. In the last few decades many reward plans and programs have cropped up to systematically reward and motivate employees, including merit pay programs, salary bonus plans, 360 degrees feedback programs, and annual performance reviews (Strickler, 2006). Each of these programs seeks to create internal or external motivation to employees to increase productivity and job satisfaction. As enablers for collaborations, rewards provide similar forms of motivation but also assist in the establishment or continuation of collaborations by providing intrinsic benefits for participation. Thus, rewards for collaboration can be either extrinsic (e.g., seed money to establish a collaboration or monetary incentive for participation) or intrinsic motivators (e.g., working well with others and receiving praise for contribution to collaboration).

Rewards are most effective when they seek to achieve either intrinsic or extrinsic motivation, because individuals are more motivated and satisfied when they receive either intrinsic or extrinsic benefits for their work. Intrinsic motivation can be described as a motivation to engage in activities that enhance or maintain a person's self-concept and positive self image. Individuals are found to be intrinsically motivated in organizations that maximize feelings of competence and self-determination (Wiersma, 1992). In organizations, intrinsic motivators include earning respect of coworkers, working well without supervision and rigid rules, and delivering results for the organization (Strickler, 2006). Rewards are then structured to capitalize on individuals' internal feelings. In collaboration, intrinsic motivation is felt when individuals are able to contribute to a collaborative team and earn respect and when the collaboration produces a beneficial product or service for the organization.

In contrast, extrinsic motivation is created by external factors, such as monetary rewards for services or work completed or praise for a job well done. Individuals are motivated, not by an internal desire, but by the external rewards granted. Common extrinsic rewards include monies for additional or exceptional tasks completed and job promotions. Rewards to enable collaboration create external incentives to participate in collaborations and remove structural barriers that prevent collaborations from taking place. For example, interdisciplinary projects that cross academic disciplines by bringing together faculty are most effective when they include "seed money" to allow groups of faculty to develop grants or pursue research projects (Frost, Jean, Teodorescu, & Brown, 2004). The same interdisciplinary teams also encounter structural barriers in the tenure and promotion process that favor individual work rather than collaborative efforts. Changing tenure and promotion policies to remove barriers to collaboration may also serve as an extrinsic motivator.

Rewards enable collaboration by linking institutional, departmental, or collaborative missions to those rewards. Connecting collaborative efforts to the institutional mission provides direct value to the work of the collaboration and establishes the significance of the work. Rewards become, not just monetary gifts or nonmonetary benefits (e.g., course releases for faculty, additional funding for offices, or additional compensation), but intrinsic motivators that provide a "value added" to the organization. Essentially, the reward is exemplified in supporting and creating positive change that fulfills the mission of the institution. In addition, connecting rewards to mission provides justification for granting rewards. In universities, where funding is becoming increasingly limited, showing the value of collaborative efforts and documenting outcomes justifies the resources required to establish reward processes.

Linking missions to rewards requires that collaborations be accountable for specific outcomes. This is achieved by establishing a system in which rewards are granted based on measuring, reviewing, and evaluating performance. Mohrman, Cohen, and Mohrman (1995) suggest that institutions establish clear rewards that are granted when specific outcomes are achieved. The nature of the outcomes varies by the type of effort but must have a measurable and identifiable outcome. For example, funding given to faculty collaborators to write grants needs to be contingent on the completion of the grant proposal and submission to the funding agency. Additional rewards may also be given by the institution if the grant is funded or a product is produced out of the collaborative effort. Establishing accountable outcomes erases the ambiguity in reward structures and helps in anticipating the difficulties that arise when giving rewards to collaborative groups.

Despite the potential of using rewards to motivate and support collaboration, the literature describes several significant challenges to the development and effectiveness of rewards to increase motivation. There is conflicting evidence regarding the effectiveness of rewards as motivation. Although some researchers argue that rewards are significant motivators, others argue that rewards have short-term effects; individuals are motivated in the short term to achieve goals and earn rewards, but in the long term motivation wanes (Strickler, 2006). Furthermore, rewards should be created based on the goal. For example, if the rewards are targeting faculty in order to promote more collaborations, establishing rewards that give faculty release time or benefits in the tenure and promotion practice is more effective than blanket rewards that do not take into account the audience and needs. Another concern and challenge noted in the literature is the internal competition that may develop as a result of a limited number of rewards. Individuals in a organization compete for the rewards, thereby creating an environment of distrust and opposition. Competition is antithetical to collaboration, which depends on mutual respect, trust, and relationship building. Rewards need to be structured to minimize competition and to reinforce the commitment and health of the collaborations. For example, many campuses have created internal grants that require faculty to collaborate with others on the campus. These grants are important in supporting collaborative work, particularly when the collaboration is just beginning. However, the increase in the number of submissions and the limited number of funds create competition among the faculty to write and collaborate on the more "fundable" projects. Thinking critically about how rewards are distributed and the ways in which unintended competition may arise between and among collaborations is crucial to the use of rewards as motivators. Information about how other campuses have developed reward structures provides additional evidence and tips for how to overcome these barriers.

## Advice and Examples from Campuses

The use of rewards to enable and reinforce collaborations has been attempted with success on several campuses. Specifically, campuses have altered the tenure and promotion process, developed incentives, and capitalized on intrinsic rewards to promote a variety of collaborations between and among faculty, staff, and administrators. Each of these reward structures is unique to the structure and needs of higher education and requires thinking beyond current structures and policies to create institutional buy-in and commitment.

### Tenure and Promotion—Extrinsic Rewards

One common facilitator of collaboration was the alteration of tenure and promotion processes, which had been modified at most campuses within the study (Boyer, 1997; Diamond, 1999; Edgerton, O'Meara, & Rice, 2005; Jacoby and associates, 2003; O'Meara, 2001). New promotion and tenure requirements allow faculty to do collaborative work without being penalized. It also demonstrates a new set of priorities on campus. The requirements allow more diverse tenure and promotion cases to move forward through the process that reflect the new institutional support for collaboration. One faculty member commented on this issue: "Rewards are critical to making the collaborative mission and philosophy come to life. If you have structures to facilitate collaboration, but not the rewards, collaboration is just not going to happen throughout the institution. Rewards signal where people's values lie." Altering rewards also socializes new faculty to an alternative approach to faculty work and attracts people to the campus who want to conduct collaborative work. The change in promotion and tenure requirements has served as a recruitment tool for many of the campuses and attracted many candidates who might not have been interested in the past (some campuses suggested, in fact, that they are obtaining more prestigious candidates). There are many faculty that are interested in interdisciplinary, collaborative learning, community-based research, and service learning who are looking for campuses that truly value collaborative work and are willing to pass up the traditionally prestigious campuses to find a campus that supports their approach to work.

In order to make changes to the promotion and tenure requirements, senior executives and faculty need to consider this a major priority (one of the other contextual conditions). This is not a system that can be altered easily or quickly. On most of these campuses, a committee or task force was charged with developing new guidelines (usually a committee of the senate or joint administrative and faculty task force) that went through the formal governance processes such as the faculty senate to the administrative ranks to the board. This process typically took several years and involved many opportunities for open discussion and campus forums. After the new requirements became official campus policy, training sessions were held to inform people of the new expanded promotion and tenure requirements. The sessions were critical because they made faculty believe that alternative cases would be supported; administrators stood firm in their support of new collaborative ways of thinking about research and teaching. They offered support to faculty in units that may not have support among faculty colleague or department chairs. On many campuses, rumors circulated about tenure and promotion guidelines that were often untrue (e.g., collaborative research will be rewarded more than individual research or the campus is lowering traditional standards by rewarding collaborative and individual efforts equally). In order to avoid misinformation being spread and having to control rumors, it is important to have the information sessions to dispel myths and misinformation. Campus leaders (both administrators and faculty) created a Web page where individuals could share their views, where updates on the process were posted, and where accurate information about the promotion and tenure requirements could be found.

Faculty and administrative leaders went to great lengths to alter reward structures and noted that it was an extremely difficult process. Administrators and faculty both shared bitter experiences with efforts to realign reward structures to value collaborative work. These efforts often resulted in administrators having to leave the campus, faculty stepping down from administrative posts, and an atmosphere of antagonism. Several administrators and faculty offered advice about how to make the process go more smoothly, hoping that others could learn from their painful mistakes and experiences. Their advice was, first, look out for resistance resulting from misinformation (e.g., individualistic work will be penalized or faculty work will be dictated by administrators). One administrator commented:

> Many faculty saw this as an attack on academic freedom, of their losing the choice of how and what they teach or research. We needed to have long conversations about how this process was about opening up a new way of doing work, not trying to control how faculty do their work. Not realizing this would be seen as an academic freedom issue or control issue really hurt us. We were politically naïve.

Second, develop a formal process for how the change in tenure and promotion will occur and ensure this process has been agreed upon by all key stakeholders. Another story demonstrates this issue:

> We established a special commission to work on changing the requirements and suddenly several groups around campus began to question the process and felt the administration was foisting this on the faculty. We stopped the process, went back and got consensus on how the new guidelines would be developed. We almost destroyed the process in moving too fast.

Leaders need to identify the key stakeholders and influential individuals on campus and make sure there is buy-in from them for the process before moving forward. They do need to agree with the notion of changing promotion and tenure requirements, but they should agree to a process for examining this issue. The preceding story demonstrates the need for patience and deliberation.

Be politically aware, be patient, and get consensus, but also, as faculty and administrators on successful campuses recommend, use resources from national organizations such as the Association of American Colleges and Universities, American Association for Higher Education (now available through Stylus Press), innovative institutions (University of Michigan has changed its guidelines, for example) and disciplinary societies that have a more interdisciplinary bent, and other outside organizations. Please see the following resources for more details (full citations are in Appendix B): Boyer (1997); Diamond (1999); Edgerton, O'Meara, & Rice (2005); Jacoby and associates (2003); O'Meara, (2001).

Examples from off-campus organizations offer models for altering guidelines and provide legitimacy for changing campus practices. Once a model of altering promotion and tenure requirements is in place, it can be tweaked to fit the particular campus context. Changing the promotion and tenure requirements is one of the most powerful ways to support collaborative work, but it is also one of the most difficult aspects of the campus to redesign.

## Incentives—Extrinsic Rewards

Another helpful lever to enable and reinforce collaborations is the use of incentives (e.g., grants, release time). Collaboration can take additional time, especially as people are beginning the process. Some minor incentives help overcome the initial time lost. Most faculty and administrators noted that over time collaboration actually takes less time and can increase capacity. But to get to the point of increased capacity, incentives provide a reason to go through the initial hard times and help make the experience less difficult.

In order to be successful, rewards need to be individualized rather than using a one-size-fits-all approach. Disciplines and units vary in terms of what might be an attractive incentive—for some it may be a mini-grant; for another it may be administrative assistance and help with grant writing. Of the extrinsic incentives, grants were mentioned most often as an enabler but varied in importance based on the groups within the institution. For faculty in the humanities and certain areas of the social sciences with limited grants and funding potential, small grants are a very successful lever for creating motivation to engage in a collaborative project. In order to devise a successful system of incentives and understand disciplinary differences at one institution, administrators conducted surveys about faculty needs and met with faculty across campus, asking them what type of incentives would best help them to engage in a collaborative project. One administrator talks about the importance talking to faculty to identify which incentives are attractive within their particular unit:

> The college was offering mini-grants, trying to get individuals more interested in conducting interdisciplinary

research. But very few people were applying and the applications were not very thoughtful. I knew people wanted to do this work, and so I went out and asked a couple of senior faculty about what would motivate them—what they really wanted was administrative support to write some major grants to NSF rather than minigrants. So we changed the competition to focus on access to administrative support. Now in the applications are pouring in and more interdisciplinary research is happening.

Incentives were typically discussed when trying to motivate faculty to participate in the collaborative projects but not often mentioned with staff. However, some supervisors set up systems whereby individuals who worked on collaborative projects were informally given some flexibility or time off to offset the additional time invested to get a collaborative project, such as a learning community, off the ground. Although most campuses are not finding it necessary to provide specific incentives to staff to collaborate, they may want to consider whether small grants or administrative support for staff could create even more creative and interesting collaborative projects. A situation in which staff see faculty receive incentives while they do not can create negative feelings between the very groups you want to collaborate.

## Merit Systems—Extrinsic

Although incentives were not mentioned as a reward for staff, merit systems are an important lever for motivating staff to consider involvement and leadership in collaborative projects. Campuses that encourage more collaborative work have altered their merit systems and annual reviews and evaluations to include credit for collaborative projects and points for the quality of involvement in these projects. In addition, bonuses and merit increases are tied to involvement with new collaborative initiatives. People are not penalized for not collaborating, but additional merit pay or bonuses are provided for involvement in a collaborative (e.g., following a supervisor's advice to join a committee that will support a collaborative).

Human resources offices have made a concerted effort to let new employees know about the value of collaboration and how it is included in annual evaluations and merit pay. Merit pay is emphasized in orientations, human resources newsletters, and listserv messages. Campus administrators are supporting human resources efforts by describing the incentives for collaboration when they meet with staff in annual evaluations, as well as during informal meetings about performance. Leaders try to make clear expectations of collaboration and how roles and responsibilities are structured to enhance collaboration—these discussions continue the socialization about the incentives and rewards for collaboration begun by human resources. In these evaluation meetings, administrators also help staff brainstorm ways to be successful in collaborative work. Some campuses have gone further and have team-based evaluation—not just individual evaluations. Within these systems, a portion of the evaluation is based on the accomplishment and success of the team. One administrator describes how she used merit pay in order to obtain more involvement by staff in collaborative efforts:

> Generally, staff are motivated to work with others across campus. But there were some people who have been on campus a long time and were set in their ways. Others had come to the campus from places where collaboration just wasn't emphasized. I realized I had two groups of people who could really benefit from emphasizing collaboration more as part of their positions. I decided the best way to do it was to change our evaluation system. Encouragement to collaborate just hadn't worked. After I implemented the new evaluation system emphasizing

and providing merit pay for collaborative involvement, these two groups really fell in line. I like to persuade people through logic or intrinsic rewards but sometimes you just have to realize it will take more.

Many campuses noted that they know it is important to move to team-based evaluations. However, because of the complicated arrangements around teamwork and partnerships (most positions are structured to involve several different teams, with individuals working a different percentage of time with various teams) and because not all employees are partnering, setting up a team-based evaluation is challenging. Campuses are asking for more guidance and support in how to think through and develop a team-based evaluation system that can work within higher education. Some administrators were aware of team-based evaluations from business or government, but none of these systems seem to work well in a higher education setting, and administrators are looking for new models and approaches.

## Intrinsic Rewards

Intrinsic rewards are also a major enabler of collaboration. Intrinsic rewards include meeting new people and accomplishing a task that could not be done alone. Many people with whom we spoke on these college campuses said that the intrinsic rewards were what really motivated them to get involved with collaborative projects and sustained their involvement over time. For example, a faculty member declared the value of meeting professors in other disciplines as rewarding; a staff member mentioned learning more about campus decision making; a junior faculty member described the value of gaining leadership skills; and an administrator in student affairs perfected his assessment skills. In addition, a staff member learned more about how universities are run and the possibilities for advancement; an associate professor recalled the first time the dean recognized his contribution to campus service; an administrator talked about getting to know faculty; and a staff member learned about how other units operate, which helped her reconsider aspects of her role and be better able to fulfill her responsibilities. These are all examples of intrinsic rewards that can accrue from collaboration. In the words of one staff member:

> Until I got involved with the new advising system where we were collaborating more directly with faculty, I hadn't actually worked with a lot of faculty. One of the major rewards out of the collaborative effort was getting to meet people across campus that I normally don't get to work with—faculty and even some academic affairs administrators. Then there was the amazing experience of seeing students who felt that the advising system really worked better. Knowing that our efforts of working together, even when it was hard, resulted in such a better outcome, it had its rewards in itself. But that was four years down the line, so the benefit of meeting new people right away helped sustain my involvement, in the short run, until I saw the impact on students.

However, you often need some incentive to get people involved with collaboration until the intrinsic rewards sustain their involvement. This is why providing initial incentives and merit increases may be particularly important for individuals who have not been involved in collaboration in the past, who have not seen the intrinsic rewards, or have only seen those individuals who had negative collaborative experiences. Also, leaders may need to provide words of praise and point out possible intrinsic benefits (such as learning a new skill or concept, honing responsibilities, and increasing visibility) until the long-term intrinsic benefits, such as the staff member seeing the impact of the new program on the students, become apparent. Campus leaders also need to make sure that they market and promote the intrinsic rewards of collaboration as they emerge so as to motivate other constituents not yet involved and to provide visibility for those who have participated. A faculty member talks about the importance of promoting intrinsic rewards:

> One of the smartest things I saw happen was that administrators took several of us out to lunch who had been involved in developing the high school outreach program. They asked us about our experiences, challenges, benefits, and how we felt about the process. It was a chance for us to really reflect about the work we were doing. One of the benefits was that I realized a lot of the rewards and benefit that had accrued from my involvement. But they took the process a step further and asked if they could share my experiences in the campus newsletter. I said sure. Suddenly I had people coming up to me saying—that sounded like a really great project and how can I get involved. So they were really savvy in identifying some of the intrinsic benefits and making these visible to the community—it generates interest by others.

The key for the institution is to make sure that when it structures collaborative activities (and does get people involved), it keeps in mind that individuals need to feel intrinsic rewards out of the experience or they are not likely to continue. As one faculty member recounted:

> People come from all sorts of different backgrounds and they may not have had particularly good experiences with collaboration in the past. For example, my early experiences were tragic, with a senior faculty member stealing my ideas and passing them off as his own. So you need to create opportunities for people to have a

good experience, to feel the many intrinsic rewards, because that will foster collaboration for the long-term when minigrants or external rewards cannot be provided, and those times always seem to come.

Institutions that are successful in creating a collaborative environment understand that they need to carefully balance a motivational strategy that initially provides incentives and other extrinsic rewards, fashions experiences in which initial intrinsic rewards can emerge (praise, learning), and points out these short-term intrinsic rewards until the long-term intrinsic rewards can emerge. So leaders must think carefully about and fashion various forms of motivation that can help people down the path of collaboration. Initially, it can be a very difficult path. Effective leaders are aware of this and provide incentives and ways for people to make this transition. Even individuals with whom we spoke who wanted to collaborate did not always do so because there were no institutional incentives for collaboration. When they saw a system of rewards in place, however, and that people were willing to alter promotion tenure requirements and evaluation processes, they saw that the institution was serious about supporting collaboration.

## Balancing Intrinsic and Extrinsic Rewards

As alluded to in the last section, institutions must carefully think through the balance of extrinsic and intrinsic rewards. Extrinsic rewards such as release time, resources, staffing, and pay increases are hard to maintain, especially at institutions that are attempting to foster widespread collaboration. These extrinsic forms of motivation tended to be used mostly initially and for innovators who are taking on greater risk. These campuses were able to take a limited set of extrinsic rewards (since resources are always finite) and strategically allocate them. They typically made three strategic choices: (1) allocate extrinsic rewards for high-profile collaborations or collaborators, (2) provide small pots of money that a larger number of people can apply for, and (3) offer rewards for collaborations that seem likely to spread or be institutionalized. By giving rewards for a couple large and visible initiatives these campuses were able to showcase successful collaborations and grab people's attention, with the potential for getting more of them interested in collaboration. But having a set of smaller extrinsic rewards ranging from a course release to short-term clerical support to small seed money, the institutions ensured that they had broader reach in fostering collaborative work. Proposals for extrinsic support and funding typically try to identify the likelihood of a collaboration being used more broadly on the campus or being institutionalized. One administrator comments on developing criteria for extrinsic rewards:

> We are really working hard to balance providing some extrinsic support for people who want to collaborate, especially because we understand how hard this work is to do initially. But we don't have many resources, like most campuses, so we have had to be particularly strategic. We've really fine-tuned the proposal criteria so that we have a good understanding of whether this person is committed to collaborative work long-term or just trying to get into some resources. The first few years, until we got this figured out, we funded projects that petered out after the resources were gone.

However, the goal was to provide extrinsic resources and support for people who were intrinsically motivated but needed some support to get something off the ground. Campuses occasionally experimented with offering rewards to individuals who were not intrinsically motivated, hoping that they would see the intrinsic benefits and continue. But they chose this path more sparingly because it was less likely to succeed.

# Challenges to Creating Rewards to Support Collaborative Work

Rewards can prove difficult to develop. Leaders struggled to find resources, to identify rewards for different groups, combat competition, and change long-supported systems of tenure and promotion.

## Finding Resources

Many reward structures require institutional resources. In some cases, rewards are monetary gifts that supplement incomes or provide "seed money" for collaborations to begin or continue. Other rewards are not directly monetary but nonetheless affect the institution's bottom line, such as time release from courses, which requires other faculty to take on additional students, or providing staff overlap in academic advising to allow an advisor to attend a meeting. These rewards do not directly cost institutions money, but indirectly they create fiscal challenges. As state allocations for public universities decrease, institutional resources become a greater challenge. To overcome the challenges, institutions need to be creative and develop a strong institutional commitment to collaboration that makes people feel intrinsically motivated to participate. Creating more intrinsic rewards that motivate individuals to become involved in collaborations despite the additional work has no fiscal impact.

## Creating a Coherent System

Another challenge is the variation of reward structures that currently exist in the university. Faculty salaries, percentage of time variations related to salaries paid for by grants, teaching responsibilities, and student advising work vary dramatically from one department to the next. Faculty in the sciences, for example, typically have more of their salary paid for by grants whereas faculty in the humanities rely more heavily on the university for their salaries. Furthermore, faculty student advising responsibilities vary between programs with undergraduate populations and those with mostly graduate students. Blanket reward structures that do not consider departmental differences may not be appealing and thereby motivating for all constituents. In addition, staff have different salary and reward systems that can vary by division. Creating reward systems to fit all these unique departmental and unit variations and differences by type of position (e.g., staff and faculty, contract and tenure track, different ranks) is an extremely complex process. Inequities can develop that might also represent legal problems, so reward systems need to be thought through carefully.

### Incorporating Multiple Constituent Interests

A one-size-fits-all approach may not work. Disciplines and units differ in terms of their current rewards structures and also in what might be an attractive incentive; for some it is a minigrant, for another administrative assistance, and for yet another help with grant writing. Of the extrinsic incentives, grants were mentioned most often as an enabler but varied in importance based on the groups within the institution. As mentioned previously, for faculty in the humanities and certain areas of the social sciences with limited grants and funding potential, offering small grants to work on a collaborative effort was a successful strategy. Other rewards may include rotating course requirements among several departments or decreasing overlap in between departments in order to free up faculty for collaborative work. Another method used to assist interdisciplinary work is to include a letter in midtenure and tenure reviews that specifically describes that work that the faculty member contributed to the collaborative team.

### Diffusing Competition

Another challenge in creating rewards to support collaborative work is the potential for resistance and competition among members of a collaborative. The literature on rewards for motivation warns that creating rewards can foster competition among individuals and teams who are competing not for intrinsic reasons (i.e., just wanting to do a good job) but for the external monies or other incentives associated with the rewards. One method suggested by Mohrman, Cohen, and Mohrman (1995) is to establish rewards that are based on the productivity of the team and not the individuals. If individuals' work on the collaborative varies, measures of individual and team performance can be combined to establish a team reward. The team can either equally distribute the rewards or establish internal criteria for distributing the rewards to the most deserving individuals. The process of reward giving may be different for each collaborative and vary according to the nature of the reward. In any case, the rewards should be established to discourage competition and encourage involvement. Although competition among collaborators does not seem to be a problem in higher education so far, it is an issue that may emerge in the future about which leaders should be aware.

### Altering Time-Honored Systems

Finally, altering promotion and tenure requirements might be much more challenging at certain institutions, particularly research universities. These institutions often resist changes until their peers have made similar changes and until disciplinary societies have altered their norms. Research universities can capitalize on changes being advocated for in a variety of disciplines. The National Academy of Sciences, the National Academy of Engineering, and Institute of Medicine, for example, have been arguing for the importance of inter- and multidisciplinary research. Their report, *Facilitating Interdisciplinary Research*, can be used on campuses to provide the logic behind changing tenure and promotion requirements. We describe the issue of disciplinary support more in Chapter Nine.

## Key Ideas

1. Scan the environment and talk to various constituent groups to understand the key intrinsic and extrinsic motivators.

2. Establish incentives that address the multiple roles of college constituents.

3. Consider a new evaluation system and merit pay for staff.

4. Review tenure and promotion policies; remove those barriers that devalue collaborative work and establish new policies that value collaborative work.

5. Allow individual departments and collaboratives to interpret and alter the dissemination of rewards.

6. Use external organizations and their models to legitimize changes in reward structures and policy changes.

7. Balance extrinsic and intrinsic rewards by being fiscally accountable and also equitable.

8. Capitalize on the intrinsic value of good collaborations by publicizing the value and success of collaborative work.

# 9

# External Pressures

*An external pressure is a force from outside the
organization that influences direction and changes.*

All organizations are susceptible to a variety of pressures from
external constituents. External pressures, such as pressures
from governmental agencies, customer expectations, and accountability movements, facilitate, enable, and may hinder collaborative
work. These external pressures can be capitalized on as mechanisms for communicating the importance and value of collaborative work to various campus stakeholders.

There are several ways that external pressures facilitate collaborations on college campuses: by mandating collaboration,
creating a sense of need or urgency, providing value and logic,
tying collaboration to quality standards, and relating collaboration to innovation, research, and development needs. The most
direct method for enabling collaboration is through federal grant
agencies and foundations tying research dollars to collaborative
efforts. As grant seeking continues to be a focus of faculty work,
faculty now find it prudent to establish relationships in order to
bring together individuals for grant-seeking activities. On campuses and within certain disciplines where obtaining grant funds
is pivotal to faculty work, this change in philosophy about obtaining funding can be capitalized on to help emphasize collaborative
work on the campus as well.

Another way that external organizations enable collaboration is by creating a sense of urgency about the need for collaboration to meet a host of goals that are important to organizations

that fund higher education. Many of these organizations are making further funding for higher education dependent on campuses' responding to calls for greater collaboration. Therefore, similar to federal grant agencies and foundations, legislatures are getting closer to mandating certain types of collaboration. Accreditation agencies create additional pressure by providing a set of standards that include collaboration, which legislatures and other groups use to judge the quality of higher education. The more that institutions of higher education are directed or mandated to collaborate or held to collaboration as a standard of quality, the stronger the message and urgency to learn how to redesign campus structures for that purpose. Finally, national disciplinary associations and societies regularly note collaboration as important to creating new and innovative research.

In addition, partnerships with communities have gained in popularity, beginning with the service learning initiatives. The majority of college campuses have a service learning initiative that promotes student engagement in community institutions and services. Partnerships between community organizations and college campuses provide the necessary infrastructure to place students in community agencies. The recent addition of a research component to these partnerships has also placed value on collaborative work that crosses the divide between student and academic affairs. Community partnerships, which have traditionally been a part of student affairs, are now requiring that faculty become involved as researchers, mentors, and community partners.

Although all of these external groups had a different form of influence that helped enable collaboration, the most important lesson is the way campus leaders combined these messages to make an undeniable case for collaboration. Administrators can and should talk about why major organizations are requiring collaboration and ask faculty to question their traditional approaches to teaching and research (without diminishing the fact that sometimes work done individually is also powerful). In sum, the major lesson from these institutions is that administrators in postsecondary education should consider capitalizing on the message from external organizations to highlight the value of collaborative work.

## Background of External Pressures

There is a large body of literature on external pressures and how they affect organizations. Organizations are constantly responding to external needs, such as pressure from professional associations, funding agencies, customers, state and federal government, and oversight agencies (e.g., accreditation agencies). One area of research that has been widely used to describe the importance of external pressures on organizations is resource dependency theory. The assumption in resource dependency theory is simply that organizations are dependent on external resources because they provide funding necessary to keep organizations operating. Higher education is influenced by state and federal governments because they accept operational funding, a nonprofit status, and state and federal aid. Postsecondary institutions vary in their dependence on state or federal funds. Some community colleges, for example, receive up to 100 percent of their operating budget from the state government whereas large research universities may receive a small fraction, potentially less than a third, of their operating budgets from state funds (Betts & MacFarland, 1995; Harbour, 2002). Yet all institutions rely on federal financial aid programs for additional student aid and on accrediting bodies that set educational standards, review individual colleges and universities, and determine whether they meet the regional standards.

Because higher education institutions receive public funding they also are subject to accountability requirements from the federal government through regional accrediting organizations.

For higher education, accrediting bodies provide the "checks and balances" on curriculum and professional preparation. As a result, accrediting bodies are another external constituent that can influence and pressure higher education institutions.

For those postsecondary institutions that do not rely heavily on state funds, primarily research universities or private institutions, external pressure also comes in the form of federal and private granting agencies, individual donors, and corporations that have a vested interest in partnering with faculty for research and development. Monies from these entities provide a substantial amount of an institution's operating budget that is not provided by state and federal funds. In addition, these monies are used for purposes that lead to patents, revenue from patents and selling of products, and indirect costs that are charged to the grants for the use of institutional resources. Often, on a variety of organizational levels (i.e., departments, individual faculty, or high-level administration), postsecondary institutions must cooperate and respond to the suggestions and considerations of those external agencies because these valuable resources allow faculty and postsecondary institutions to continue to operate.

Corporations and industry also attempt to influence colleges and universities and have a stake in their direction. This sector receives the graduates of colleges and universities and has expressed interest over the years in the curriculum and professional offering of campuses. Many community colleges are also partnering with local industries to offer specialized training for regional workforce needs. Increasingly businesses are partnering with colleges and universities to create research centers, and colleges are now providing the research and development arm for these companies. Over the years, business and industry has had an increasing influence on the curriculum of certain college campuses (Slaughter & Rhoades, 2004).

In addition to resource dependency theory and the external pressures described above, the professional organizations and societies of faculty constitute another external influence. In many organizations, groups of employees are considered professional if they are characterized by the following criteria: (1) their occupation performs a crucial social function, (2) which requires considerable skill; (3) development of those skills requires substantial education; (4) during education, socialization into professional values is obtained; and (5) considerable freedom is granted in daily job tasks that require individual judgment (Hoyle, 1982). Faculty are linked to institutional and national academic cultures and are highly skilled and autonomous. Furthermore, faculty are linked to professional organizations, which also influence higher education and its practices. Every academic discipline and field has a society that defines professional values for that group and offers forums for setting standards such as conferences and working groups. Not only faculty but staff also participate in professional organizations that guide their professional practice, such as the National Association of Student Personnel Administrators, National Association of Student Financial Aid Administrators, or the Association of American Colleges and Universities. The purpose of these groups is to create standards that cross institutions and establish practice for the entire field wherever it is practiced. Because the standards for various professional groups are set outside of individual institutions, external groups play a significant role in shaping the work of many administrators and staff.

To summarize, external pressures arise when organizations require resources from the external environment and when external constituents have a vested interest in the success of the organization. Higher education institutions, by virtue of their history as public entities that serve the public good, have many external pressures, such as accrediting bodies, granting agencies, and state and federal governments. Moreover, the employees of postsecondary institutions are, for the most part, professionals who move between organizational and disciplinary norms and are heavily influenced by external pressures from their professional fields. Collaborations within colleges and universities are susceptible to these external pressures. On the one hand, external constituents can provide the funds and guidance necessary to foster collaborations (e.g., interdisciplinary projects). On the other hand, external entities may pose additional barriers by creating competition for grant dollars between faculty and by imposing disciplinary values that may be antithetical to the college and that negatively affect the creation of collaborations that bring together faculty and staff from various discipline and functional areas of the university. What is important is that champions and leaders of collaboration understand that these external pressures can be used to help create more collaborative environments. As noted in the introduction, it is these very organizations—government, foundations, and corporations— that have already realized the importance of collaboration and have been applying pressure to higher education.

Many commentators have suggested that external forces are increasing in higher education (Boyer, 1987; Kezar, Chambers, & Burkhardt, 2005; Slaughter & Rhoades, 2004). For much of its history, postsecondary institutions were mostly autonomous from state and federal regulations. After World War II, greater federal regulation was put in place as state coordinating boards were formed (Slaughter & Rhoades, 2004). With the advent of federal financial aid (and state financial aid) and the dramatic rise in federal research dollars, increasing regulation, control, and impact from federal and state sources emerged. In very recent years, concerns about college costs, accountability related to student outcomes and learning, and ethical concerns over conflict of interest for research have created even greater scrutiny and pressure from external sources (Kezar, Chambers, & Burkhardt, 2005). This trend seems likely to continue, and external pressures will continue to be important levers for creating change on college campuses related to collaboration.

## Advice and Examples from Campus

The main advice from campuses that have created a supportive environment for collaborative work is to identify and capitalize upon all of the various sources of external pressure. In short, these campuses made sure they were familiar with professional organizations that encourage collaborative work, academic societies in which discussions about interdisciplinary work are strong, professional literature supportive of collaboration, and the private and public agencies that fund collaborative research, government organizations that support collaboration, accreditation agency criteria related to collaboration, and various corporations and industries promoting partnerships.

Campus change agents who determined which of the external groups had more influence on campus were strategic in invoking external messages. In addition, they spoke with various subgroups of faculty and staff in order to understand which external bodies they found to be more influential. For example, research universities are driven by disciplinary societies and research funding organizations; institutions with a history of not meeting certain accreditation standards may be greatly influenced by this process as they try to improve performance; campuses with a strong staff might appeal to national professional organizations; faculty in the sciences are more influenced by the National Science Foundation and the National Institutes of Health. Successful leaders were aware of the relative importance of external pressures related to institutional context and campus constituents. Invocation of multiple external pressures is usually necessary to create enough support among a critical mass of people on any campus to move forward.

### Creating Dialogue Related to All These External Pressures

Because collaboration is such a difficult transition to make, external pressures are needed to overcome institutional inertia and disciplinary silos. One of the ways to overcome institutional inertia is to create a message that is pervasive and powerful to influence administrators, faculty, or staff who are resistant. Leaders on the successful campuses we studied actively capitalized on messages from external groups and were persistent in creating dialogue (retreats, all-campus or school meetings, and public talks) about the external environment and pressures for collaboration. One administrator described how the campus leaders were using external conversations to enable collaboration:

> We know that people read professional materials and reports, know what's going on in national trends, but often do not translate that into their workplace. So, we create dialogues about changes in the workplace, new accreditation standards, and the like and make that connection for people. The feedback I have heard from people across campus is that these conversations work to create collaboration.

In addition to the important process of synthesizing various external messages and creating dialogue about them, campus leaders talked about specific ways that they capitalized on the messages of each specific external group. These approaches are described next.

### Disciplinary and Professional Societies

In recent years, some disciplinary and professional societies have been emphasizing collaboration, thereby creating a source of support for those interested in collaboration. Disciplinary and professional societies have been so persuasive that they have been able to transform the view of faculty who were previously uninterested. Every campus that we visited was aware of and tapping into the support provided by the professional societies. Some campuses were using resources that have been published by some of the academic societies, such as *Facilitating Interdisciplinary Research,* published by the National Academy of Sciences, the National Academy of Engineering, and Institute of Medicine. As one faculty commented:

> Even though our president and provost had been talking about the potential of interdisciplinary research, it wasn't until we started a reading group related to the publication of *Facilitating Interdisciplinary Research* that faculty seemed interested or got on board. Professional societies often have a much greater influence than leaders on campus, especially at more research-driven institutions.

---

*Facilitating Interdisciplinary Research:* **Summary of Key Report That Should be Used to Guide Campus Efforts and Gain Support**

*Facilitating Interdisciplinary Research* examines current interdisciplinary research efforts and recommends ways to stimulate and support such research.

Advances in science and engineering increasingly require the collaboration of scholars from various fields. This shift is driven by the need to address complex problems that cut across traditional disciplines and the capacity of new technologies to both transform existing disciplines and generate new ones. At the same time, however, interdisciplinary research can be impeded by policies on hiring, promotion, tenure, proposal review, and resource allocation that favor traditional disciplines.

This report identifies steps that researchers, teachers, students, institutions, funding organizations, and disciplinary societies can take to more effectively conduct, facilitate, and evaluate interdisciplinary research programs and projects. Throughout the report key concepts are illustrated with case studies and results of surveys of individual researchers and university provosts undertaken by the Committee on Facilitating Interdisciplinary Research (NAS, IOM, & NAE, 2005).

Another campus has a forum on collaboration in research and teaching. They asked each discipline and field to bring in information from their professional society related to interdisciplinarity or other forms of collaboration. Faculty brought in information from the American Association for the Advancement of Science, the Society for Anthropological Sciences, and the Society of Human Behavior and Evolution. Suddenly, faculty across campus realized that many disciplines were promoting collaborative work and these were not isolated ideas—there was a real power in bringing together all the work of different professional societies.

In addition to support from specific disciplinary or professional societies, a variety of associations have emerged that specifically focus on supporting interdisciplinary work, such as the Association for Integrative Studies and the Society for Literature, Science, and the Arts. There are now specific journals devoted to interdisciplinary studies as well. Here is an example of how campus leaders capitalized on these disciplinary societies. A provost sent several of her deans to the Association for Integrative Studies, a society devoted to promoting interdisciplinary research. At this conference, these individuals had the opportunity to identify some of the best practices of working within an interdisciplinary fashion. One of the deans reflected on this experience:

> It's really hard to imagine different ways to make connections among various disciplines both in research and teaching, especially after years of being socialized within a particular discipline. The provost really wanted the deans to brainstorm on ways to get more synergy between the units. Having had the opportunity to attend this conference really moved our thinking forward.

Many professional staff organizations are also emphasizing collaboration, such as the National Association of Student Personnel

Administrators, the American and College Personnel Association, the Association of American Colleges and Universities, the National Association of College and University Business Officers, the American Council on Education, and other groups that support administrators and staff on campus. Each of these groups has publications promoting the importance of cross-campus collaborative work such as *Greater Expectations* (AAC&U, 2002) or *Learning Reconsidered* (Keeling, 2004). Many of these associations also have conferences that have collaboration as part of the theme. For example, the American Association of Colleges and Universities has an integrative learning conference. Campuses are taking advantage of the publications, conferences, and professional networks available through the organizations to socialize new staff members to the value of collaboration and are using these conferences as a way to recruit staff to take leadership on their own campuses and providing professional development opportunities for existing staff. One staff member recalls how sending a team of staff to one of the national conferences helped fundamentally change their approach to programming:

> We had always developed programs pretty much in isolation of each other. I was doing leadership programs, Tim was doing multicultural programming, Jean did study skills on academic support, and everybody was sort of working in isolation like that. Our director sent us off to an ACPA conference and told us to attend some of the sessions related to collaboration. There must have been forty or fifty sessions at least. When we returned to campus, Jane, our director, brought us together and asked us to summarize some of the ideas we learned about collaboration and how we might rethink our work. I know I wouldn't have had ideas to share if I had not gone to this conference. It really helped to shape my thinking in new ways. Also, I have gone to conferences before, but

having us all focus on an issue and learn together about a topic was meaningful.

We heard story after story about the value of getting off campus and hearing about new ideas from professional groups.

### Federal Grant Agencies and Foundations

Disciplinary and professional associations and societies play a substantial role in supporting and valuing collaboration among faculty and staff. Federal grant-giving agencies that provide a large portion of research and development funds for the sciences are often trendsetters because they have the ability to establish guidelines for grant applications. One faculty member commented that

> The pressure from the National Science Foundation has changed the nature of faculty work on many campuses. I was always inclined toward collaboration, but usually my colleagues were uninterested and, in fact, actively against working with community agencies, other fields across campus, and the like. But now, grants encourage collaboration and people have become accustomed to the benefits—the increased dissemination of results, better studies, etc.—so now things are much easier, but it has taken time. I have been at this twenty-eight years and have only recently seen the groundswell of change. In large measure, the change I see on this campus is that we now pay attention to and channel those external messages around campus.

This observation is echoed on many college campuses across the country, which are responding to grant funding initiatives that encourage interdisciplinary teams to come together and collaborate on the grant proposal and subsequent project. Campuses are also changing their internal processes to align with and support these calls for collaboration. For example, since the National Institutes of Health is encouraging collaboration for grant proposal submission, institutions are rethinking their own support for grants. Some institutions now provide seed money as well as administrative assistance to bring together faculty across disciplines to write collaborative grant proposals. Institutions may also consider internal competitions between groups of faculty to put forth one institutionally sponsored proposal with the expectation and requirement of faculty from several disciplines. Furthermore, many campuses are responding to the calls of collaboration from government and private funding agencies by implementing campus-based grant programs that require at least two individuals from different departments and colleges (e.g., engineering and education) to collaborate on the development of a project. External pressures are changing the nature of internal grant processes in the hopes of changing habits so that campuses can compete for larger national grants.

Not only are federal agencies requiring collaboration, but private foundations are also emphasizing it. Many foundations have noticed that their grant dollars are not having the impact they wanted. A variety of foundations including PEW Charitable Trusts, the Ford Foundation, the Rockefeller Foundation, the Carnegie Foundation, the Jim and Ann Casey Foundation, and other major foundations and organizations across the country are requiring collaboration across units on college campuses, among college campuses, and between colleges and community agencies and other sectors. The Center for Philanthropy and Public Policy at the University of Southern California has charted this trend in fostering collaboration in order to maximize the impact of foundation dollars. Greater collaboration and partnerships can increase the complexity of the findings, bring together more expertise across the country, and connect important groups that are needed to contribute to complex social problems.

## Accrediting Bodies

Accrediting and state agencies have been stressing collaboration, especially around the area of assessment. The pressure from accrediting bodies is a major source of support for administrators and faculty, who believe in collaborative work. An unsatisfactory accreditation report can have a significant effect on institutional reputation and can create an incentive to conduct work in new ways. Many of the problems identified within the accreditation reports can be associated with lack of collaboration: weak communication, fragmented learning experience, uncoordinated service offerings, unclear and disconnecting governance processes, and low morale. One campus talked about how their accreditation report that cited very poor communication among units was jeopardizing institutional effectiveness. Because an external agency called attention to poor communication and the fragmented nature of the campus, leaders committed to a long-term process to redesign their campus to enhance coordination and communication through more internal partnerships.

In addition to some problems cited in accreditation reports that are related to lack of campus collaboration, many of the accreditation bodies are now emphasizing collaboration as part of their core values and beliefs about institutional effectiveness. For example, the Middle States Commission on Higher Education lists a commitment to cooperation, flexibility, and openness as important to institutional accreditation reviews. Organizations that are more hierarchical and fragmented often lack the ability to work together, adaptability, and open communication. Accreditors also cite the importance of higher education being responsive to the needs of community and to social changes (again, these can be achieved through greater collaboration with external groups). Their documents on the characteristics of excellent organizations include many references to partnerships and collaborations as tools for being more effective institutions. Several campus constituents made comments similar to this one about the emphasis on collaboration among accreditors:

> Whether you are on an accreditation team or whether they are coming to your campus, you realize that when people think about quality in this country, they think about more coordinated efforts. And most campuses just do not operate that way. So to sit back and look at campuses, you realize we are fundamentally out of alignment with other sectors that have been working to create more team-based approaches.

Western Association of Schools and Colleges emphasizes collaboration between faculty and administrators in its model of educational effectiveness. Each region in the country is emphasizing the importance of student learning outcomes and the ways the campuses need to work in a coordinated fashion across campus constituents to truly understand and measure student learning. A faculty member describes how the accreditation process on the campus has created many more conversations and collaborative projects:

> Assessment is one of those areas where people definitely recognize the need to collaborate and the emphasis among accreditors to actually demonstrate what students are learning has been pivotal in having our campus think about other ways we might need to collaborate. After the campuswide committee we created an assessment. We also created a technology initiative which brought faculty, administrators, and staff from across campus together. The pressure from accreditors to look at assessment now has us rethinking many of our processes.

## Business and Industry

Business and industry is another influential constituent that has applied external pressure to encourage collaboration. These sectors have communicated that collaboration is important for graduates entering the workplace. The pressure from business had a more dramatic effect on certain disciplines and professional fields, such as engineering, which had transformed its curriculum on the majority of campuses visited. One faculty member talked about emphasizing collaboration based more on the needs and concerns of local industry:

> We have a round table with engineering firms in the area at least once a year. One of the issues that had been discussed for a few years was how graduates from our institution were competent in the content but that they lacked adequate skill for being successful engineers in the workplace. They didn't have the communication skills to work with other members of the team and did not work well in the team environment which characterized most engineering firms. Although this came up, we hadn't really done anything to change our instruction or our program. The firms really challenged us to make this a priority and over the next few years we fundamentally transformed our curriculum, and the program emphasizes working in teams both in the classroom and outside the classroom. We changed our model of advising and mentoring to a more collaborative approach. Pretty soon we were beginning to touch all of the aspects of the program, rethinking our underlying assumptions. We now serve as a model for other professional schools across the country and are helping other units across campus who want to make a similar change.

As this story suggests, many professional schools and programs on college campuses are serving as role models for other units and divisions. Business, engineering, social work, public policy, and education, among other units, are often more in touch with external groups who have expressed a desire for higher education to integrate collaboration into the curriculum and model collaboration for students. Some campuses (or schools and colleges within the campus) have created advisory groups made up of important external constituents with the goal of tapping this influence in order to create more collaboration on the campus. One administrator noted how they use the strategy:

> Let's face it, faculty often ignore some of the messages we are trying to send about institutional effectiveness and student learning. I think that they believe we are caught up in fads. So what made a big difference on our campus is that we were creating guidelines that each school needed to have an external advisory board. We knew once we got some of these groups talking to the faculty—people that they cared about, related to their research and professional field or discipline—that they could have a bigger impact.

Business and industry are also demanding more partnerships with universities for research and development and fueling innovation, which are key to the national economy. Collaboration is a focal point for innovation which often requires multiple groups and different perspectives to address new technologies and new problems creatively. These partnerships also create funding streams for the campus and are another pivotal lever for making faculty, administrators, and staff see the value of collaboration. Many campuses were strategic in pointing out these partnerships as successful laboratories for innovation. They pointed out that the campus needs the same research and development units that bring together the best expertise from across campus to address complex problems of attrition and student support as well.

## State Legislatures

State policymakers and legislatures have also been strong advocates for collaboration on a variety of fronts and for different purposes, including improving K–12 education through college and school partnerships, working with business and industry related to workforce development, partnering with community agencies to address social problems, collaborating between institutions to share best practices as well as resources, and engaging in internal collaboration for institutional effectiveness and cost savings. Diminishing resources at the state level provide incentives for divisions and units to work together to preserve important programs and initiatives. Many state legislatures have been sending the message that campuses cannot keep doing business as usual and that they need to think more about being more efficient, creating some cross campus offices, coordinating more among groups, and restructuring; that is, getting rid of unnecessary hierarchies and bureaucratic structures. One faculty member described a story of how messages from the state affect public institutions, in particular:

> We started to have these conversations in each of our departmental meetings: "Did you see the editorial in the paper about cutting funds for higher education?" The next month we would be talking about the budget shortfall. And then the week after, over coffee, about accountability concerns from the state and their concerns about institutional effectiveness. These used to be things we just hoped administrators would magically take care of. But things have shifted and faculty need to wake up and realize we need to change the way we do our work. This is what administrators had been saying

for several years, and reading about it in the paper and talking about it at our meetings made it hit home.

Organizations that support state policymakers such as the Education Commission of the States have been emphasizing a variety of different collaborative ventures in higher education, particularly college and school partnerships and more information sharing between colleges. The Western Interstate Commission on Higher Education sees its mission of sponsoring more collaborations between and within institutions related to student exchanges, technology, workforce development, or risk management. Although much of the focus of state organizations is on collaboration between institutions, the emphasis and importance of collaboration is used by leaders on many campuses to foster more internal collaboration. One campus leader describes how the administration uses some of their experiences with external collaboration to support more internal collaboration:

> We got involved with a collaborative to share technology knowledge and pool our resources to buy the latest technology. Our access to cutting-edge technology became apparent to people on campus. One of the things I did, was I began talking about how we would not have this benefit if we had not collaborated, and this is why we have been emphasizing collaboration as part of our mission and strategic planning. When people can actually see the results of collaboration and how it helps them—they finally get it.

State legislatures and policymakers have shown an interest in educational collaborations by mandating that the different sectors (K–12 and higher education) engage in formal partnerships. For example, the State of Georgia has the Georgia P–16 Council that provides coordination and leadership for all educational sectors

188 ORGANIZING HIGHER EDUCATION FOR COLLABORATION

across the state. The council is comprehensive in that it includes elected officials, individuals from the community, and representatives from public schools and postsecondary institutions. The work of the council is mandated by the state, and the council members report to the governor. Wyoming also has a state-mandated collaboration between K–12 schools and higher education under the auspices of the Wyoming P–16 Education Council. The mission of the council is to improve all educational systems through coordination, communication, and evaluation of all educational sectors. They achieve this goal through the development of a shared vision, program coordination, and coherence in policies. The fact that these states have mandated and funded these large-scale collaborations illustrates the commitment that legislatures and policymakers have toward a collaborative ethic in all education systems and sectors.

### Community Agencies and Groups

External pressure to collaborate also comes from community and social agencies. Although these organizations typically do not have a great deal of influence or power on colleges and universities, they are beginning to have more of a voice because legislatures are emphasizing the need for higher education to be more responsive to the problems in schools (by encouraging GEAR programs and other P–16 partnerships), workforce development, poverty, immigration, and local problems of violence or safety. Some legislatures are considering attaching performance funding to benchmarks around community impact and outreach. Already many legislatures are asking for reports and documentation about higher education outreach. Campuses that are successful in fostering collaboration realize that this is another source of support for efforts to create greater collaboration through service learning projects, community-based research, or community and university partnerships. Leaders on these campuses brought political and community leaders to speak to faculty and staff about community needs and the changing relationship with legislatures who are demanding more evidence of community outreach from higher education.

## Challenges to Communicating External Pressures

There are many opportunities to capitalize on external pressures to promote collaboration in higher education institutions; however, there are also many challenges.

### Managing Multiple Conflicting Messages

One of the major challenges is sifting through the multiple and often conflicting messages from external pressure groups to focus and create successful collaborative efforts. Although federal granting agencies may value collaborative work, the grant-seeking process is competitive and often requires that only one proposal be submitted from each university. Therefore, internal competitions between collaborative groups often occur in order to evaluate and vote on one institutionally supported grant proposal. This competition may be antithetical to collaboration, particularly when faculty compete against each other.

### Fighting Faddishness

Another challenge mentioned by several campuses is that naysayers on campus may suggest that the campus leaders are merely following the latest trends of external groups that are not close enough to the mission of their specific campuses. Some campuses might see that they have a very specialized or traditional mission that should not be affected by changes in the higher education landscape or societal changes. Faddishness is a difficult criticism to lodge against all the external groups mentioned, but some groups such as legislatures or businesses can sometimes be easier to pigeonhole as responding to the latest whim or trend. There are always going to be traditionalists on campus that suggest that changes recommended by external groups have or could corrupt higher education. However, this criticism is important because there have been external pressures that have created problematic changes on campus such as rampant commercialization and ethical challenges such as conflicts of interest. In recent years, businesses and government have encouraged higher education to focus much more narrowly on economic goals, which one of us has critiqued (Kezar, 2004).

### Changing Demands from External Groups

Granting agencies and other external groups change their priorities from time to time, and it is often difficult for postsecondary institutions to anticipate the changes. When a granting agency releases a request for proposals that requires collaboration, the institution is forced to gather a large number of faculty to work on a grant proposal. The relationship building required for successful collaboration is often impossible, given the time constraints of grant writing in combination with the various faculty responsibilities. Using a group of faculty who already collaborate regularly may assist in overcoming the relationship building required for successful collaboration; however, overuse may overwhelm faculty, who may not be able to take on any additional projects. Furthermore, when additional offices are required, such as offices in student affairs, the time sensitivity of student enrollments, federal financial aid, advising, and other student needs make it difficult for these offices to participate at particular times during the year. One suggestion for overcoming this challenge is to bring different groups of faculty together to brainstorm on future projects to build relationships that will be needed for future grant development. These groups should also include individuals from other academic and student affairs offices who may also be needed for grant development.

## Matching Pressures to Mission

Moreover, not all external constituents value collaborative work in the same way. It is the challenge of administrators to understand and communicate the messages from external constituents to the larger institution and to relate these messages to the mission and values of the institution. Interpreting the messages helps campus constituents understand in what ways collaborative efforts are valued by external agencies relative to institution-specific missions and values. Relating external pressures to the overall campus mission is important, but the external pressures need to be considered alongside the campus culture and different constituent groups. For example, leaders need to relate the value of collaborative work espoused by accreditation agencies to the mission of the college and describe how each individual faculty member can include collaborative work within academic programs.

Another challenge concerns articulating those extra pressures and messages within an existing organizational mission and an existing value system. The history and traditions of the higher education institution may be entrenched in departmental silos and individualistic faculty work. The external pressures that place value on collaborative work may stand in direct contrast to the mission and values of the organization. Therefore, a major challenge is articulating the ways in which collaborative work benefits the organization, as well as how it benefits the traditional mission. As we suggest in this book, organizations may need to consider more drastic ways to restructure and undergo a culture shift, but these shifts take time, whereas the external pressures are more immediate. In the short term, institutional leaders may consider communicating with the external constituents (e.g., state legislators or accreditors) to create an understanding of how the institution is responding to pressures to conduct more collaborative work while also respecting the institutional mission and value system. In this regard, the interaction with external pressures is not a one-way street. Institutions are not being required to respond only to those external constituents; rather, a dialogue needs to be created between the external pressures and the institutions to create an understanding of how collaborative work can be integrated. Furthermore, administrators can slowly and symbolically articulate the value of collaborative work through internal monies given for short-term collaborative projects or grant development, partnerships between academic disciplines or individual faculty and student affairs offices, and interdisciplinary degree programs to bring together faculty from multiple disciplines under the umbrella of an academic program. Each of these initiatives creates a sense of value and begins to transform the mission of the institution to align itself with collaborative work that is being communicated and required by external constituents.

The challenges of managing the multiple and sometimes conflicting external pressures and priorities, falling into a faddish and false sense of change and urgency that turns people off, responding to calls for collaboration without having systems in place, and creating processes that are more aligned with collaborative work while still being trapped in some conventional structures are real, and campuses need to be aware of these issues.

## Key Ideas

1. Capitalize on external pressures regarding collaborative work to foster collaboration within the institution.

2. Evaluate and interpret external pressures in relation to the institutional context (mission and values of the institution), as well as aligned to particular campus constituencies.

3. Create dialogues with external constituents to facilitate an understanding of how collaborative work can be fostered within the institution.

4. Send faculty and staff to off-site conferences that reinforce collaborative work.

5. Read publications from professional societies that describe the importance of interdisciplinary research and teaching.

6. Read accreditation reports for problems related to collaboration.

7. Set up advisory boards of external groups from the community, business, and political groups to inform campus operations.

8. Establish faculty collaborative networks to build relationships that can be called upon to respond to grant agencies that require faculty from multiple disciplines (see also Chapter Six).

9. Provide institutional funds as well as opportunities to bring together groups of faculty and staff in anticipation of the external pressures for interdisciplinary work and collaboration (see also Chapter Six).

# 10

# Learning

*Definition: Learning is the cognitive process of acquiring new skills or knowledge. Specifically in this book, it refers to both developing an awareness of the benefits of collaboration and acquiring the skills necessary to effectively collaborate.*

Not all individuals understand the definition or nature of collaboration. Whereas values communicate the need for collaborative work, learning leads to an understanding of the nature of collaboration and development of the skills necessary to practice it. The most important aspect of learning, in the framework of this study, is communicating the need and importance of collaboration. But learning also serves several important roles in fostering collaboration (or learning how to collaborate).

In some organizations, such as nonprofits that regularly partner with other organizations, the value of collaboration is well established. But in higher education, the first step in learning is understanding the importance and benefits of collaboration. In this setting, learning promotes collaboration when individuals learn about the value, nature, and importance of collaboration. The history of higher education and its focus on individualistic faculty work does not naturally lead to an understanding of the value of collaborative work. Collaboration is unlikely if faculty and staff on college campuses do not learn about the benefits and advantages of collaboration for their own work performance and for organizational effectiveness. Furthermore, engaging in the process of learning about collaboration can create a common philosophy linked to the mission of collaboration. As noted in earlier chapters, linking the institutional mission to collaborative efforts is one way to promote collaboration around the institution.

As mentioned previously, learning also promotes collaboration by giving people the necessary knowledge and skills to collaborate. But people from institutions with successful collaborations in our study emphasized that the learning process that they went through provided them with context-based knowledge about how to collaborate in their particular settings. They warned that generic information about the skills of collaboration would not have been as helpful in enabling them to collaborate. Rather than generic skills about how to collaborate, collaborators shared very content-specific information about how to work with particular individuals and units on campus, structures that needed to be negotiated, particular incentives available on campus, and the range of perspectives on collaboration within indifferent pockets of the institution, for example. Although campuses mentioned some formal processes that helped enable collaboration, such as symposia or luncheons at which information from successful collaborators was presented, institutions did not mention bringing in trainers or consultants with expertise in collaboration to help them learn skills or gain knowledge about the collaboration process. Instead, campuses found that tapping the local expertise of pioneering collaborators, who understood the organizational contexts and how collaboration unfolds on the campus, were the most successful approaches to learning. Also, rather than during formal learning sessions, they found that much of the learning happened as people within the network interacted informally as part of their day-to-day work.

Another way that learning about collaborative work supports and enables it is by helping people understand challenges that they might face and how to overcome them. Often this happens initially through the network of collaborators. The pioneering network of collaborators can help generate needed learning to help redesign systems to support collaboration and to identify problems in the redesign. This was similar to the Mohrman, Cohen, and Mohrman model (1995), where learning played a role in designing collaborative systems as people tested new designs and altered and changed aspects based on proven practices. The troubleshooting work of the network was critical in helping to sustain collaboration. However, as opposed to the Mohrman, Cohen, and Mohrman model, in which experimental structures or networks were commonplace, once changes were made to redesign campuses they became formalized quite quickly and without redesign.

## Background of Learning

There are several different types of learning that are usually referred to in the literature on collaboration: learning about the process of collaboration itself, learning about people within the collaborative relationship, learning the skills to collaborate, mastering the ability to overcome interpersonal dynamics and conflict, rethinking organizational processes, and developing a new and better understanding of the organization(s) as collaborative work requires people to view their organizations in new ways.

First, collaborations require individuals and organizations to learn about the process of collaboration itself and the issues that may arise in attempting to foster collaborative work. For example, in Mohrman, Cohen, and Mohrman's (1995) learning model for intra-organizational collaboration, an organization must lay the foundation by reading resources, collecting data, visiting other organizations to learn about the process of collaboration, and diagnosing and assessing their own performance, perhaps identifying organizational issues affecting collaboration. Analyzing other organizations and having conversations about the barriers and challenges to collaboration creates an opportunity for organizations to learn about collaboration and avoid the common challenges that prevent collaborations from moving forward.

Collaborations, according to Mohrman, Cohen, and Mohrman, are continuously learning and should solicit feedback in order to evaluate their effectiveness. For example, a collaborative team can conduct periodic discussions with team members to see whether their goals are achieved and whether the team members are still dedicated to their collaborative efforts and mission.

Second, learning must also occur within the collaborations: learning about other types of people and their perspectives. Relationships are key to moving the collaboration forward, as well as the learning that occurs between partners as they negotiate and become familiar with each other (Ring and Van de Ven, 1994). Mohrman, Cohen, and Mohrman (1995) suggest that individuals within collaborations need to be open to learning. Individuals must be willing to acquire new knowledge, develop an understanding of different ways of viewing the world, and develop interpersonal and conflict resolution skills. As many faculty and staff come together from multiple disciplines and professional fields that have different theoretical and philosophical perspectives, people's willingness to learn and to understand these disparate perspectives serves as an important foundation for successful collaborations.

Third, people who collaborate are better served over the long term if they learn the skills of being a good collaborator. These skills include how to negotiate perspectives, improve interpersonal intelligence, manage one's own emotions, facilitate meetings, retain flexibility, assist in reaching a consensus, respect others, manage conflict, and practice active listening. The ability to resolve interpersonal conflicts that sometimes arise from group dynamics within collaborations is another useful skill to learn.

In addition to an understanding of the content of work, Mohrman, Cohen, and Mohrman (1995) suggest that collaborations also require learning about the process of the work. Inherent in collaborative work is an understanding of how work is to be completed. For example, faculty in the hard sciences work on long-term projects with many individuals in a laboratory setting whereas faculty in the social sciences typically work alone in social settings and on projects that are more short term (three to five years). If faculty from the hard sciences and social sciences work together on a collaborative project, their expectations for the duration of the project, the ways of working together, and the setting will all need to be negotiated, which will require compromise and learning about each other's cultures and processes. Another example would be an academic and student affairs collaboration project. Since these two groups may not have a lot of experience working together, they might approach certain processes differently. Academic affairs staff tend to have longer meetings that may not be as goal driven, whereas student affairs staff may have a specific agenda and shorter meetings, which also may include more interpersonal time. Academic and student affairs staff must each learn how the other conducts their work and develop a process that works for both groups. Without learning about each other's processes, it is difficult to advance and work together.

Finally, collaborators are more successful if they learn about and become knowledgeable about the larger organizational processes and structures in which they conduct their collaborative initiative. Individuals can facilitate collaborative work if they understand levers (e.g., rewards, senior administrators, and networks) within the organizations that support them. For example, faculty working in a collaborative project, discussed previously, will need to understand support services and processes within the higher education institutions in order to complete the project. These processes may include institutional review boards, reward structures, and ways to disseminate funds. Although we all work in organizations, we often do not broadly understand how the organization operates because of its siloed nature. Collaborative processes require that we learn about an organization cross-functionally.

Once collaborators understand areas for learning (e.g., how to be a collaborator, broader understanding of the organization), to be successful they also need to understand conditions that might affect the learning process within the collaboration. Doz (1996) argues that several components, starting with a set of initial conditions (task definition, partner's routines, interface structure, and expectation of performance, behavior, and motives), either facilitate or hamper learning processes. Task definition and expectation performance refers to the understanding of the task that the collaboration is attempting to achieve; partners' routines, behavior, and motives are the skills and processes that each partner brings. Essentially, each of the initial conditions defines how the partners will work together, how they will accomplish the task, their skills, and the motives or goals of each partner. If each of these initial conditions is met, the collaboration has an increased chance of being successful, both in its goal and in the learning process. And in collaborations, there needs to be an understanding of the values, goals, and expectations of each individual in order for the learning process to move forward. So it is not enough just to know areas where learning must occur, it is also important that to be aware of factors that could hamper and facilitate learning. An obvious condition is the difficulty of the collaborative task. The learning required for conducting interdisciplinary teaching for creating learning communities is quite extensive, and new collaborators may need to move at a slower pace. In contrast, bringing people from across campus into a committee to study retention who have already been working on issues of retention may not require as much learning, as all groups have already been focused on the task of retention.

Once the initial conditions are met, learning must also occur on several fronts—environment, task, process, skills, and goals—for the collaboration to move forward (Doz, 1996). If this learning occurs as the collaboration unfolds, then a process of evaluation about the efficiency, equity, and adaptability of the alliance can be undertaken. After evaluation there are usually some adjustments that result in revised conditions related to task definition, partner's routines, interface structures, and expectations of performance. For Doz, the key aspect of the evolution is a learning process that occurs within the evaluation and re-adjustment process.

Finally, Mohrman, Cohen, and Mohrman (1995) argue that modeling values and norms are required for a successful, collaborative organization. They suggest that the lack of experience with collaborative work within an organization requires that leadership teams spearhead the learning process, solicit feedback, and model collaborative processes.

## Advice and Examples from Campuses

Campuses offered four main suggestions for those who hope to create a more collaborative environment on how learning can be harnessed to move collaboration forward. They recommended (1) spreading informal knowledge through on-campus networks, (2) offering a few formal information-sharing sessions in which people can learn more about the process and skills of collaboration, (3) identifying models of collaboration for observation, and (4) tailoring learning opportunities to the constituent group and institutional culture.

### Formal and Informal Learning Processes

Although the literature on collaboration emphasizes the importance of formal training sessions to help collaborators learn the skills and process of collaboration, within higher education much of this information is shared in more informal ways (e.g., passing out materials, word of mouth). However, these campuses utilized both. In addition to the informal situations, there were formal learning processes (workshops, luncheons, speaker sessions) that helped individuals learn about the nature and value of collaborations in which they learned about the benefits and logic of collaboration. The formal and informal processes promoted learning about the process of collaboration itself and collaboration skills (usually through modeling, which is discussed in a later section), about transforming processes, and about how to overcome challenges in collaborating. This section describes both the informal and formal learning processes.

Learning was used by change agents as a strategy for informing people of the benefits of collaboration in order to motivate people to conduct collaborative work. Leaders often used formal processes, such as sharing research on the advantages of collaboration and distributing data from the National Science Foundation on partnerships, and they held forums and workshops on various forms of collaboration they were trying to encourage to help people understand the benefits. One administrator's comments epitomized the stories of many individuals: "After a symposium was given, I got messages from twenty-five faculty who told me they were fundamentally rethinking their work and it was the evidence presented about the benefits of collaboration that convinced them." So occasionally holding some formal event such as a symposium can be beneficial.

As campuses became more sophisticated, collaborators often needed to understand how to transform what had been individualistic processes to meet the needs of a collaborative process or how to overcome challenges that emerged in a collaborative process. One of the best formal ways for educating others was to host a luncheon or workshop that focused on best practices or examples of successful collaboration on campus.

Symposia and forums often brought in speakers related to one of the collaborative projects to help people learn and overcome challenges. For example, one campus that was beginning a more collaborative budgeting process brought in the chief financial officer of another campus who was already operating within this new model and asked him to describe the benefits and some of the challenges they faced. The dialogues also provided opportunities for leaders to gauge understanding among faculty and staff, as well as any barriers and resistance (increasing administrators' own learning). One administrator describes how hosting a symposium helped him address some resistance to the collaborative project:

> As we started the research institutes, I knew that some faculty were uncomfortable and I could not get them to describe their hesitation. And maybe they weren't even able to articulate the issues at the time, but as we started to discuss the benefits and challenges of inter-disciplinary research they were better able to articulate some concerns they had with potential weaknesses in interdisciplinary research, faculty teaching outside their areas of expertise, or budgetary concerns. Unless we are able to sit down and develop trust between each other and learn more about the initiative, I'm not sure we would have been able to address these concerns and they would have lingered for a long time, perhaps making the initiative fail.

Another formal way of sharing information is assembling individuals who are from collaborative projects to describe what they are learning and what best practices they can share with others. An administrator describes how senior administrators held a session for different collaborators across campus:

> One of the most successful ways that we created learning was by hosting an annual forum for individuals who were working on collaborative projects to share ideas. We also invited individuals who were interested in creating a collaborative project to listen in. They shared ideas about key faculty and staff who can be helpful and like collaborative work [essentially educating people about

the campus network], ways to kick off the planning process, how they developed a common purpose, ways to motivate people [appealing to values and incentives], shared publications and resources, accounting difficulties, problem units and ways to negotiate with them, and talked about ways to maintain resiliency in the face of antagonists. And they generally had fun as well!

One of the important roles of change agents and senior executives is to monitor and be aware of various collaborative projects and to know when ones have gone particularly well. These projects are sources of learning for the campus. Change agents need to meet with these groups to find out what they learned as the collaboration unfolded and to ask this group if they would be willing to host a session for others on campus. If this experience can be archived in some way—either in a newsletter or some campus document that can be handed out to others at a later time—this can also help to maintain this learning, even if some members of the collaborative leave. So change agents can help the campus by monitoring, identifying, and capturing learning from collaborative activities that can be formally shared with people on campus through hosting an event or informally shared through conversations in the network. A faculty member comments on the way she tapped into the informal network to learn about ways to move a collaborative forward:

> We were running into some problems with the research institutes. There was some concern about budgeting and I asked around among some other people who participated in establishing the assessment office. Their feedback about how to handle some of the budgeting problems I was dealing with helped. So tapping into those who have gone before you is really important to address challenges that emerge.

As these stories demonstrate, the information session on collaboration helped individuals and groups learn all aspects necessary to be successful in collaboration as noted by Mohrman, Cohn, and Mohrman (1995). These aspects included dealing with conflict, managing interpersonal dynamics, working with different groups on campus, developing successful collaboration processes, creating data and resources to support collaboration, and achieving better understanding of the overall organization.

## Modeling Collaboration

Modeling collaboration as a technique to help people learn the specific skills of collaboration is another informal process that the campuses used. Modeling collaboration can take many forms, including creating campuswide teams, opening up cabinet meetings to a broader constituency, including constituents from across campus in planning the process, involving faculty and staff and fundraising efforts, working interactively with all of the senior staff (rather than through a provost), asking for input on budgeting processes, and a variety of others.

Once faculty and administrators understood the benefits of collaboration and felt compelled to begin changing the way they work, they looked for successful models to follow. Sometimes senior executives served as models; other times it might be programmatic examples. For example, a strong interdisciplinary center on campus can serve as a model for rethinking work or perhaps a member of the network of individuals who already does collaborative work can be the model. Most campuses—even ones that have not become conducive to collaboration yet—will have pockets of collaboration that can be called upon to be role models. One staff member commented on the importance of modeling and learning to collaborate:

> When I came here, I had never worked in a collaborative environment. I thought, of course I know how to collaborate, it was just never encouraged. But I noticed I had

> picked up so many individualistic working patterns, it
> was hard to break. I also realized as I watched people
> work collaboratively that I learned new skills—how to
> integrate multiple members' feedback, how to listen for
> consensus points, how to facilitate conflict resolution,
> how to make people feel included, and other skills that
> I might not have realized were important to succeed in
> collaborative work.

As this quote demonstrates, faculty, staff, and administrators often think they know how to collaborate, either through an innate skill or because it is something they learned in the past. Yet given that so few organizations operate in a collaborative manner, people need to learn or relearn how to collaborate in most workplaces. But again, in this instance, modeling processes were more organic, not something that people constructed or devised; rather, modeling tended to be informal rather than programmatic.

In addition to helping them learn collaboration, modeling helped faculty and staff view collaboration as a priority. Faculty and staff are looking for and learn from examples of senior executives modeling collaboration. They observe details of how senior executives collaborate: do they build trust, do they listen to the feedback, how do they build relationships, and do they seem to really believe in collaboration? Each person interviewed noted that if the senior leadership simply tell you collaboration is important but they do not practice it, you are unlikely to believe and follow their encouragement. One faculty member commented:

> I have been on several campuses and I have heard presidents talk about collaboration before, and seen that it
> wasn't really valued, because they did not practice it,
> and, therefore did not realize the needed supports that
> have to be put in place like rewards or resources. But
> when I arrived here, the president and provost modeled
> collaboration and provided real support, such as the new

institutes. So I saw that in practicing it, they believed
it and would support it institutionally as well. I think
those two go hand in hand.

The senior administrators on these campuses embodied the collaboration that they hoped to foster; this also provided an example
of healthy collaboration for people to follow and learn from.

Many individuals interviewed saw a relationship between the
modeling of collaboration and the senior administrators' willingness to create campus systems and a culture in support of collaboration. They also believed that senior executives who modeled
collaboration were better able to sympathize with challenges that
emerge in collaboration and are better able to help brainstorm
solutions to keep collaborative projects moving forward. Faculty
and staff were wary of senior executives who only spoke about but
could not model collaboration:

> Without adequate experience collaborating, there is
> this false naïveté that it is really easy to collaborate and
> there is no recognition about the way that institutions
> inhibit collaboration until you've actually tried to do it.
> And senior executives have a much easier time, granted.
> But they will still experience the difficult interpersonal
> dynamics and they acquire a better sense of what they're
> actually asking people to do. They're also much more
> likely to provide incentives and think about restructur-
> ing. So you're willing to follow a leader who has that
> kind of knowledge. I'm not going down the path of the
> naïve leader chasing collaboration who doesn't know
> that much about it.

## Constituent-Focused and Aligned with the Campus Mission and Values

To successfully teach people the benefits or introduce them to the
skills and processes of collaborative work, one needs to approach

the task with the constituents in mind. People in the humanities might be compelled by a quotation by the philosopher Hannah Arendt that "excellence occurs in the company of others." For a chemist, empirical data about the outcomes of collaborative versus individual efforts might be convincing, whereas another individual may have to experience collaboration before he or she can be aware of its benefits. Individual, disciplinary, and other differences need to be taken into account when helping individuals learn about collaborative work. As one campus official noted:

> You need to be multimodal and use the language of various disciplines and be aware of different learning styles. Collaboration is more intuitive to certain disciplines, personality styles, and individual preferences, so you need to move beyond a limited group and help all people see collaboration as important. We usually miss out on these people because we go with people who intuitively understand you and already have the skills.

In addition to being sensitive to particular groups and individuals on campus who might have different interests or perspectives that will make them open to learning about collaboration, change agents also need to be sensitive to differences in organizational culture and how learning opportunities should be designed to capitalize on the unique mission and values. On a campus with a strong teaching mission, sessions on learning to collaborate might focus on the specifics of team teaching and learning communities. Change agents who attend these sessions can extrapolate broader lessons of collaboration from these examples of team teaching and learning community. People are learning the skills of collaboration, but within the context of issues they care the most about and already understand deeply. For example, a group of faculty who are interested in promoting environmentalism across campus may come together in a collaborative group in order to create campus buy-in from multiple departments and offices. Although the faculty are not intentionally setting out to collaborate, the fact that they need support across the institution leads them to a collaborative experience in which they are able to learn new skills.

## Challenges of Learning

Learning, a process that would seemingly be smooth in higher education, was difficult to create based on the complex subcultures and different groups on campus.

### Lack of Expertise in Collaboration

One of the major challenges in using learning to promote collaboration is the assumption that the campus has some internal expertise and has had some pioneering efforts from which to learn. Some campuses that are very early on in the process may not have this level of local knowledge to tap into. Change agents on these campuses may need to consider having outside consultants and trainers who work with the campus to brainstorm some of the ways they might move toward collaborative work. However, the example of these campuses show that the most relevant information is context based. The advice from consultants should be matched with internal, contextual knowledge. Also, if the training sessions offered by consultants do not have the desired impact in terms of preparing people for successful collaboration, campus constituents should not become cynical or frustrated, but rather should try to identify how this learning can be grounded in the context of the specific campus. But campuses with limited experience with collaboration will have less knowledge to draw on to help the overall campus learn how to collaborate.

### Difficulty in Matching Learning to Various Constituents

Another challenge is to identify the best learning approaches for various campus groups. Creating learning within the higher education context is one of the most significant challenges because there are so many different groups and subcultures with very different perspectives. Faculty, staff, and administrators all have subcultures that rely on different shared values and perspectives. Establishing the need and urgency of learning about collaborative work requires that administrators and others appeal to a variety of value sets. People in our study mentioned that learning opportunities should be customized to the various groups on campus, thus requiring an awareness of the various cultures that exist on campus and developing learning opportunities that match each faculty discipline and staff professional orientation (from business officers to academic affairs to student affairs). If these groups are networked together and communicate, then creating a customized message and communicating it through this network seems more likely to be successful. This again suggests the pivotal role of networks to expand collaboration. Learning opportunities can be developed by various members of the networks and customized by individuals who understand their own constituent group best.

The multiple cultures and constituents on college campus also presented the challenge of collaborators having to learn many different perspectives in order to be successful in their efforts to work with others across campus. In other organizations, where one or two different constituent groups might exist, understanding and learning different perspectives is not a great challenge. Colleges and universities are significantly challenged in creating learning processes to enable collaboration because of the multiple constituents. In addition, colleges and universities will need to spend more time in learning about ways to negotiate conflicts, and conflict is more likely to emerge with all of the differing perspectives.

### Learning Relevant to Campus Needs

Creating learning that matches the institutional context is another challenge campuses faced. Most of the campuses in the study already had some type of network of individuals who collaborate and work on collaborative projects. As a result, more informal processes of learning were focused on modeling collaboration. However, one can imagine campuses where there are few collaborators, little opportunity for informal learning, and no opportunities for modeling, where, as a result, formal learning experiences may be required. As noted earlier, change agents should be aware that they must match learning opportunities to the phase of the campus (how far it has moved along toward being more collaborative, e.g., teaching why collaboration is important early and later focusing on skills of collaboration), as well as its institutional culture (teaching versus research culture, for example). Some campuses easily matched learning opportunities to campus culture, but it is easy to imagine that some campuses may not find this an intuitive process and it could present a challenge. Other institutional differences are also significant when thinking about challenges to learning. Larger campuses with many different cultures and groups will find themselves overwhelmed, so leaders on some campuses suggested picking one or two significant and influential constituent groups to target first. But size and complexity of cultures was not the only issue. Whether the culture of the campus is more political or collegial was also a factor. Change agents were optimistic about more collegial campuses and noted that appealing to the shared values could make the learning process less challenging. Political campuses need to proceed more slowly, as the benefits of collaboration have to be identified for different interest groups on campus.

## Key Issues

1. Use campus networks to create informal learning opportunities about collaboration skills and knowledge.

2. Establish formal sessions to capitalize on the learning among pioneering collaborators and invite those interested in collaborating.

3. Monitor, identify, and archive important learning that emerges from campus networks and collaboration pioneers in newsletters and other documents.

4. Encourage people to watch successful collaborators and make sure change agents are aware of collaborative projects that can serve as a role model.

5. Match learning opportunities to constituent interests and predilections. Be aware that the pace of learning may be impeded by the sheer number of different interest groups on a campus.

6. Planners of learning opportunities should keep in mind the institutional phase and campus culture.

# Part III

## Conclusion
### *Bringing the Strategies Together for Collective Action*

In Chapters Eleven and Twelve, we bring together the various features of organizational context into a comprehensive model. Although it is important to examine each feature separately to thoroughly understand it, each of the features is highly interrelated. Values can be used to rethink mission, integrating structures help create networks, rewards can help bring integrating structures into fruition, learning can lead to new values, and external pressures can help provide funding for rewards. In Chapter Eleven, we present a model for how the various elements of organizational context unfold over time to create an environment for collaborative work. Although we do not describe all possible interrelationships between the context features, we do describe the common path taken by the four campuses to help leaders see how they can strategically design a process for creating a collaborative work environment. In addition, this model demonstrates how institutions move, over time, to a collaborative context, through a three-phase process. One does not build a campus that supports collaboration without going through a deliberate and lengthy process.

Chapter Twelve outlines the various ways that external groups can support campuses in moving to a collaborative context. Accreditors, state legislators and policy staff, professional associations, and others can provide support to make higher education a sector more open to collaborative work. The norms of higher education will be changed more rapidly if external groups provide support for this type of work. In recent years, as demonstrated in Chapter Nine, these groups have been extremely helpful in shifting the work of postsecondary institutions toward greater collaboration through incentives, encouragement, and mandates. We also describe the roles that internal constituents such as faculty, staff, and administrators can play in creating support for on-campus collaboration. This collective action can create a new postsecondary sector in which collaboration is not as difficult and becomes much more commonplace.

# 11

# Developing a Collaborative Context

## Toward a Developmental Process

It is critical for leaders to understand that a collaborative context will not emerge overnight and that they need to guide the campus through a series of stages that will help them eventually move to being supportive of collaborative work. In this chapter, a three-stage model is presented that can be used by leaders to develop a collaborative context by identifying their current status or stage and moving to the next phase (see Figure 11.1). The three-stage developmental model that emerged from the study includes (1) building commitment, (2) commitment, and (3) sustaining commitment. Campuses may differ in the time it takes for them to go through any particular stage. Some campuses may have great support for collaboration already and can move through stage one quite quickly. For example, there are campuses where great support has already emerged for learning communities or interdisciplinary research, and they can use this support for one collaborative arrangement in order to build support for others.[1]

What do these three stages entail and how does each phase contribute to advancing campuses toward an environment that supports collaboration? The first stage has four elements: external pressure, learning, values, and a network. In stage one, *building commitment*, the institution uses ideas and information from a variety of sources—related to the values, evidence of beneficial outcomes of collaboration, and external pressure or messages about the importance of collaboration—to convince members of the campus of the importance of collaborative work. The network

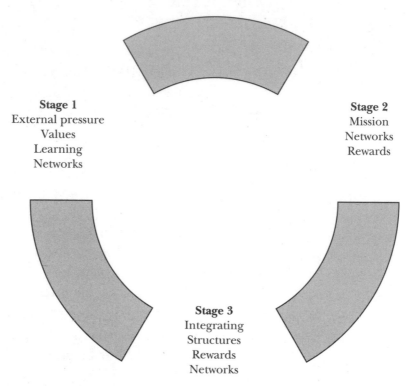

**Stage 1**
External pressure
Values
Learning
Networks

**Stage 2**
Mission
Networks
Rewards

**Stage 3**
Integrating
Structures
Rewards
Networks

**Figure 11.1    Stage Model of Collaboration in Higher Education**

and those in positions of authority help communicate the new collaborative values, external messages or pressure that supports collaboration, and learning.

In the second stage, *commitment*, senior executives demonstrate support by reexamining the mission, vision, and educational philosophy of the campus, and leadership emerges within the network to make the commitment real and tangible. The leadership within the network provides momentum and energy to build commitment by a broader mass of people on campus. In stage two, a sense of priority is created. The third stage, *sustaining*, includes the development of new or redesigned integrating structures and processes and rewards to support the collaborations. Without the overall institution undergoing some macrolevel changes to support collaboration, major initiatives have difficulty being sustained. The network again emerged in this stage as important to help brainstorm and overcome problems and barriers faced in sustaining collaborative efforts.

Throughout this model, senior executives and change agents are critical for identifying these contextual features and appropriately using them to encourage change. Therefore, we refer to these actors throughout. Change agents can be anyone on campus: faculty, staff, students, alumni, and so forth. We do mention senior executives specifically in some sections because they may be the only individuals with the authority to execute a change in mission or rewards. However, any change agents can encourage a senior executive toward these changes. In fact, we often found that change agents persuaded and influenced administrators and senior executives to consider change. But certain context features can only be accessed by senior executives, so we point out the aspects where they have specific responsibility. This model is captured in Figure 11.1.

## Stage One—Building Commitment to Collaboration

The model begins with a sense of priority from change agents who listen to cues from external groups and identify a set of values to support collaboration. Three elements are critical for building commitment: values, external pressure, and learning. These elements together helped campuses build a story in support of a new way of conducting work; each one alone was insufficient for building commitment. The development of a set of values relates to the importance or value of collaborative work, which creates a new norm or operating philosophy for individuals. As noted earlier, the three value systems most often described on campuses were being student centered, innovative, and egalitarian. These provided a logic for why individuals and groups should collaborate.

Campuses' leaders and change agents identified messages from external groups that supported collaborative work and created public forums for discussion of new accreditation and foundation guidelines, business and industry proposals, and federal agency initiatives. Without a compelling external argument for why collaboration is necessary, it is unlikely to occur. Faculty, staff, and administrators described stories of failed efforts of trying to create a context for collaboration, and a main factor was failure to build a case of the external support.

Some individuals on campus were compelled by the values of collaboration, others by external pressures, but an equal number of people needed to be convinced of the benefits of collaboration—they needed evidence. Learning was used by change agents as a strategy for informing people of the benefits of collaboration in order to motivate people to conduct collaborative work. Leaders passed out research on the advantages of collaboration, National Science Foundation data on partnerships, and held forums and workshops on various forms of collaboration they were trying to encourage, helping people understand the benefits. An appeal to people's hearts and minds and influential groups all appeared significant for changing the overall context, since people are motivated by very different factors. The specifics of these external messages and aspects of learning were already described in earlier chapters on the importance of relationships, learning, and external pressures.

In order to better understand what a story or message might sound like, we provide an example:

Innovation and creativity—our campus has always been on the cutting edge. We are not bound in tradition, our values have long supported different ways of thinking about teaching and learning. There are many external constituents who also believe that innovation/creativity is crucial to our nation's future economy and social success. Look at the many new National Science Foundation projects focused on creativity as a guide for collaborative work. We too, as a college, need to come together more and use our collective expertise to develop teaching and learning experiences that are best suited for today's generation of students and for the new world the technological age will live in. Let us look at some data from cognitive science about how complex social problems can be better addressed through bringing together expertise across different areas of knowledge. Also, data on student learning and how students who socially construct knowledge together reported stronger outcomes on critical thinking and problem-solving. We need to learn together about the benefits of more collaborative approaches—so we can help our students learn to be the innovators for the next century and so that we can serve as a model of innovation for colleges and universities across the country.

Or

In a more globalized and interdependent world, our students will need to learn in a more networked and connected fashion. How are we working together as faculty to connect various areas of knowledge? How do we have students working together so they can be prepared for the more team-oriented environment of the future? Our own campus has a tradition of being an egalitarian place where we actively involve students, staff, and faculty throughout the campus in decision making. Although we have a rich tradition of breaking down traditional bureaucratic and power structures, these have not always translated in having us create teaching and learning experiences or support environments for students that emphasizes a team or collaborative approach. A variety of recent national reports from higher education associations such as Greater Expectations provide us with information and data about these global trends; we should all read and use these resources to think about our collective responsibility within our egalitarian values to create the connected learning environment of the future.

As these examples demonstrate, every campus created its own unique story, based on its distinctive values and its history and traditions. As a result they adapted to different external pressures, focused on different benefits, and used different and distinctive data.

The campus network is pivotal for communicating these messages and in spreading the story. Values or external pressures articulated only from "on high" among senior executives, or learning proclaimed by a few believers, was not sufficient to build commitment. What made the story, created through the values and external messages, work is that the story elements were fed into an existing network that transferred the ideas around campus but also provided additional validity because peers were supporting the notion and ideas distributed through the network. There needs to be a critical mass of people on campus that are interested in change and supportive of campus initiatives; it is helpful if they are interested in collaborative work, but this element is not necessary. As noted in Chapter Six on networks, campuses tend to use a host of strategies over time to build networks. Most had the networks in place before they endeavored to move toward creating a collaborative context. They also noted how a history of trust and mutual respect helps in fostering the type of network that is dedicated to advancing the campus collaborative initiatives and helping redesign the campus.

Let's look at the campus with the commitment to an egalitarian ethic ("Egalitarian College"),[2] who had worked on developing their compelling message tied to external globalization trends and using many of the national higher education reports. Although they had a commitment to egalitarianism through their values, they had not been operating in a collaborative fashion. But their values provided them with some existing norms and support for more collaborative work. Change agents crafted a message that they thought would be appealing to members of the campus. Some of these change agents were senior executives, and others were faculty and staff on campus who were part of the campus network and already tended to work in collaborative ways. Senior executives began to include information about their new collaborative aspiration or story in speeches, campus announcements, and newsletters, but many people were aware that a human touch was needed to make this message more powerful. The senior executives appealed to members of the campus network already invested in collaborative work to also talk about the new collaborative message. Their network was a relatively small group of people because the campus was not large itself; there were eight faculty who met on occasion to discuss their common interest in interdisciplinary research and teaching. There were also ten staff members—some quite new and some who had been on campus awhile who were excited about trying some new campus processes and had even experimented with a few, including a first-year interest group that operated as a learning community. Some of these experiments had already created some interest in collaborative initiatives among staff and faculty and had garnered attention to this network. As a result, these individuals were already visible on campus. But the members of the network were not universally admired, and some faculty and staff felt this work was quite threatening by breaking traditional ways of doing things. This sense of threat that can emerge among more traditional faculty and staff was also typical of the experience of tapping into the networks of innovators who had already embraced collaboration. Although this group was pivotal to helping advance collaborative initiatives, its presence was difficult, challenging, and controversial on some campuses.

Egalitarian College did not use only the network of innovators to communicate the message and story about collaboration. Like many other campuses, it decided to tap a more general group of staff and faculty who had been pulled into campuswide work through committees, open meetings, forums, and events, and who might have been antagonists of collaborative initiatives at times—they could be seen as more disinterested advocates for the new campus direction. Some campuses strategically chose to work with this broader network of individuals and asked them to help convince others about the new direction the campus might take.

The advantages of working with individuals already committed to collaborative work is that they understand the message that campus leaders are trying to communicate and also have the enthusiasm about spreading the message. As noted earlier, the disadvantages are that some people may see this group as self-interested in a collaborative direction that would provide more rewards and support for work they are interested in. The advantage of working with a more general network of faculty and staff is that these individuals appear to be unbiased or disinterested—not invested in an initiative that is supportive of a personal interest. Staff and faculty may be more open to influence from this general network. However, the members of a general network may not always be as invested in spreading the message as other individuals with a deep commitment to a specific form of collaboration such as learning communities, and they may not always clearly articulate the vision or direction because they are not as closely tied to it. Egalitarian College, like many other colleges, used both of these networks in attempts to spread the message. Each college or university needs to decide, based on its own institutional culture, campus politics, time, and energy, which groups and individuals are best for spreading the message about collaboration.

Some change agents reading this book might believe that smaller campuses do not need to rely on networks because their small size makes them much more open to influence either by senior executives or a few influential individuals. Although it is true that larger campuses are much more dependent on networks to influence people throughout the campus, smaller campuses also rely on networks to help spread the message about the need to become a more collaborative context.

## Stage Two—Commitment to Collaboration

Building commitment only brought the campuses to believing that a new way of organizing work might better benefit the campus. The next step was to move from commitment to action. Given all of the competing demands on people's time, making more time to redesign processes and do work in new ways will never happen that easily. Three conditions help solidify the commitment to building a collaborative context and help move toward action: mission, rewards, and network (leadership).

Senior executives have access to a variety of levers that help solidify commitment, such as rethinking the institutional mission. In stage two, the main work of senior executives was revising the campus mission statement and making sure that people were discussing the new mission and vision, and creating a sense of priority on campus. Senior executives became vocal about the new direction for the campus and the new way work was being done. Had people not felt that the senior executives made this a priority issue, most said they would not have gotten involved (and would have avoided certain collaborative efforts that were not deemed a priority). Senior executives also had many specific mechanisms they could access to solidify commitment in addition to their spoken dedication. These included incentives, rewards, hiring, and modeling. A significant lever that emerged in stage two was rewards. A sense of priority was developed by seeking out and creating new rewards for involvement in collaboration. These rewards ranged from altering tenure and promotion standards to creating minigrants to including merit in staff annual reviews. Similar to how the mission supports collaboration, rewards demonstrate priorities and put the philosophy of collaboration into practice. Furthermore, support from senior executives needs to be maintained into stage three; because they control resources, they are usually the only ones with the ability to alter rewards and create integrating structures to support collaborative efforts.

The third condition that was needed to solidify commitment and move into action was that the campus network was mobilized as a source of leadership. Most campuses made a commitment around creating a collaborative context because of a dedicated set of individuals, who continue to make the work of the campus more collaborative. Interviewees kept mentioning the dynamic energy, enthusiasm, and momentum that individual leaders within the network bring to a collaborative effort. In the words of one interviewee:

> Well, it keeps coming back to the distributed leadership on campus that is part of that "critical mass" I was speaking about earlier. What has made certain collaborations work? I can see the various people in my mind over time, those who were the dedicated leaders. When the grants went away, senior leadership turned to new strategic plans, etc. These people kept watch over the initiative and enabled it to succeed.

We heard comments like this on each campus—that there were key individuals who moved the campus past ideas, visions, and mission to implementation. They were the driving force to make sure that commitment translated into action. This same leadership, within the network, is also critical in stage three, where the collaborations are sustained and institutionalized. Change agents who help implement are especially important when rewards run out or senior executives turn to the next priority.

## Stage Three—Sustaining Collaboration

In order to sustain the collaboration, more formal elements needed to be put in place. The main elements that emerged for sustaining a context of collaboration on college and university campuses were integrating structure, rewards, resources, hiring, and formalizing the network. Sustained collaboration seems highly dependent on the redesign of campus systems, including computing systems, divisional meetings, rewards and incentives, the creation of new structures such as institutes, and new relationships. This finding mirrors the work on collaboration in other fields of study and within other sectors (such as business or government), in which the concept of redesign also emerged. These organizations have spent several years already trying to develop a commitment to work collaboratively, and their experience of "what it takes" seems to match the experience of leaders in higher education—sustained change means rethinking overall organizational structures, processes, and design.

As noted earlier, each campus had developed particular integrating structures that appeared most important for helping to create an environment that supports collaboration—a central unit(s) for collaboration, a set of centers and institutes, cross-campus teams, presidential initiatives, and new accounting, computer, and budgetary systems—by helping to integrate work and facilitate cross-functional activities. These new structures were supportive of each other and solidified the new way of working collaboratively. The centralized unit orchestrated existing collaborative activities and helped bring new initiatives to the fore. The new accounting processes ensured that divisions and departments could easily exchange money on joint research projects or full-time equivalents for team teaching. The new institutes provided a physical space for collaborative projects to flourish. Cross-campus teams provided ongoing mechanisms for communication and for coming together on shared work.

Rewards and incentives also played a critical role in sustaining collaboration. Structures provided the logistical support, but rewards and incentives provided motivation and external value. By far the most important reward system to focus on for faculty was the promotion and tenure requirements. If the tenure and promotion system supported collaboration, the members of campus felt the context of collaboration would be fully sustained. Yet on one campus that had changed tenure and promotion requirements, there was fear that the new provost was not committed to the principles as articulated. Campus leaders believed that the change would be sustained because other structures, processes, and systems had been redesigned. This same campus felt hope that the collaborative context would be sustained because the mission statement reinforced this work, other senior executives were committed, and campus processes were overwhelmingly collaborative.

Incentives, in terms of grants or administrative support, were also critical in sustaining collaboration. Many individuals were interested in engaging in collaborative work (interdisciplinary research, learning communities, etc.), but they felt it impossible to transition to a new way of working without some relief from their day-to-day activities. Many individuals we spoke with mentioned that the overwhelming pace of being in an institution with dwindling funds and increasing responsibilities made the notion of fundamentally changing work difficult. However, at each of these institutions, funds had been drawn away from the regular operating budget (or grants obtained) to support people in moving to collaborative work. Resources need to be available to support collaborations; hiring and restructuring were also key for sustaining collaboration. If adequate human resources cannot be made available, eventually people stop doing collaborative work on top of their existing work. Change agents knew that positions and roles had to be carefully constructed to provide the right infrastructure for the long term.

Networks were also critical in sustaining the collaborative context in two ways. First, they maintained and generated more collaboration on campus. People noted how "collaboration built upon itself." Relationships developed through participation in one collaboration led to other activities and ongoing connections and a greater degree of formality to the network. One campus described its story of how collaboration spawns collaboration:

> We had brought together a campuswide team to kick off our new first-year experience program that included constituents all across campus. The process was really successful and there was a lot of energy around thinking about other collaborative projects. Our vice president

for student affairs, the dean of engineering, three faculty members, and director of experiential learning started having side conversations about rethinking orientation and developing a new leadership program. Three years later, we have two new programs in place and it all started when the campuswide committee was charged with a whole different agenda.

Second, after the collaborations are in place and obstacles encountered, members of the network can work together to cull expertise or relationships needed to overcome barriers. For example, it was the campus network on one campus that helped determine that change was needed in their accounting and computer systems and that identified new options for the campus to use. On another campus, the network was responsible for creating the idea of a centralized unit to facilitate collaboration. The story at another campus also demonstrates the problem-solving skills of the network, which helped sustain further collaboration:

We have long had a commuter center, but many of us felt it was not really accomplishing its goal. A key group of interested people began to meet to try and rethink the goal. We brought in a much larger group that represented more interests across campus, but we did not understand the student concerns as deeply as we needed to in order to make the center work. A faculty member remembered an earlier study that had been done and he brought a copy in; no one seemed to have it except him. Another member of the team had a student who as a project had interviewed several students. Anyway, in the end through the team and their collective contacts we got the information we needed to truly make the changes needed.

Creating new structures or rewards to support collaboration was a monumental task and often met with failure. It was usually the networks that created the intellectual resources to overcome barriers and resistance to new structures and processes on campus.

Because leaders play such a pivotal role, leadership changes can have an impact on the process of moving toward and sustaining a collaborative environment. If the mission statement has been recently changed, and there is a turnover in the president, this could affect the way that the mission is translated into practice and on the budget. A new leader might come in and question the collaborative reward system and undo many of the changes that have been made. However, the reason for embedding collaboration in the mission, rewards, and structures of the institution is to make it more difficult for individual leaders to alter the overall environment.

The model itself is a heuristic device. Although mission is very important in stage one on most campuses and rewards or integrating structures are key in stage three, this does not mean that these elements may not be important in other stages. Rewards may be needed to solidify commitment on some campuses. However, the model suggests the way that these elements tended to play out on most campuses. In the next section, we describe more about why the model may have unfolded in this way and how this represents key lessons for higher education leaders about how to make collaboration work.

## Key Lessons for Making Collaboration Work in Higher Education

Higher education exhibits some distinctive features in the way that a collaborative context can be developed. Some of these distinctions are described in this section.

The developmental model (remember, development merely means phases or paths taken to reach a more collaborative context) that emerged in higher education shared some of the features of the MCM model described in Chapter Two (see Figures 11.1 and 11.2).

Phases:

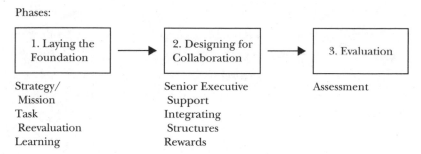

Figure 11.2    Mohrman, Cohen, and Mohrman Model

First, many of the contextual conditions are similar to those found in the corporate sector: mission, senior executive support, integrating structures, rewards, and learning. In addition, two of the most important conditions mirrored the MCM model—mission and integrating structures. However, other elements were important in higher education that were not mentioned or played a minor role in MCM, including values, external pressure, and the network. These differences help uncover important areas for leaders to be aware of as they approach this task.

Both had three phases, yet they differed in emphasis and focus. The laying-the-foundation phase of the MCM model resembled the building-commitment phase that was identified within this study. However, the case that needs to be built for conducting work in a collaborative fashion was much more pronounced in the higher education setting. The history and traditions of long-standing institutions such as colleges and universities are less flexible to change than other sectors with shorter histories and less-entrenched norms. The second phase of the MCM—designing for collaboration—is similar to the third phase of the higher education model that emerged in this study, with the emphasis on putting organizational features into place that will ensure collaboration is maintained in the future. The third phase of the MCM developmental model, evaluation, did not exist within the higher education setting, as most institutions have not solidified collaboration to the extent that some businesses have, and evaluation and accountability mechanisms are much more pronounced in the business culture than in higher education (although this is changing). The differences that emerged within the higher education context are important to take into consideration when working within this specific context to develop support for collaboration.

### Building Commitment in Higher Education Takes Time

First, "building commitment" was extremely important within the higher education context but was not relevant within the MCM model. All campuses within this study mentioned the importance of stage one and noted they could never have reached stage three without attention to building the case for collaboration. The importance of stage one (building commitment) might be the result of the differences in management and hierarchical structures between corporate and higher education settings. In the corporate setting, where there is more control and the management can mandate a change in the environment, there is likely to be less need to persuade and articulate the reasons that collaboration is necessary. Also, mission and task reevaluation were not the beginning contextual elements for creating a context of collaboration within the higher education model. Unlike corporations, where collaboration can be mandated from the hierarchy, creating a collaborative context within higher education requires that parties need to be convinced of the importance of the commitment. Also, the multiple stakeholders suggest there may be fewer agreed-upon ways of doing work and that changes in work conditions need more involvement of various constituents.

### Importance of Collecting Outside Ideas and Appealing to Values and External Pressures

In higher education, leaders need to develop a story or narrative to support why collaboration is important that takes into account the specific history and mission of the campus. Change agents described external pressures, outside ideas, values (sometimes even bringing in new or external values), and a philosophy about why collaborative work is needed to help build the case. Furthermore, campus leaders and change agents identified messages from external groups that supported collaborative work and created public forums for discussion of new accreditation and foundation guidelines, business and industry proposals, and federal agency initiatives.

Internal values also provided a compelling logic for collaboration. Values were used by each campus to illustrate the alignment of collaboration with other deeply held beliefs. In addition to values, a philosophy aligning collaboration to the mission (noted in the section on mission) was a powerful lever. Embracing a philosophy of collaborative learning provided a form of logic or persuasion for why collaboration was critical to the work of teaching, research, and learning. But an internal story needed support from external sources; these conditions were interrelated. Faculty, staff, and administrators described stories of past failed efforts on their campus or on other campuses of trying to create a context for collaboration, and a main factor contributing to failure was not building a case of external support or not capitalizing on internal values or demonstrating the benefits of collaboration.

The business or governmental sectors did not have to make the extensive arguments about why collaboration was necessary or beneficial—collaboration was accepted logic and intuitive to their employees. External pressures or values might be needed less in government and business because there are more internal drivers related to the bottom line of making money or serving the public that motivate people to embrace collaboration. In addition, the logic of collaboration has been used within these sectors for a long time period and it has become part of the internal logic by now. Also, as noted above, this difference might be the result of the differences in management and hierarchical structures between corporate and higher education settings. In the corporate setting, where there is more control and the management can mandate a change in the environment, there is likely less to be the need to persuade and articulate the reasons for collaboration. The importance of a network for convincing people about the value of collaboration is also probably related to fewer management controls and hierarchical arrangements. Grassroots efforts and ownership are needed to create motivation within the higher education setting. Members of the higher education context are likely to be motivated by people, more so than goals, management, or rewards that are more the hallmark of the business world.

### Relationships and Network Building

Relationships and networks appear extremely important within the higher education context both as features that enable collaboration and factors that propelled the development of the context from individualized to collaborative work. Leaders and change agents in higher education emphasized and spoke about the influence of specific individuals and groups (and their values and commitments) and deemphasized rewards—evaluation, for instance—in comparison to other sectors that have been studied. Because higher education institutions are professional organizations in which individuals are greatly influenced and persuaded by peers, and rewards are less important than prestige, this may account for why networks and relationships are a key lever (Birnbaum, 1991; Kezar, 2001b). The importance of relationships suggests that more mechanisms that allow people to interact such as communal dining areas or retreats that bring people together are needed in higher education institutions. Also, campuses need to be attentive to the way they work to support and nourish networks on campus. Having a center or institute responsible for creating cross-campus events is a helpful structure for nurturing networks. This does not suggest that rewards and incentives were unimportant, however, just less emphasized than other settings.

## Relationships and Informal Learning as Central to Movement Forward?

Another difference in the developmental process is that higher education institutions do not appear to advance through phases based on learning but based on well-developed relationships. Other models (Doz, 1996; Mohrman, Cohen, and Mohrman, 1995) emphasize that the move to a collaborative context happens because institutions learn new behaviors and the pivotal work to be done is learning to advance from one stage to the next. Instead, in higher education, relationships serve to build commitment and circulate the reasons that collaborative work should be conducted. The network provided the needed leadership, energy, and momentum to conduct work in new ways. The network members served as role models for members of the campus to observe as they embarked on collaborative ventures. The network supported collaborative work by helping overcome barriers that emerged. In some ways, relationships helped create learning, so learning was not unimportant to the development of the new context, but learning tended to happen within the context of the networks, informally and through modeling rather than through training sessions, as is often emphasized in other contexts. Again, higher education leaders need to focus more on the learning that comes from informal relationships, modeling, and meetings. These interactions have the potential to spontaneously and organically create learning.

## Senior Executives' Role

Sense of priority among senior executives emerged uniquely in the higher education setting and diverged from how it is described in the corporate model by Mohrman, Cohen, and Mohrman (1995). For example, in the MCM model, they refer to management structure and roles and more directive ways that executives changed the environment. On campuses, leaders typically tried to lead discussions around mission rather than changing the mission, write concept papers with others' input, create opportunities for faculty and staff to interact, and fund incentives and development opportunities. Although some processes were more directive, such as rewards or creating integrating structures, these were typically created in consultation. In the higher education setting, management had less control over which collaborations emerge and in designing the features of a collaborative activity. Faculty and staff were the point of emergence for many collaborations, and the authority to develop collaborations was delegated to these groups. Also, there is more emphasis on senior executives' building commitment for people to engage in collaboration through networks, rather than dictating the need to collaborate. Yet this context feature (sense of priority from senior executives) was similar to the corporate sector in that it served an enabling role in altering rewards and creating integrating structures, actions critical to sustain collaboration.

## A Model for Creating a Collaborative Context in Higher Education

By combining the findings from this study of higher education settings (importance of relationships and networks, values, and external pressures) with the elements that mirrored the Mohrman, Cohen, and Mohrman model (mission, integrating structures, rewards, and one modified feature: learning) a new model for enabling higher education collaboration emerged, which has been presented in this book. Armed with the experiences of these campuses, institutional leaders can now work to foster a philosophy about the importance of collaborative work, fashion a narrative using the words of external groups about the necessity of collaboration that takes into account disciplinary and other types of differences on campus, more intentionally develop campus networks and grassroots leadership, create a centralized unit to foster collaboration, bolster resources for faculty development activities, and work to alter computing, management, and accounting systems.

The interplay of the various strategies in the new higher education model of collaboration and ways that campuses look different as a result of the re-organization are brought to life with examples and stories from the campuses in the study.

## Notes

1. All the elements described in this chapter—for example, mission or integrating structures—have already been discussed in other chapters. We bring these elements together in this chapter into a model demonstrating how all the individual elements work together. We do not repeat the detail of each contextual element but suggest readers return to the individual chapters for this information if necessary.

2. This is a pseudonym given for a campus in the study.

# 12

# A Collective Responsibility

## *What Can Various Constituents Do to Support Collaboration on Campus?*

One of the main lessons learned from the study of campuses that support collaboration is that this is a collective responsibility. These campuses realize that it is difficult to do it on your own and that reaching out to groups and individuals who can support their vision is critical for moving forward. Likewise, those in positions of authority cannot do this alone; they are dependent on campus networks, external constituents, and campus champions and change agents. External groups, too, need to appeal to individuals and groups on campuses who have influence, some of whom may have formal authority and others who do not. The network depends on external groups and those in authority to help provide support and enable their work. This chapter focuses on the role that various groups and individuals can play in re-organizing campuses in order to collaborate. We also recommend ways that groups might better work together to achieve their mutual goals.

## Foundation Directors and Government Funders

Faculty and administrators are very attentive to cues from external groups that provide funding. Much of the support that exists on campus for more collaborative work is the result of foundation and government support for interdisciplinary work and for cross-sectorial collaboration. Other sources of support include philanthropic organizations and individuals who contribute additional funding for single projects or departments. However, we also noted that campuses are also trying to manage different cues from outside funding sources. Sometimes a foundation mandate may be out of sync with a state commission or federal request for proposal. An example of this problem is a foundation that might require work with a local nonprofit for a funding opportunity whereas a government agency might require work with a state commission or group. Instead of advocating for greater connections between sectors, in mandating which groups with whom they must collaborate, foundations and government officials may be creating requirements that are too complex for universities to successfully manage as they begin collaborative work. Although it is natural for different groups to have varying priorities, it would help if external agencies that work with and fund colleges and universities would annually meet or find a forum for communication in which they could discuss priorities and develop an agenda that sets a clear message about the ways that campuses can best work collaboratively. Therefore, more collaboration among external funding groups, themselves, would help shape an agenda for higher education with fewer mixed messages.

## Leaders of Disciplinary Organizations

Leaders within some disciplinary associations have also played a significant role in moving interdisciplinary teaching or research to the forefront of encouraging learning communities or partnerships with student affairs. However, disciplinary societies may believe that there is a conflict between the historical discipline-specific structure and collaboration. Disciplines are historically organized in departments that maintain faculty power. On some campuses, more collaboration might lead to less power for disciplinary groups and the dissolution of some disciplines; this might not lead disciplinary groups to see the advantages in encouraging collaboration on campus.

None of the campuses we spoke with had eradicated any disciplines or had plans to. Working in a collaborative way does not naturally lead to decreased disciplinary power or influence. Some campuses may choose to go that route, but it was not our experience within the campuses we studied. Usually collaborative campuses with limited disciplinary power were campuses that had never had strong disciplinary power, such as Evergreen State or California State University Monterey Bay. Also, on many campuses collaboration did not challenge existing structures of knowledge production and dissemination and focused more on working across units. But we recognize that some disciplinary leaders may read this book and feel it is against their self-interest to foster and adopt these ideas. We hope that disciplines read carefully the logic of collaboration and realize that in advocating for collaboration we are not suggesting there is no value in disciplinary knowledge. Disciplinary knowledge is a powerful building block that may be more powerful when leveraged with other disciplines as well. Transdisciplinary knowledge (working beyond existing frameworks) does challenge the power of disciplinary knowledge more than interdisciplinary or multidisciplinary research. Thus, we can understand the trepidation among some disciplinary groups to transdisciplinary work.

Yet we hope that disciplinary societies and their leaders can begin to more actively discuss the potential of other ways of organizing knowledge and to some degree challenge existing paradigms and arrangements. Professional administrative groups such as student affairs have reexamined their professional boundaries and in some instances leaders are advocating for different campus arrangements that better meet the needs of students, even if this ends up disempowering student affairs. In order to move forward to enable collaboration, disciplinary societies and academics need to ask the hard questions of which knowledge structures best support research and student learning and be courageous enough to change existing structures if they are not suited best to meet the goals. One question a campus might address is this: How is specialization fragmented or interdisciplinary knowledge limited, for example? Without the support of disciplinary societies, collaboration on campus will struggle to become fully institutionalized—especially those that involve faculty. The challenge to involve faculty was apparent even on campuses committed to collaboration.

In addition, disciplinary societies could encourage new ways of training collaborative faculty (Ward, 2003; Weidman, Twale, & Stein, 2001). A variety of practices within graduate education should be reexamined. Some of the following practices might help develop and socialize faculty to be better able to conduct collaborative work. Rather than having one-on-one mentoring with faculty, the doctoral process could involve group mentoring and advisement. Several faculty members could potentially work with several different graduate students in a learning community. Also, graduate programs could include more group and community events. For example, there are a few graduate programs that have biweekly opportunities to meet as a group and discuss common books and readings. Furthermore, graduate students could jointly work on research projects. Although this has become a more common practice in the sciences, the social sciences and humanities would benefit by including more collaborative opportunities for research and work. Finally, teaching can become a more public process and graduate students could share ideas about developing their teaching skills and observe each other teaching, thus beginning to conceptualize all their work in more public and collaborative ways (Weidman, Twale, & Stein, 2001).

## National and Professional Associations

National organizations have already played a significant role in helping campuses rethink their work and focus more on collaboration. *Powerful Partnerships* and *Greater Expectations* were developed by major higher education associations, and these groups have made an ongoing commitment to foster collaboration. For example, the Association of American Colleges and Universities annually hosts a conference focused on collaborative leadership and shared responsibility for learning. Campus leaders who want to consider ways to do more cross-functional and collaborative work have a forum that they can attend to develop their own skills and their staff.

We encourage national associations to maintain this focus on collaboration and for certain professional associations that have not made this a focus among their membership to make this a commitment. For example, collaboration has not been a major centerpiece of the presidential serving organizations such as the American Council on Education, the American Association of State Colleges and Universities, or the National Association of State and Land Grant Universities. As noted earlier, those in positions of authority are extremely important to creating a collaborative context. Support from the top is less likely to occur nationally unless the presidential serving associations engage in leading the move to a collaborative context. Also, leadership development for chairs and deans that happens on college campuses or within national or regional professional development should also focus on collaboration. For example, the American Council on Education's department chair workshop might include a session on the benefits and challenges of collaboration. Provosts who organize events for deans and department chairs should try to encourage individuals who create and host these events to read books like this.

The National Association of College Business Officers, Association for Institutional Researchers, Society for University Planning, and other professional groups might have a one-time conference or article in a newsletter about collaboration, but many of these associations have not made collaboration a priority. It would be helpful if other associations representing these more specialized professional groups would also examine their commitment to working cross functionally and to increasing the effectiveness of their membership.

## Accreditors

It is a difficult time for accreditors with the department of education officials calling for a major overhaul of the system or completely abandoning accreditation. To recommend that accreditors try to take on any responsibility for encouraging collaboration will surely be difficult at this time. However, the accreditation system has been influential in creating collaboration, unintentionally for the most part. Although accreditation does not formally endorse or encourage collaboration, the areas that it examines—from effectiveness to efficiency to communication to shared governance to learning outcomes—all tend to be enabled by collaboration. Furthermore, many accreditors require a collaborative process for engaging in the self-study process. Middle States Regional accreditors require a cross-campus team that represents different institutional constituents to work on the report. Through the processes they require for self-study, they are reinforcing collaboration. They might even be more intentional in emphasizing how these accreditation teams structured for addressing institutional analysis need to be in place all the time, not just for self-studies.

It might be helpful for the regional accreditation agencies to examine their standards and procedures to identify whether including collaboration in some way might not improve some of the processes they follow. They may want to develop some guidelines about ways to encourage collaboration, some benchmarks for areas to examine related to collaboration (perhaps using this book as a framework for considering this work), and other ways to more systematically and intentionally bring collaboration into the accreditation process. Many campus leaders mentioned how having collaboration more deliberately mentioned in the accreditation report would be helpful. Although it was often alluded to, because it is not formally part of the standards or benchmarks, it is not highlighted in the same way as other issues. Campus leaders supportive of collaboration would benefit from more direct language around the benefits of collaboration.

## Government Officials

Although our work does not suggest a pivotal role for government officials and agencies (unlike the importance we found for getting national associations or disciplinary societies involved), there is still some collective government responsibility for fostering collaboration. We already noted the important role of encouraging collaboration in grant and project proposals, but there are also several other major areas that the government can help to encourage collaboration. Perhaps most important, the government does play a part in the accreditation and accountability processes that govern postsecondary institutions. Whatever accountability measures are put in place, it would help if some parameters around quality processes were also examined. Although achieving desired outcomes is the most important role of accountability standards and systems, the processes for meeting goals and outcomes are also important to examine, especially if certain processes can achieve more learning goals and produce deeper and richer outcomes. Therefore, encouraging collaboration standards within accreditation or other accountability processes would be helpful for making postsecondary institutions make support of collaboration a higher priority.

Another role of the government in support of collaboration concerns state coordinating boards, which often function as oversight committees for all institutions of higher education within a state. These coordinating boards vary in their degree of influence as well as their mission, but each has an opportunity similar to associations and foundations to express support for collaborative activities. For example, several state coordinating boards serve as curriculum oversight committees, approving all curricular changes within state institutions. These coordinating boards can require or suggest interdisciplinary curricula and collaboration from multiple departments in creating academic programs. By using their influence as oversight committees, state coordinating boards have an opportunity to support collaborative practices within higher education.

## Students and Alumni

In addition to the government and philanthropic agencies, groups closely associated with institutions have an opportunity to encourage collaboration. In the last few decades, state funding for higher education has decreased, which has necessitated many institutions seeking out alumni financial support. As alumni provide monies, become more involved in the institution, and serve on committees or boards, their influence has increased, a situation that provides an opportunity for this group to identify the value and need for collaborative practices. It might be helpful for alumni to express their interest in academic programs, research, and student services that are conducted in a collaborative fashion. In addition, the push toward student affairs and a focus on the holistic education of students have given students more voice in the practices of college and universities. You may find students who serve on governing boards and as advisors to the president. With the influence of the students, similar to alumni, comes an opportunity for students to advocate for increased collaboration.

## Business and Industry Stakeholders

Business and industry can be a role model for how to conduct collaborative work. Although other sectors can provide funding, standards, or exert influence, business can play a unique role in demonstrating how collaborative work can be best executed and provide models and procedures. When engineering firms are invited to campus, they can discuss the current trends in civil engineering as well as the benefits of engineering teams that work cross-functionally. Since this sector is farther ahead in creating a collaborative environment, it can be helpful for offering direct and concrete examples or models for campuses to follow, as well as advice on challenges. Business leaders should share the latest research on cross-functional teams, new ways to think about team-based rewards and accountability systems (quite prevalent in business now), or forums that have been successful helping senior executives learn to model collaboration.

The importance of this role cannot be underestimated. So few campuses are supportive of collaborative work that the normal networking among institutions is unlikely to yield successful solutions. Although this book provides advice on how to create collaboration, the business sector will be an ongoing and dynamic source of support as campuses take the journey to be more collaborative. Campus leaders and change agents should reach out to business leaders, and business leaders should offer their expertise. Business leaders should be aware that collaboration unfolds a bit differently in higher education, as outlined in the developmental model. By being aware of some of these differences, they can better offer advice and keep these ideas in mind when they collaborate to develop a research and development park with a campus.

## Educational Leaders

In the end, the major responsibility for creating collaboration falls to a host of educational leaders on college campuses—from the faculty and staff on campus who support collaborative work to the individuals with influence who choose to champion collaboration to those in authority who have become enlightened about the benefits and necessity of collaborating. The responsibilities of these groups have been described in many chapters, but we summarize them here so the truly collective responsibility among many members of campus from all levels is clear.

### Members of the Campus Network and Change Agents

1. Create ideas for restructuring the campus
2. Connect people on campus who are like minded
3. Develop proposals to change promotion and tenure and evaluation systems
4. Brainstorm ways to overcome barriers
5. Instill the logic of collaboration among others
6. Create learning opportunities related to collaboration
7. Create and foster a value system that supports collaboration
8. Help create mechanisms to sustain the network
9. Keep people resilient within the network
10. Model collaboration

### Influential Individuals without Formal Roles of Authority

1. Instill the logic of collaboration among others
2. Connect people on campus who are like minded
3. Support proposals to change promotion and tenure and evaluation systems
4. Help people overcome personality conflicts
5. Encourage people to attend symposia, reading groups, and seminars on collaboration
6. Make people aware of external pressures and voices

### Individuals in Positions of Authority on Campus

1. Include collaboration in the mission statement and strategic planning documents and articulate the mission and plans widely—in other words, articulate a commitment
2. Support restructuring plans

3. Create integrating structures

4. Create mechanisms that help foster a campus network

5. Change promotion and tenure requirements

6. Support collaboration in the budget process

7. Hire people who support collaboration or a specific initiative

8. Hold people accountable for collaboration

9. Help people overcome personality conflicts

10. Frame and package various external constituencies that support collaboration into a compelling message

11. Support learning opportunities for collaboration

12. Model collaboration

13. Set up a task force to examine campus values and alignment with collaboration

Part of shared responsibility is making sure that senior administrators and executives do not create a top-down environment that might make people resistant to collaboration. Senior executives need to recognize that while many of the aspects of the redesign fall under their responsibility, they need to be careful not to be perceived as creating a top-down environment that might create resentment of the collaborative efforts, and of course undermine the very collaboration they are trying to create. This is why modeling collaboration and working very closely with a leadership team are so important to breaking down the perception that senior executives are foisting collaboration on the campus. Also, working closely with the network of individuals already supportive of collaboration can spread out some of the responsibility for this work. Senior executives need to understand that although they have been delegated authority over meeting the mission, hiring, or resource allocation, these processes are opportunities to demonstrate collaboration rather than to exert their individual authority. They need to temper urges to manage too strongly as individuals, especially as resistance emerges, which often brings people to act quickly as individuals to defend their choices.

Working together, however, higher education leaders can work with the other groups noted in this chapter to create a compelling process for changing the very foundation of college campuses. But this work across sectors between higher education and business or government or foundations will not come easily. Why? Because higher education is not the only system in which collaboration has proven difficult.

## Paradox Comes Full Circle

What can enable more collaboration in higher education? Part of the answer is that more groups need to work collaboratively to foster and facilitate multidisciplinary learning communities, or university and community partnerships. The more that these various elements of support can work together to create greater synergy, the more powerful the message to individual campuses and the sooner such work will be institutionalized. However, as the beginning premise of this book suggests, collaboration is extremely difficult because not only are our organizations based on principles and structures antithetical to collaboration, so are our larger systems of government, foundations, disciplinary societies, and the like. So, the challenges exist within all parts of the system. Leaders within various sectors—from government to nonprofits to business—will be more successful encouraging collaboration if they can acknowledge their own challenges in collaborating, learn from these experiences, and try to be role models for higher education—a system that is even more embedded in an ethic that prevents collaboration.

Leaders also need to recognize the challenges that higher education faces—outlined within this book. Higher education has a history of entrenched practices—specialization, departments, loose coupling, rewards systems, and bureaucratic structures—that pose a challenge in trying to support collaboration. Moreover, each organizational structure (e.g., mission, rewards, learning) that requires change has specific challenges that must be addressed. For example, rewards require valuable and often unavailable resources, the incorporation of multiple constituent groups, and the challenging of time-honored systems. Higher education institutions can overcome these internal challenges, but they cannot do it alone. To expect collaboration, without helping institutions become aware of and overcome these barriers, is to set higher education institutions up for failure. Other sectors can be better stewards by understanding how paradoxical collaboration is within the higher education setting and stepping in as a partner to help campuses overcome and wrestle with these challenges. Becoming a campus that values collaboration while also valuing the important traditions of disciplines is a challenge and a paradox. However, as seen with Collaborative University, institutions of higher education are able, with a focused effort and help from external sources, to overcome the paradox and become a campus that values individual and collaborative efforts.

# Appendix A: Methodology

The research questions pursued were (1) What are the organizational features (structure, processes, people/relationships, learning, rewards, and culture/values) that facilitate the process of internal collaboration related to learning-oriented initiatives in higher education institutions? (2) What organizational features are most important: structure, processes, people and relationships, learning, rewards, or culture and values? The unit of analysis was the overall institution, rather than specific collaborations, which has been the emphasis in earlier studies.

## Sample

The project used intrinsic case sampling, which is undertaken because the case(s) illustrate a particular issue, not because the case represents other cases (Stake, 1994). It also used unique case sampling, which entails the identification of cases based on a particular set of characteristics (extensive collaboration and organizational context features) that they share to better understand the distinctive phenomenon that emerges within these cases (Stake, 1994). Uniqueness is more important than representation or generality. The special cases examined were four institutions that demonstrated high levels of intra-organizational collaboration. Institutions were chosen if they demonstrated they were conducting collaboration across a host of areas, not just in one area. The assumption was that a single collaboration or two might not reflect organizational features but only individual leaders. The main forms of internal collaboration operative within these institutions were interdisciplinary teaching and research, learning communities, community-based learning, team-teaching, student and academic affairs collaboration, and cross-functional teams.

Institutions were nominated by the American Association for Higher Education, a national association that worked to create change within colleges and universities. These preliminary nominations were based on reputation and working knowledge of these institutions—essentially nomination by experts. Approximately thirty institutions were nominated from all over the country.

After nomination, institutions were contacted and asked to fill out a brief survey (just for selection purposes, not data collection—each institution filled out the survey) and institutional members were interviewed to determine the depth and perceived quality of the collaboration. Criteria used to examine depth and quality included (1) number of collaborative initiatives, (2) restructuring or redesign efforts to help facilitate collaboration, (3) reputation for collaboration among peer institutions, and (4) perception of employees of depth and quality of collaborations on their campus in comparison to their peer institutions. The institutions that were strongest in these criteria were chosen for study.

Another selection criteria was that the institutions chosen were "typical" higher education institutions (without significant funding to leverage partnerships and collaboration) and were non-elite. Many studies of collaboration or partnerships focus on models of excellence among elite or high-profile organizations and the findings are often not transferable to other settings with more limited resources. Thus, although these cases were studied because they are unique in their ability to create a context supportive of collaboration, the researchers wanted the institutions not to be so unique in terms of resources that other institutions would feel that the lessons learned from these campuses would not have relevance.

The type of institutions examined was held constant. Four public comprehensive institutions were explored, since this is among the largest sectors and one mostly directly affected by recent budget cuts. These institutions are in even greater need for strategies for collaboration. The institutions shared several similar characteristics of this sector—most were in urban areas, serve around twenty-five thousand students, and have large numbers of commuter students. But they also differed in meaningful ways that help the reader understand that the model operates across different types of contexts. For example, two campuses had faculty oriented toward teaching whereas two had faculty more oriented toward research. Some people hypothesize that faculty oriented toward teaching are more likely to collaborate or that it is easier in that environment to create collaboration (Ramaley, 2001). Because of the depth needed to examine this complex phenomenon and the interest in interviewing an assortment of individuals on campus, four institutions were chosen for investigation. The number of institutions did allow for patterns to be determined across exemplary institutions, while still maintaining the needed depth.

## Data Collection

Multiple methods were used to collect data, including interviews, document analysis, and observation, a practice that is common to case study methodology (Stake, 1994). Prior to the campus visits, documents were reviewed, such as institutional planning documents and cross-campus committee and accreditation reports. Approximately twenty interviews were conducted at each site. The interviewees were identified through an institutional representative, usually the provost, as individuals who had knowledge of, or experience with, a host of collaborative activities. A mix of faculty from various disciplines, administrators, and staff from across various divisions was interviewed. Snowball sampling was used, and people interviewed were asked for the names of others to interview. Because collaboration occurs within so many different areas on these campuses, to have an accurate picture, researchers needed to speak with people across different collaborative ventures to ensure that an organizational feature was not specific to any one collaborative activity but was used across collaborative activities. Because faculty, staff, and administrators often have varied perspectives about organizational life, it was also important to ask individuals across the institution for their perspective on what organizational features enabled collaboration—to ensure that the views were commonly held and not reflective of their specific positioning within the institution. The study also examined differences by position for meaningful differences.

One-on-one interviews were conducted, which were tape-recorded and a transcript of each interview developed. Follow-up interviews or e-mails were sent to individuals who appeared to have a particular insight or to clarify information from the interviews, observation, or document analysis. Observation of various collaborations (e.g., meetings of the groups or activities such as an interdisciplinary research symposium), where possible, was also conducted to triangulate institutional members' perceptions.

The researcher explored which aspects of the organizational context were observed to be the most important for facilitating collaboration, specifically focusing on those features identified in the literature: structure, processes, people and relationships, learning, rewards, values, and culture. The research used several sources of data to examine these issues, as noted above: (1) perceptions of members of the institution, (2) observation of collaborations, and (3) official documents related to the collaboration and the campuses.

## Data Analysis

Data analysis proceeded following case study techniques outlined by Merriam (1998) and thematic analysis outlined by Boyatzis

(1998). All transcripts were read an initial time for themes that emerged (inductive) as well as the themes brought to the study from the model and literature (deductive). Transcripts were then coded according to the inductive (four initial inductive codes emerged) and deductive (twelve initial deductive codes) theme codes. Secondarily, field notes and documents were also reviewed and coded. Two students and one colleague also reviewed the data in order to add credibility to themes developed. They read the literature used to frame the study, which was used to develop the deductive codes. Transcripts were read independently and coding compared. Where there were differences noted, the team negotiated the interpretation.

The main items that facilitated collaboration were documented and then the researcher attempted to determine which conditions seemed to be playing a more significant role. This analysis was based on the following criteria: (1) examination of the interview question related to what they felt were the most significant features that enabled collaboration; (2) review of answers to individual questions and notation of times they felt that condition was more important than others; (3) comments from a person on campus who seemed to have particular insight into the workings of the campus—they tended to be people with a long history or new on the campus having been at several other campuses for comparison; and (4) triangulation by the researcher, based on information from document analysis, interview data, and observation.

## Trustworthiness and Limitations

Credibility was ensured through triangulation, multiple readers of transcripts, and member checking (Yin, 1993). Multiple sources of data ensured trustworthiness; in particular, observations, field notes, and documents by the researcher were carefully compared to interview data (triangulation of data). Different interviewees' perspectives were also used to ensure credibility (which is why thirty individuals were interviewed per institution). Multiple people reviewed the data and compared themes. A set of deductive themes, noted above, were compared to inductive themes that emerged. This process was followed to ensure credibility and dependability of the themes. Finally, several individuals interviewed were selected to review interpretations of the contextual conditions that were important as well as the model (member checking).

In terms of limitations, the sample for the study represents an attempt to find institutions with high levels of quality collaboration occurring. Because quality was perceptual and based on people inside and outside the institution claiming these were of high quality, it is difficult to say whether they are empirically high quality. In addition, the findings are reflective of people's perceptions about how a process unfolded and are reliant on memory. Two campuses had been operating in this manner for over a decade. The researcher was not on the campuses at the time of the change to a collaborative environment and had to rely on perceptions and opinions. Yet when there was disagreement or differing perceptions, the researcher had to make judgments about the way events unfolded, using trends in the data and triangulation with documents to make such judgments. Finally, the model presented in the book may only be reflective of comprehensive institutions and needs to be explored within other institutional types for fit. Future research should examine institutional differences. The same organizational conditions may be used, but they may vary in importance and priority.

# Appendix B: Resource Guide

*Resources on Collaborative Teaching and Learning and
Developing an Educational Philosophy Related to
Collaborative Learning*

Barkley, E., Cross, K. P., & Howell Major, C. (2004). *Collaborative learning techniques: A handbook for college faculty.* San Francisco: Jossey-Bass.

Bruffee, K. A. (1998). *Collaborative learning: Higher education, interdependence, and the authority of knowledge.* Baltimore: Johns Hopkins University Press.

Thousand, J. S., Nevin, A. I., & Villa, R. A. (2002). *Creativity and collaborative learning: The practical guide to empowering students and teachers.* Baltimore: Brooks.

Bosworth, K., & Hamilton, S. J. (Eds.). (1994). *Collaborative learning: Underlying processes and effective techniques. New Directions for Teaching and Learning.* San Francisco: Jossey-Bass.

Smith, B. L., & McCann, J. (Eds.). (2001). *Reinventing ourselves: Interdisciplinary education, collaborative learning, and experimentation in higher education.* Bolton, MA: Anker.

Sagor, R. (1992). *How to conduct collaborative action research.* Alexandria, VA: Association for Supervision and Curriculum Development.

Harris, T., & Browne, R. (2007). *Collaborative research and development projects: A practical guide*. Berlin: Springer-Verlag/Berlin and Heidelberg: GmbH.

## Resources on Computing, Accounting, and Technology

1. EDUCAUSE Web site: http://www.educause.edu/

2. Enrollment management software:

   a. AACRAO has several committees dedicated to admissions and enrollment management. We recommend that those who are members contact the individuals on those committees for more information. Committees may be found at http://www.aacrao.org/forms/committee/CommitteeFormPublic/search?action=find&year=2008

   b. Swanson, R. M., & Weese, F. A. (Eds.). (1997). *Becoming a leader in enrollment services: A development guide for the higher education professional*. Washington, D.C.: AACRAO Publications.

   c. College Entrance Examination Board. (1980). *Undergraduate admissions: The realities of institutional policies, practices, and procedures*. Princeton, NJ: College Board Publications.

   d. Although we do not wish to advocate any one product or service, there are several companies offering services; for example, Noel Levitz: https://www.noellevitz.com

## Resources for Changing Tenure and Promotion Guidelines

Boyer, E. L. (1997). *Scholarship reconsidered: Priorities of the professoriate*. Princeton, NJ: Princeton University Press, Carnegie Foundation for the Advancement of Teaching.

Diamond, R. M. (1999). *Aligning faculty rewards with institutional mission: Statements, policies, and guidelines*. San Francisco: Jossey-Bass.

Edgerton, R., O'Meara, K., & Rice, R. E. (Eds.). (2005). *Faculty priorities reconsidered: Rewarding multiple forms of scholarship*. San Francisco: Jossey-Bass.

Jacoby, B., & Associates. (2003). *Building partnerships for service learning*. San Francisco: Jossey-Bass.

O'Meara, K. A. (2001). *Scholarship unbound: Assessing service as scholarship for promotion and tenure*. New York: Routlege Farmer.

# References

Adler, P. S. (2001). Market, hierarchy and trust: The knowledge economy and the future of capitalism. *Organization Science, 12*(2), 215–234.

Allen, J., James, A. D., & Gamlen, P. (2007). Formal versus informal knowledge networks in R & D: A case study using social network analysis. *R & D Management, 37*(3), 179–196.

American Association for Higher Education, American College Personnel Association, NASPA: Student Affairs Administrators in Higher Education. (1998). *Powerful partnerships: A shared responsibility for learning.* Washington, D.C.: Author.

American College Personnel Association (ACPA). (1994). *The student learning imperative: Implications for student affairs.* Washington, D.C.: Author.

Ancona, D. G., & Caldwell, D. F. (1992). Bridging the boundary: External activity in performance in organizational teams. *Administrative Science Quarterly, 37*, 634–665.

Arnold, G. B. (2004). Symbolic politics and institutional boundaries in curriculum reform: The case of National Sectarian University. *The Journal of Higher Education, 75*(5), 572–593.

Arreola, R. A., Theall, M., & Aleamoni, L. M. (2003). *Beyond scholarship: Recognizing the multiple roles of the professoriate.* Paper presented at the annual meeting of the American Educational Research Association. Chicago, IL.

Ascher, C. (1988). *School-college collaborations: A strategy for helping low-income minorities*. Washington, D.C.: Office of Educational Research and Improvement. (ERIC Document Reproduction Service No. ED 308258.)

Association of American Colleges and Universities (AAC&U). (2002). *Greater expectations: A new vision for learning as a nation goes to college*. Washington, D.C.: Association of American Colleges and Universities.

Astin, A. (1993). *What matters in college?* San Francisco: Jossey-Bass.

Astin, A. W., & Astin, H. S. & Associates. (2001). *Leadership reconsidered: Engaging higher education in social change*. Battle Creek, MI: W. K. Kellogg Foundation.

Austin, A. E. (2000). *The collaborative challenge*. San Francisco: Jossey-Bass.

Austin, A. E., and Baldwin, R. G. (1991). *Faculty collaboration: Enhancing the quality of scholarship and teaching*. (ASHE-ERIC Higher Education Report No. 7). Washington, D.C.: The George Washington University.

Axelrod, R. (2001). *Partnerships for development*. Ann Arbor: World Bank.

Bar On, B. (1994). *Engendering origins: Critical feminist readings of Plato and Aristotle*. Albany: State University of New York Press.

Barkley, E., Cross, K. P., & Major, C. W. (2004). *Collaborative learning techniques: A handbook for college faculty*. San Francisco: Jossey-Bass.

Barringer, B. R., & Harrison, J. S. (2000). Walking a tightrope: Creating value through interorganizational relationships. *Journal of Management, 26*(3), 367–403.

Beecher, T. (1989). *Academic tribes and territories*. Buckingham, U.K.: Oxford University Press/SRHE.

Bensimon, E. M., & Neumann, A. (1993). *Redesigning collegiate leadership: Teams and teamwork in higher education*. Baltimore: Johns Hopkins University Press.

Betts, J. R., & McFarland, L. L. (1995). Safe port in a storm: The impact of labor market conditions on community college enrollments. *The Journal of Human Resources, 30*(4), 741–765.

Birnbaum, R. (1991). *How colleges work.* San Francisco: Jossey-Bass.

Birnbaum, R. (1992). *How academic leadership works: Understanding success and failure in the college presidency.* San Francisco: Jossey-Bass.

Birnbaum, R. (2000). *Management fads in higher education.* San Francisco: Jossey Bass.

Bloland, P. A. (1997). *Strengthening learning for students: Student affairs collaborations and partnerships.* Greensboro, NC: ERIC Counseling and Student Services Clearinghouse.

Boardman, C., & Bozeman, B. (2007). Role strain in university research centers. *The Journal of Higher Education, 78*(4), 430–463.

Boardman, C. P., & Ponomariov, B. L. (2007). Reward systems and NSF university research centers: The impact of tenure on university scientists' valuation of applied and commercially relevant research. *The Journal of Higher Education, 78*(1), 51–70.

Bohen, S. J., & Stiles, J. (1998). Experimenting with models of faculty collaboration: Factors that promote their success. In S. H. Frost (Ed.), *Using teams in higher education: Cultural foundations for productive change.* New Directions for Institutional Research, no. 100. San Francisco: Jossey-Bass, pp. 39–56.

Bok, D. (1986). *Higher learning.* Cambridge, MA: Harvard University Press.

Bolman, L. G., & Deal, T. E. (1997). *Reframing organizations: Artistry, choice and leadership* (2nd ed.). San Francisco: Jossey-Bass.

Bosworth, K., & Hamilton, S. J. (1994). *Collaborative learning: Underlying processes and effective techniques* (J-B TL Single Issue Teaching and Learning). San Francisco: Jossey-Bass.

Bourassa, D. M., & Kruger, K. (2001). The national dialogue on academic and student affairs collaboration. *New Directions for Higher Education,* no. 116. San Francisco: Jossey-Bass, pp. 9–38.

Boyatzis, R. E. (1998). *Transforming qualitative information.* Thousand Oaks: Sage.

Boyer, E. L. (1987). *The undergraduate experience in America.* New York: Harper & Row.

Boyer, E. L. (1997). *Scholarship reconsidered: Priorities of the professoriate.* Princeton, NJ: Princeton University Press, Carnegie Foundation for the Advancement of Teaching.

Bozeman, B., & Boardman, C. (2004). The NSF engineering research centers and the university-industry research revolution: A brief history featuring an interview with Erich Bloch. *Journal of Technology Transfer, 29,* 365–375.

Bradshaw, T. K., Kennedy, K. M., Davis, P. R., Lloyd, L., Gwebu, N., & Last, J. A. (2003). Science First: Contributions of a university-industry toxic substances research and teaching program to economic development. *The Journal of Higher Education, 74*(3), 292–320.

Braxton, J. M., & Hargens, L.L. (1996). Variation among academic disciplines: Analytical frameworks and research. In J. C. Smart (Ed.), *Higher education: Handbook of theory and research; 11,* 1–46. New York: Agathon Press.

Bridges, D., & Husbands, C. (Eds.). (1996). *Consorting and collaborating in the education marketplace.* (ERIC Document Reproduction Service No. ED394174.)

Brisbin, R. A., & Hunter, S. (2003). Community leaders' perceptions of university and college efforts to encourage civic engagement. *The Review of Higher Education, 26*(4), 467–486.

Brown, F. (2000). *Collaborative community endeavors: Their numbers, natures, and needs.* Seattle: Human Services Policy Center, University of Washington. (ERIC Document Reproduction Service No. ED453949.)

Bruffee, K. A. (1998). *Collaborative learning: Higher education, interdependence, and the authority of knowledge.* Baltimore: Johns Hopkins University Press.

Buskens, V. W. (2002). *Social networks and trust.* New York: Springer.

Button, K., et al. (1996). Enabling school-university collaborative research: Lessons learned in professional development schools. *Journal of Teacher Education, 47,* 16–20.

Cabrera, A. F., Crissman, J. L., Bernal, E. M., Nora, A., & Pascarella, E. T. (2002). Collaborative learning: Its impact on college students' development and diversity. *Journal of College Student Development, 43*(2), 20–34.

Chafee, E. E. (1998). Listening to the people we serve. In W. G. Tierney (ed.), *The responsive university: Restructuring for high performance.* Baltimore: Johns Hopkins University Press.

Chickering, A. W., & Gamson, Z. F. (1987). Seven principles for good practice in undergraduate education. *AAHE Bulletin, 39*(7), 3–7.

Christensen, L., McNair, L., Patterson, J., & Wade, S. (1998). *Professional partnerships in polyphonic voice.* Baltimore, MD: National professional development school conference. (ERIC Document Reproduction Service No. SP038239.)

Clark, B. R. (1983). *The higher education system: Academic organization in cross-national perspective.* Berkeley: University of California Press.

Clark, B. R. (1991). The fragmentation of research, teaching, and study: An explorative essay. In M. A. Trow & T. Nybom (Eds.), *University and society: Essays on the social role of research and higher education.* London: Jessica Kingsley.

Cohen, S., & Brand, R. (1993). *Total quality management in government.* San Francisco: Jossey-Bass.

Cohen, M. D., & March, J. G. (1976). *Leadership and ambiguity: The American college president.* New York: McGraw-Hill.

Cole, R. E. (1999). *Managing quality fads: How American business learned to play the quality game.* New York: Oxford University Press.

Conway-Turner, K. (1998). *Women's studies in transition: The pursuit of interdisciplinarity.* Newark: University of Delaware Press.

Corden, R. E. (2001). Group discussion and the importance of a shared perspective: Learning from collaborative research. *Qualitative Research, 1*(3), 347–367.

Creamer, E. G. (2003). Exploring the link between inquiry paradigm and the process of collaboration. *Review of Higher Education, 26*(4), 447–465.

Damanpor, F. (1996). Bureaucracy and innovation revisited: Effects of contingency factors, industrial sectors, and innovation characteristics. *Journal of High Technology Management Research, 7*(2), 149–173.

Davenport, T. (1993). *Process innovation: Reengineering work through information technology.* Boston: Harvard Business School Press.

Denison, D. R., Hart, S. L., & Kahn, J. A. (1996). From chimneys to cross-functional teams: Developing and validating a diagnostic model. *Academy of Management Journal, 39,* 1005–1023.

Diamond, R. M. (1999). *Aligning faculty rewards with institutional mission: Statements, policies, and guidelines.* San Francisco: Jossey-Bass.

Diamond, R. M., & Bronwyn, A. E. (2004). Balancing institutional, disciplinary and faculty priorities with public and social needs: Defining scholarship for the 21st century. *Arts and Humanities in Higher Education, 3*(1), 29–40.

Doz, Y. L. (1996). The evolution of cooperation in strategic alliances: Initial conditions of learning processes. *Strategic Management Journal, 17,* 55–83.

Eckel, P., Kezar, A., & Lieberman, D. (1999). Learning for organizing: Institutional reading groups as a strategy for change. *AAHE Bulletin, 25*(3), 6–8.

Edgerton, R., O'Meara, K., and Rice, R. E. (Eds.). (2005). *Faculty priorities reconsidered: Rewarding multiple forms of scholarship.* San Francisco: Jossey-Bass.

EDUCAUSE. (N.d.). Retrieved December 17, 2007, from http://www.educause.edu/

*EDUCAUSE Quarterly.* (2008). Current issues survey report, 2008. *31*(2).

Ehrenberg, R. G. (2006). *What's happening to public higher education?* Portsmouth, NH: Greenwood Press.

Eickmann, P. E. (1996). A systematic approach to fostering an academic and student affairs interface. *NASPA Journal, 26,* 40–44.

Eisenstat, R. A., & Cohen, S. G. (1990). Summary: Top management group. In J. R. Hackman (Ed.), *Groups that work (and those that don't): Creating conditions for effective teamwork.* San Francisco: Jossey-Bass.

Engstrom, C. M., & Tinto, V. (2000). Developing partnerships with academic affairs to enhance student learning. In M. J. Barr, M. K. Desler, & Associates (Eds.), *The handbook of student affairs administration*. San Francisco: Jossey-Bass.

Ewell, P. T. (1998). Achieving high performance: The policy dimension. In W. G. Tierney (Ed.), *The responsive university: Restructuring for high performance*. Baltimore: Johns Hopkins University Press.

Eyler, J., & Giles, D. (1999). *Where is the learning in service learning?* San Francisco: Jossey-Bass.

Ferren, A. S., & Stanton, W. W. (2004). *Leadership through collaboration: The role of the chief academic officer*. American Council on Education/Praeger Publishers.

Frankham, J., & Howes, A. (2006). Talk as action in "collaborative action research": Making and talking apart teacher/researcher relationships. *British Educational Research Journal, 32*, 617–632.

Fried, J. (2000). *Steps to creative campus collaboration*. Washington, D.C.: National Association of Student Personnel Administrators.

Frost, S. H., & Jean, P. M. (2003). Bridging the disciplines: Interdisciplinary discourse and faculty scholarship. *Journal of Higher Education, 74*, 119–149.

Frost, S. H., Jean, P. M., Teodorescu, D., & Brown, A. B. (2004). Research at the crossroads: How intellectual initiatives across disciplines evolve. *The Review of Higher Education, 27*(4), 461–479.

Fuller, T.M.A., & Haugabrook, A. K. (2001). Facilitative strategies in action. *New Directions for Higher Education, 116*, 75–88.

Golbeck, J., & Hendler, J. (2006). Inferring binary trust relationships in web-based social networks. ACM *Transactions and Internet Technology, 6*(4), 497–529.

Goodlad, J. (1993). School-university partnerships and partner schools. *Educational Policy, 7*, 24–39.

Googins, B. K., & Rochlin, S. A. (2000). Creating the partnership society: Understanding the rhetoric and reality of cross-sectoral partnerships. *Business and Society Review, 105*(1), 127–144.

Guba, E. and Lincoln, Y. (1999). Naturalistic and rationalist enquiry. In J. Keeves and G. Lakomski (Eds.), *Issues in educational research*. Amsterdam: Pergamon.

Hagadoorn, J. (1993). Understanding the rationale of strategic partnering: Interorganizational modes of cooperation and sectoral differences. *Strategic Management Journal, 14*, 371–385.

Hammer, M., & Champy, J. (1993). *Reengineering the corporation: A manifesto for business revolution*. New York: Harper Business.

Harbour, C. P. (2002). The legislative evolution of performance funding in the North Carolina Community College System. *Community College Review, 29*(4), 28–49.

Harris, T., & Browne, R. (2007). *Collaborative research and development projects: A practical guide.* New York: Springer.

Haskins, M. E., Liedtka, J., & Rosenblum, J. (1998). Beyond teams: Toward an ethic of collaboration. *Organizational Dynamics, 26*(4), 34–50.

*Higher education and school reform: Creating the partnership*. (1991). Denver, CO: State Higher Education Executive Officers Association. (ERIC Document Reproduction Service No. ED337110.)

Hirsch, D. J., & Burack, C. (2001). Finding points of contact for collaborative work. *New Directions for Higher Education*, no. 116, San Francisco: Jossey-Bass, pp. 53–62.

Holland, S., Gaston, K., & Gomes, J. (2000). Critical success factors for cross-functional teamwork in new product development. *International Journal of Management Reviews, 2*(3), 231–259.

Hoyle, E. (1982). The professionalization of teachers: A paradox. *British Journal of Educational Studies, 3*(2), 161–171.

Hursch, B., Hass, P., & Moore, M. (1983). An interdisciplinary model to implement general education. *Journal of Higher Education, 54*(1): 42–59.

Hyman, R. E. (1995). Creating campus partnerships for student success. *College and University, 72*(2), 2–8.

Jacoby, B., and Assoc. (2003). *Building partnerships for service learning.* San Francisco: Jossey-Bass.

Jassawalla, A. R., & Sashittal, H. C. (1999). Building collaborative cross-functional new product development teams. *Academy of Management Executive, 13*(3), 50–63.

John-Steiner, V. (2000). *Creative collaboration.* New York: Oxford University Press.

Johnston, B., Wetherill, K., High, H., & Greenebaum, H. (2002). Teacher socialization: Opportunities for university-school partnerships to improve professional cultures. *The High School Journal, 85*(4), 23–39.

Kanter, R. M. (1996). Collaborative advantage: The art of alliances. *Harvard Business Review,* 96–108.

Katz, J. S., & Martin, B.R. (1997). What is research collaboration? *Research Policy, 26,* 1–18.

Keeling, R. P. (Ed.). (2004). *Learning reconsidered: A campus-wide focus on the student experience.* Washington, D.C.: National Association of Student Personnel Administrators & the American College Personnel Association. (ASHE-ERIC Higher Education Report No. 2.)

Keig, L., & Waggoner, M. D. (1994). *Collaborative peer review: The role of faculty in improving college teaching.* Washington, D.C.: George Washington University, School of Education and Human Development.

Keith, K. M. (1998). Conclusion: The responsive university in the twenty-first century. In W. G. Tierney (Ed.), *The responsive university: Restructuring for high performance.* Baltimore: Johns Hopkins University Press.

Kennedy, D. (1997). *Academic duty.* Cambridge: Harvard University Press.

Keyes, L. C., Schwartz, A., Vidal, A. C., & Bratt, R. G. (1996). Networks and nonprofits: Opportunities and challenges in an era of federal devolution. *Housing Policy Debate, 7,* 201–229.

Kezar, A. (2001a). Organizational models and facilitators of change: Providing a framework for student academic affairs collaboration. *New Directions for Higher Education*, no. 116. San Francisco: Jossey-Bass, pp. 63–74.

Kezar, A. (2001b). *Understanding and facilitating organizational change in the 21st Century: Recent research and conceptualizations* (Report 28: 4). Washington, D.C.: ASHE-ERIC Higher Education Reports.

Kezar, A. (2003a). Achieving student success: Strategies for creating partnerships between academic and student affairs. *The NASPA Journal, 41*(1), 1–22.

Kezar, A. (2003b). Enhancing innovative partnerships: Creating a change model for academic and student affairs collaboration. *Innovative Higher Education, 28*(2), 137–156.

Kezar, A. (2004). Obtaining integrity? Reviewing and examining the charter between higher education and society. *The Review of Higher Education, 27*(4), 429–459.

Kezar, A., Carducci, R. C., & Contreras-McGavin, M. (2006). *Rethinking the "l" word in higher education: The revolution of research on leadership* (ASHE Higher Education Report, 31:6). San Francisco: Jossey-Bass.

Kezar, A., Chambers, T., & Burkhardt, J. (Ed.). (2005). *Higher education for the public good: Emerging voices from a national movement.* San Francisco: Jossey-Bass.

Kezar, A., Hirsch, D., & Burack, K. (Ed.). (2001). Understanding the role of academic and student affairs collaboration in creating a successful learning environment. *New Directions for Higher Education*, no. 116. San Francisco: Jossey-Bass.

Kidwell, R. E., Mossholder, K. W., & Bennett, N. (1997). Cohesiveness and organizational citizenship behavior: A multilevel analysis using work groups and individuals. *Journal of Management, 23*, 775–793.

Kingston, W. (1995). Innovation or bureaucracy? *Creativity and Innovation Management, 4*(3), 184–194.

Knefelkamp, L. L. (1991). *The seamless curriculum. CIC Deans Institute: Is this good for our students?* Washington, D.C.: Council for Independent Colleges. (ERIC Document Reproduction Service No. ED356720.)

Kolins, C. A. (1999). *An appraisal of collaboration: Assessing perceptions of chief academic and student affairs officers at public two-year colleges* (Doctoral dissertation, The University of Toledo, 1999). Dissertation Abstracts International, 60(11).

Kuh, G. D. (1996). Guiding principles for creating seamless learning environments for undergraduates. *Journal of College Student Development, 37*(2), 135–148.

Kuh, G. D. (1999). Setting the bar high to promote student learning. In G. S. Blimling & E. J. Whitt (Eds.), *Good practice in student affairs.* San Francisco: Jossey-Bass.

Kuh, G. D. (2006). Making students matter. In J. C. Burke (Ed.), *Fixing the fragmented university: Decentralization with direction* (pp. 235–264). San Francisco: Jossey-Bass.

Kuh, G. D., Douglas, K. B., Lund, J. P., & Ramin Gyurmek, J. (1994). *Student learning outside the classroom: Transcending artificial boundaries.* Washington, D.C.: The George Washington University, Graduate School of Education and Human Development. (ASHE-ERIC Higher Education Report, No. 8.)

Kuh, G. D., Kinzie, J., Schuh, J. H., & Whitt, E. J. (2005). *Student success in college: Creating conditions that matter.* San Francisco: Jossey-Bass.

Kuh, G. D., & Whitt, E. J. (1988). *Invisible tapestry: Culture in American colleges and universities.* Washington, D.C.: ASHE-ERIC Higher Education Report Series (Vol. 1).

Lattuca, L. (2001). *Creating interdisciplinarity: Interdisciplinary research and teaching among college and university faculty.* Nashville, TN: Vanderbilt University Press.

Leiderman, S., Furco, A., Zapf, J., & Goss, M. (2004). *Building partnerships with college campuses: Community perspectives.* Washington, D.C.: Council for Independent Colleges.

Lenning, O., & Ebbers, L. (1999). *The powerful potential of learning communities.* Washington, D.C.: ASHE-ERIC Higher Education Report Series.

Liedtka, J. M. (1996). Collaborating across lines of business for collaborative advantage. *Academy of Management Executive, 10*(2), 20–34.

Loan-Clark, J., & Preston, D. (2002). Tensions and benefits in collaborative research involving a university and another organization. *Studies in Higher Education, 27*(2), 169–185.

Lockwood, A. T. (1996). *School-community collaboration.* Washington, D.C.: Office of Educational Research and Improvement. (ERIC Document Reproduction Service No. ED426479.)

London, M., & Walsh, W. B. (1975). The development and application of a model of long term group process for the study of interdisciplinary teams. *JSAS Catalog of Selected Documents in Psychology, 5,* 188.

Love, P. G., & Love, A. G. (1995). *Enhancing student learning: Intellectual, social, and emotional integration.* (ASHE-ERIC Higher Education Report, No. 4.) Washington, D.C.: The George Washington University, Graduate School of Education and Human Development.

Loy, D. R. (2002). *A Buddhist history of the west: Studies in lack.* Albany: State University of New York Press.

Martin, J., & Murphy, S. (2000). *Building a BETTER BRIDGE: Creating effective partnerships between academic affairs and student affairs.* Washington, D.C.: National Association of Student Personnel Administrators.

Mattessich, P., and Murray-Close, M. (2001). *Collaboration: What makes it work.* St. Paul, MN: Amherst H. Wilder Foundation.

Mattila, E. (2005). Interdisciplinary "In the making": Modeling infectious diseases. *Perspectives on Science, 13*(4), 531–553.

Merriam, S. (1998). *Qualitative research and case study applications in education.* San Francisco: Jossey-Bass.

Miller, N. J., Besser, T., & Malshe, A. (2007). Strategic networking among small businesses in small US communities. *Small Business Journal, 26*(6), 631–665.

Mohrman, S., Cohen, S., & Mohrman, A. (1995). *Designing team based organizations: New forms for knowledge work*. San Francisco: Jossey-Bass.

Muraskin, L., & Lee, J. (2004). *Raising the graduation rates of low-income college students*. Washington, D.C.: The Pell Institute for the Study of Opportunity in Higher Education.

Murphy, K., Cifuentes, L., & Shih, Y. (2004). Online collaborative documents for research and coursework. *TechTrends, 48*(3), 40–44.

National Academy of Sciences, Institute of Medicine, and National Academy of Engineering (2005). *Facilitating interdisciplinary research*. Washington, D.C.: National Academies Press.

National Association of Student Personnel Administrators (NASPA). (1997). *Principles of good practice for student affairs*. Washington, D.C.: Author.

Nesheim, B. E., Guentzel, M. J., Kellogg, A. H., McDonald, W. M., Wells, C. A., & Whitt, E. J. (2007). Outcomes for students of student affairs: Academic affairs partnership programs. *Journal of College Student Development, 48*(4), 435–454.

Neumann, G. A., & Wright, J. (1999). Team effectiveness: Beyond skills and cognitive ability. *Journal of Applied Psychology, 84*, 376–389.

Newell, W. H. (1994). Designing interdisciplinary courses. In J. T. Klein & W. G. Doty (Eds.), *Interdisciplinary studies today*. New Directions for Teaching and Learning, 35–42. San Francisco: Jossey-Bass.

Newell, W. H. (Ed). (1998). *Interdisciplinarity: Essays from the literature*. New York: College Entrance Examination Board.

Newell, W. H., & Green, W. J. (1982). Defining and teaching interdisciplinary studies. *Improving College and University Teaching, 31*(1), 22–30.

Noel Levitz (n. d.). Retrieved December 17, 2007. https://www.noellevitz.com/Our+Services/Recruitment/Enrollment+and+Revenue+Mgmt/Support+and+software.htm

Oliver, C. (1990). Determinants of interorganizational relationships: Integration and future directions. *Academy of Management Review, 15*(2), 241–265.

O'Meara, K. A. (1997). *Rewarding faculty professional service.* Boston: Graduate College of Education University of Massachusetts Boston.

O'Meara, K. A. (2001). *Scholarship unbound: Assessing service as scholarship for promotion and tenure.* New York: Routlege Farmer.

O'Meara, K. A. (2003). Believing is seeing: The influence of beliefs and expectations on posttenure review in one state system. *The Review of Higher Education, 27*(1), 17–43.

On, B. B. (1994). *Modern engendering: Critical feminist readings in modern western philosophy.* Albany: State University of New York Press.

Osborn, R. N., & Hagedoorn, J. (1997). The institutionalization and evolutionary dynamics of interorganizational alliances and networks. *Academy of Management Journal, 40*(2), 261–278.

Osborne, D., & Gaebler, T. (1992). *Reinventing government.* Reading, MA: Addison-Wesley.

Osguthorpe, R. (1999). *The role of collaborative reflection in developing a culture of inquiry in a school-university partnership: A U.S. perspective.* Montreal, Quebec, Canada: Annual meeting of the American Educational Research Association. (ERIC Document Reproduction Service No. HE033078.)

Palmer, C. L. (2001). *Work at the boundaries of science: Information and the interdisciplinary research process.* Boston: Kluwer.

Parker, G. (1990). *Team players and teamwork.* San Francisco: Jossey-Bass.

Pascarella, E. T., & Terenzini, P. T. (2005). *How college affects students: A third decade of research.* San Francisco: Jossey-Bass.

Paulus, P. B., & Nijstad, B. A. (2003). *Group creativity: Innovation through collaboration*. New York: Oxford University Press.

Philpott, J. L., & Strange, C. (2003). "On the road to Cambridge": A case study of faculty and student affairs in collaboration. *The Journal of Higher Education*, 74(1), 77–95.

Potter, D. L. (1999). Where powerful partnerships begin. *About Campus*, 4(2), 11–16.

Rafferty, C. (1994). *Promoting multi-site collaborative inquiry: Initial efforts and challenges*. Paper presented at the annual AERA conference in New Orleans, LA.

Ramaley, J. (2001). Why do we engage in engagement. *Metropolitan Universities*, 12(3), 13–19.

Reagans, R., Zuckerman, E., & McEvily, B. (2004). How to make the team: Social networks vs. demography as criteria for designing effective teams. *Administrative Science Quarterly*, 49(1), 101–133.

Rice, E., Sorcinelli, M. D., & Austin, A. E. (2000). *Heeding new voices: Academic careers for a new generation*. Washington, D.C.: American Association for Higher Education.

Ring, A., & Van de Ven, A. (1994). Developmental processes of cooperative interorganizational relationships. *Academy of Management Review* 19(1), 90–118.

Romero, M. (2000). Disciplining the feminist bodies of knowledge: Are we creating or reproducing academic structure? *NWSA Journal*, 12(2), 148–162.

Russell, B. (2004). *History of western philosophy* (2nd ed.). New York: Routledge.

Sabel, C. (1992). Studied trust: Building new forms of cooperation in a volatile economy. In E. Pyke & W. Sengenberger (Eds.), *Industrial districts and local economic integration*, pp. 215–249. Geneva, Switzerland: ILO.

Salter, L., & Hearn, A. (1996). *Outside the lines*. Montreal: McGill-Queen's University Press.

Sandholtz, J., & Finan, E. (1998). Blurring the boundaries to promote school-university partnerships. *Journal of Teacher Education, 49,* 13–25.

Saxton, T. (1997). The effects of partner and relationship characteristics on alliance outcomes. *Academy of Management Journal, 40,* 443–461.

Schein, E. H. (1985). *Organizational culture and leadership.* San Francisco: Jossey-Bass.

Schroeder, C. C. (1999a). Collaboration and partnerships. In C. S. Johnson & H. E. Cheatham (Eds.), *Higher education trends for the next century: A research agenda for student success.* Washington, D.C.: American College Personnel Association.

Schroeder, C. C. (1999b). Forging educational partnerships that advance student learning. In G. S. Blimling & E. J. Whitt (Eds.), *Good practice in student affairs.* San Francisco: Jossey-Bass.

Schroeder, C. C. (1999c). Partnerships: An imperative for enhancing student learning and institutional effectiveness. *New Directions for Higher Education,* no. 87, San Francisco: Jossey-Bass, pp. 5–18.

Schroeder, C. C., Minor, F. D., & Tarkow, T. A. (1999). *Learning communities: Partnerships between academic and student affairs.* Greensboro, NC: ERIC Counseling and Student Services.

Schroeder, C. S., & Hurst, J. C. (1996). Designing learning environments that integrate curricular and co curricular experiences. *Journal of College Student Development 37,* 174–181.

Schuh, J. H. (1999). Guiding principles for evaluating student and academic affairs partnerships. *New Directions for Student Services,* no. 87. San Francisco: Jossey-Bass, pp. 85–92.

Schuh, J. H., & Whitt, E.J. (Eds.). (1999). Creating successful partnerships between academics and student affairs. *New Directions for Student Services,* no. 87. San Francisco: Jossey-Bass.

Scott, J. (2000). *Social network analysis.* Thousand Oaks: Sage.

Selke, M. (1996). *Cultural analysis of school-university partnerships: Assessing dynamics and potential outcomes.* Paper presented at the Annual AACTE conference in Chicago, IL.

Senge, P. (1990). *The fifth discipline: The art and practice of the learning organization.* New York: Doubleday.

Sirotnik, K., & Goodlad, J. (1988). *School-university partnerships in action: Concepts, cases, concerns.* New York: Teachers College Press.

Slaughter, S., & Rhoades, G. (2004). *Academic capitalism and the new economy: Markets, state, and higher education.* Baltimore, MD: Johns Hopkins University Press.

Smith, B. L., & McCann, J. (Eds.). (2001). *Reinventing ourselves: Interdisciplinary education, collaborative learning and experimentation in higher education.* Bolton, MA: Anker.

Smith, D. G. (1982). The next step beyond student development: Becoming partners within our institutions. *NASPA Journal, 19*(4), 53–62.

Smith, J., & Wohlstetter, P. (2004). *Understanding the different faces of partnering: A typology of public-private partnerships.* Paper presented at AERA in San Diego, CA.

Sobol, M. G., & Newell, M. K. (2003). Barriers to and measurements of the diffusion of technology from the university to industry. *Comparative Technology Transfer and Society, 1*(3), 255–276.

Sorenson, D. (1998). *School-university partnerships: Collaboration among autonomous cultures.* St. Louis, MO: Annual meeting of the University Council for Educational Administration. (ERIC Document Reproduction Service No. SP038394.)

Stake, R. (1994). *The art of case study research.* Thousand Oaks: Sage.

State Higher Education Executive Officers (SHEEO). (2003). *Student success: Statewide P–16 systems.* Boulder, CO: Author.

Stein, R. B., & Short, P. M. (2001). Collaboration in delivering higher education programs: Barriers and challenges. *The Review of Higher Education, 24*(4): 417–435.

Stewart, G. L., & Manz, C. C. (1995). Leadership for self managing work teams: A typology and integrative model. *Human Relations, 48*, 747–770.

Strickler, J. (2006). What really motivates people? *Journal for Quality and Participation, 29*(1), 26–28.

Swanson, R. M., & Weese, F. A. (1997). *Becoming a leader in enrollment services: A development guide for the higher education professional.* Washington, D.C.: American Association of Collegiate Registrars and Admissions Officers.

Teitel, L., (1991). *Getting started: Issues in initiating new models for school and university collaborations.* Boston, MA: Annual Conference of the Eastern Educational Research Association. (ERIC Document Reproduction Service No. ED356219.)

Thelin, J. R. (2004). *A history of American higher education.* Baltimore: Johns Hopkins University Press.

Thompson, V. A. (1965). Bureaucracy and innovation: Special issue on professionals in organizations. *Administrative Science Quarterly, 10*, 1–20.

Thousand, J. S., Nevin, A. I., & Villa, R. A. (2002). *Creativity and collaborative learning: The practical guide to empowering students and teachers.* Baltimore: Brookes.

Tierney, W. (2002). Mission and vision statements: An essential first step. In R. Diamond (Ed.), *Field guide to academic leadership.* San Francisco: Jossey-Bass.

Tierney, W. G. (1988). *The web of leadership: The presidency in higher education.* Greenwich, CT: JAI Press.

Tierney, W. G. (Ed.). (1998). *The responsive university: Restructuring for high performance.* Baltimore: Johns Hopkins University Press.

Timar, T., Ogawa, R., & Orillion, M. (2004). Expanding the University of California's outreach mission. *The Review of Higher Education, 27*(2), 187–209.

Timpane, M., & White, L. (1998). *Higher education & school reform.* San Francisco: Jossey-Bass.

Tjosvold, D., & Tsao, Y. (1989). Productive organizational collaboration: The role of values and cooperation. *Journal of Organizational Behavior, 10*(2), 189–195.

U.S. Department of Education. (2006). *A test of leadership: Charting the future of higher education.* Washington, D.C.: Author.

Wasserman, S., & Faust, K. (1994). *Social network analysis: Methods and applications.* Cambridge, England: Cambridge University Press.

Ward, K. (2003). *Faculty service roles and the scholarship of engagement.* San Francisco: Jossey-Bass. (ASHE-ERIC Higher Education Report Series, 29: 5.)

Weick, K. E. (1991) The nontraditional quality of organizational learning. *Organization Science, 2*(1), 116–124.

Weidman, J., Twale, D., & Stein, E. (2001). *Socialization of graduate and professional students in higher education.* San Francisco: Jossey-Bass. (ASHE-ERIC Higher Education Report Series, 28: 3.)

Westfall, S. B. (1999). Partnerships to connect in- and out-of-class experiences. In J. H. Schuh & E. J. Whitt (Eds.), *Creating successful partnerships between academic and student affairs* (pp. 51–61). San Francisco: Jossey-Bass.

Whetten, D. A. (1981). Interorganizational relations: A review of the field. *Journal of Higher Education, 52*, 1–28.

Wiersma, U. J. (1992). The effects of extrinsic rewards on intrinsic motivation: A meta-analysis. *Journal of Occupational and Organizational Psychology, 65*, 101–114.

Wingspread Group on Higher Education. (1993). *An American imperative: Higher expectations for higher education.* Racine, WI: Johnson Foundation.

Wohlstetter, P., Malloy, C., Hentschke, G., & Smith, J. (2004). Improving service delivery in education through collaboration: An exploratory study of the role of cross-sectoral alliances in the development and support of charter schools. *Social Science Quarterly, 85*(5), 1078–1096.

Wohlstetter, P., Smith, J., & Malloy, C. (2005). Strategic alliances in action: Toward a theory of evolution. *The Policy Studies Journal, 33*(3), 419–442.

Wood, D. J., & Gray, B. (1991). Toward a comprehensive theory of collaboration. *Journal of Applied Behavioral Science, 27*(2), 139–162.

Yin, R. K. (1993). *Applications of case study research.* Beverly Hills, CA: Sage.

Younglove-Webb, J., Gray, B., Abdalla, C. W., & Purvis Thurow, A. (1999). The dynamics of multidisciplinary research teams in academia. *The Review of Higher Education, 22*(4), 425–440.

# Index